W9-DHM-177

# Unity and Plurality

# Unity and Plurality

## Mission in the Bible

**Lucien Legrand**

*Translated from the French by
Robert R. Barr*

ORBIS BOOKS

Maryknoll, New York 10545

The Catholic Foreign Mission Society of America (Maryknoll) recruits and trains people for overseas missionary service. Through Orbis Books, Maryknoll aims to foster the international dialogue that is essential to mission. The books published, however, reflect the opinions of their authors and are not meant to represent the official position of the society.

This is a translation of *Le Dieu qui vient: la mission dans la Bible*, © 1988 by Desclée, Paris. English translation by Robert R. Barr copyright © 1990 by Orbis Books, Maryknoll, New York 10545
All rights reserved
Manufactured in the United States of America

**Library of Congress Cataloging-in-Publication Data**

Legrand, Lucien, 1927-
   [Dieu qui vient.  English]
   Unity and plurality: mission in the Bible / Lucien Legrand; translated from the French by Robert R. Barr.
     p.  cm.
   Translation of: Le Dieu qui vient.
   Includes bibliographical references and index.
   ISBN 0-88344-692-8
   1. Missions—Biblical teaching.  2. Christianity and culture.
3. Christianity and other religions.  4. Catholic Church—Missions.
5. Missions—Theory.  I. Title.
BV2073.L4413   1990
266'.001—dc20

                              90-38940
                                CIP

# Contents

**Foreword**                                                                    ix

### PART ONE
### THE OLD TESTAMENT                                                            1

**1. A Preliminary Question**                                                    3
Various Points of Departure      3
Must We Choose?      5

**2. Twin Poles of Israel's Mission**                                           8
*Election*
Election      8
Particularism?      9

**3. Twin Poles of Israel's Mission**                                          15
*The Nations*
Psalms of the Reign, and Psalms of Zion      15
Second Isaiah      18
Gathering of the Peoples      20
A Decentralized Universalism?      22

**4. Some Conclusions and Some Questions**                                     28
A Basic Hermeneutic Problem: Development or Pluralism?      28
Gathering of a People: Come!      30
A People *in Via*: Go!      35
The God Who Comes      37

### PART TWO
### THE GOOD NEWS OF JESUS                                                     39

**5. "The Gospel of Jesus Christ"**                                            41
Preliminary Questions      42
Messenger of the Good News      43
In Galilee: A Limited Mission Field      48

A Particularistic Discourse?     54
Eschatological Gathering of the Peoples     55
The Gathering Begins     59
The Gospel: The Power of God     62

6. **The Risen Christ**                                       68
Overview     68
The Accounts of the Sending: Variations     74
Conclusion     82

7. **Some Reflections on Jesus and His Mission**     85

### PART THREE
### *THE PRIMITIVE CHURCH AS A MISSIONARY CHURCH*     89

8. **"In Jerusalem, throughout Judea ..."**                   91
The Missionary Project of the Book of Acts     91
"In Jerusalem ..."     95
The "Twelve Apostles"     98
Peter     102
Conclusion     104

9. **Paul**                                                  107
Paul in the Acts of the Apostles     107
Paul as Seen Through His Own Eyes     115
From Paul to Luke: Constants and Variables     124

10. **The Gospel of John as a Missionary Synthesis**         131
The Prologue     132
The Book of Signs     134
The Book of Glory     138
The Great Missionary Prayer of John 17     141
Conclusion     143

### PART FOUR
### *CONCLUSIONS AND QUESTIONS*     147

11. **The Ways of Mission**                                  149
Diversity     149
Convergences     152
Questions     154
Israel or the Mongols?     156
Conversion of Mission     159

**Epilogue** 163

**Notes** 167

**Index of Scriptural References** 183

# Foreword

The reading of the biblical texts proposed in these pages has germinated and grown up along pathways of mission. The pilgrimage it reflects has actually been a number of different journeys, distinct but intertwined:

- The modern pilgrimage of this great land of India, which received me during the first years of its independence and recovered pride, and which has ever since been engaged in a titanic struggle—proportionate to its continental dimensions—to preserve its unity, conquer its poverty, and assure its progress, while still maintaining its cultural authenticity;
- The journey of twentieth-century humanity, sovereign of new techniques that have opened unsuspected horizons, but helpless to solve its conflicts, close its economic and social gaps, or surmount its racial and cultural divisions;
- The journey of the church and its mission, with their increased openness to human efforts and struggles, hopes, and sorrows;
- A personal journey, at once human and spiritual, through all the years of the adventure upon which I was cast by my missionary vocation.

In more concrete terms: In 1953, after having completed, at Paris, Rome, and Jerusalem, the standard curriculum for an advanced degree in biblical studies, I left for India. I had been assigned to various biblical apostolates in that land—teaching, translation, dialogue, and so on. I had heard the call of Asia by way of the events of World War II. Far in the distance, beyond the European conflict, one could feel the world shift eastward—toward Japan, which had so suddenly and devastatingly appeared on the scene as a great world power; toward India, which, rather more attractively, manifested, in the person of Mahatma Gandhi, the spiritual power of truth; toward China, which, in immense somersaults, was embarking on a revolution of dimensions that matched its gigantic size. It was in Asia that the future of the world would be played out. It was to Asia, then, that one must carry the Christian faith. After all, young Christians sang, in those years, that they wished to "win the world for Jesus Christ!"

Then came contact with Asian reality. The first priority was to study an Indian language. It was an absorbing, fascinating task. Through that language, and through the reading and contacts that this new tool gradually made possible, an entire world opened to me, with its civilization and its philosophy, its way of seeing things, its way of organizing its thought, society, and life. Through the vocabulary, expressions, and proverbs of that language, one could perceive the religious impregnation of the whole of life. Through my human encounters, I discovered a dignity in human relationships and a dignity in suffering, an instinctive nobility, the product of thousands of years of tragic vicissitudes and spiritual growth. One cannot live in India without feeling its spell. But the experience of this seduction was both ravishing and disquieting. Was I not betraying my vocation in allowing myself to be fascinated by the world I should be converting? Furthermore, even to go out into the street was to feel swallowed up by its enormous throngs, to become an infinitesimal drop in an ocean of humanity. Did the church I represented really have the capacity to gather up all of these masses' suffering and anguish, vitality and hope, yes, spiritual wealth?

In the beginning, the conquest of the world for Jesus Christ seemed a beautiful and noble enterprise. But in the course of my contact with these realities, doubt crept in. Were these people, whom I had found so winning, really so "pagan"? And my church and I—what were we, amidst this world that went so far beyond us? Had I not set myself an impossible, futile task? I thought of Jeremiah's complaint: "You duped me, O Lord, and I let myself be duped . . ." (Jer. 20:7). My doubt became agony. All unawares, I was Jacob battling the Angel. I did not know it, but I was wrestling with God. It was God who, in these troubling experiences, was beckoning to me, calling me. I was the primary one that God wanted to convert. I had come in the name of a conquering faith, and God wanted me to learn to receive. I had come with full hands, and God reached out hands to me filled with the wealth that the divine largess had broadcast among the nations, and specifically, among this people to whom I had been sent.

I was making this personal faith pilgrimage in the company of an Indian church that had embarked on a search for its own identity. The search had begun with pioneers like Pére Monchanin and Abhishiktananda (Le Saux), to mention only the dead and only those known in France. But we could cite name after name. And especially, we could refer to the broad current of reflection in which the church of India is steeped today. The search for an Indian theology has ceased to be the isolated contribution of a few original minds. It has become a vast movement of study, reflection, and prayer, with its special moments of sometimes adventurous, always fruitful, interdisciplinary encounters. If this movement has as yet produced no coherent synthesis comparable with that of the theology of liberation, it is doubtless because the task in India is even greater than it is elsewhere. Perhaps never in the history of the church has the Christian faith encountered a culture so solid and so comprehensive, a religion so living and as profoundly mystical, as it has in today's India. The only parallel might be in the encounter with the Greek world. But the Greece of the first Christian centuries had lost its liberty and was entering upon its decline, while the last hundred years in the history of India have been the century of independence and great renewal, the age of Ramakrishna, Vivekananda, Aurobindo, Mahatma Gandhi, and Vinobha Bhave, to limit ourselves to figures of the past.

For that matter, this Indian authenticity has never been the monopoly of professional theologians. This theological quest would be a vain one unless it sought its roots in the toils, the trials, and the hopes of daily life. I have been fortunate enough to share the life of poor peasants of a village of the Dekkan, to be accepted into the fabric of their community, to live their problems, their prayer, and their struggle with poverty, drought, ignorance, and disease. I have found far more inculturation here than I have in books. Cultural authenticity has not emerged from an academic effort to connect faith with culture. Cultural authenticity has been the visceral fidelity of the inmost Indian soul. It has been no veneer: it is life.

Nor has it been only Christians who have lent their ears to the Indian echoes of the voice of the gospel. Numerous non-Christians have done so, as well—for example, the physician I knew who, while remaining completely faithful to Hinduism, had devoted to a study of Jesus any leisure left over from the busy practice of his profession. He had composed a thick manuscript, whose content might well have shocked a Christian whose christological formulas were the traditional ones of received Western theology, but which was no less surprising in its reverence, humility, and fervor. Another example would be a biblical prayer group with which I was acquainted, made up entirely of non-Christians. Still another would be the young people I have happened to meet on long train trips, so eager to compare their Hindu prayer and faith with mine. They were not theologians or philosophers. They have only spoken of their lives. Through them, God has been addressing me, and asking me to learn to listen, as well.

Indeed, God was challenging the entire church in the same way. To have experienced mission in the latter half of the twentieth century is to have taken part in the great forward march of the church during and after Vatican II. It would be hazardous in the extreme to attempt to draw up the balance sheet of this still too recent phenomenon. Somewhat subjectively, and only from the viewpoint of mission in India, I should single out six elements:

1. A *return to the word of God*, a word received in faith, celebrated in the liturgy, and shared among believers in the church and with all women and men in mission.

2. A *presence to human beings*, not in the form of a capitulation to the world, but by way of a prolongation in that world of the role of the Servant, addressing to it the prophetic message of conversion and perceiving in it the signs of the times and the "seeds of the Word" (cf. Vatican Council II, *Ad Gentes*, no. 11; Paul VI, *Evangelii Nuntiandi*, no. 53).

3. The *theology of liberation* has been a particularly meaningful element of this presence to human beings. The gospel is the Good News of the liberation of the oppressed (Luke 4:18). Salvation is the restoration of the image of God in which human beings have been created, and which has

been distorted by all forms of slavery and misery. The Second Vatican Council did not explicitly anticipate these perspectives; but ten years later, Paul VI's "Apostolic Exhortation on Evangelization in the Modern World" cited "peoples ... engaged with all their energy in the effort and struggle to overcome everything which condemns them to remain on the margin of life: famine, chronic disease, illiteracy, poverty, injustices in international relations and especially in commercial exchanges, situations of economic and cultural neo-colonialism," and asserted that the church had "the duty of assisting the birth of this liberation, of giving witness to it, of ensuring that it is complete. This is not foreign to evangelization" (Paul VI, *Evangelii Nuntiandi*, no. 30).

4. The *reintegration of mission into ecclesiology* and the reestablishment of ecclesiology on the foundation of the local church. Mission is the church in its very dynamism, and the church is the people of God in a given place and the concrete circumstances of this existence. But there is also the other side of the coin: the local community is the church only if it is "on mission"—focusing not on its own, internal problems, but on other human beings, focusing elsewhere, in a world that calls it and challenges it.

5. The *changing political and religious situation*, terminating in the loss to the West (if indeed it ever possessed it) of its place as the umbilicus of the world and of Christianity. Too long had mission pursued the lines of force of world politics, moving from the West to the East, and from the North to the South. These entanglements, of such doubtful legitimacy, have now been dissolved. Missionaries in Asia no longer represent a supposed political and economic superiority. Too, they know that they are no longer the representatives of a "Christian world": Christendom had doubtless entered upon its decline long before the dawn of the twentieth century; but the evidence of this decline is now so striking that it needs no further elaboration. We need only cite the new freedom that mission has received from this circumstance.

6. As mission no longer originates with a Christian world, so neither does it continue to address a "pagan world." It addresses this world that God has so loved (John 3:16), a world where the invisible divine perfections have never ceased to be in evidence (Rom. 1:20). Vatican II adopted this theme and proposed a program of *dialogue with non-Christians*. Evangelization and dialogue have sometimes been seen as standing in a relationship of opposition. But does not evangelization in dialogue mean that evangelization must be engaged in with love—that is, with respect—and be able to sense the breath of the Spirit across this world and these nations that God loves?

•

Proclamation of the word and call to conversion; but the witness of one's life, as well; and then dialogue, and a struggle for the development and liberation of human beings: this was the broadened panorama of mission proposed in the Decree of Vatican Council II *Ad Gentes*, and the apostolic exhortation of Pope Paul VI's *Evangelii Nuntiandi* following the 1974 Synod of Bishops. It was not a matter of rationalizing the acceptance of failure, or of camouflaging with pompous terms the demobilization of mission. It was a matter of exploring and exploiting, in the light of God's word and the experience of the churches, the depths and breadths of mission itself. Mission is not a limited, specialized activity. It has as many faces as the dynamism of a church "on the move" in the world and in history. History testifies to this variety of missionary commitments. Thérèse of Lisieux in her Carmel earned the title of Patron Saint of Missions. Charles de Foucauld, in the silence of his hermitage in the midst of the Sahara and of Islam, was certainly not in retreat from mission. The first missionaries to Korea, martyred the moment they set foot in that land, without so much as having had the opportunity to learn the language, or Bishop Marion-Brésillac and the first missionaries of Africa, prostrated by fever a few weeks or months after having broached the Dark Continent, were scarcely examples of surrender. In other ways, but just as genuinely as "conquistadors of faith" like St. Paul and St. Francis Xavier, they were witnesses of mission. They only reflect other aspects of the "reality of evangelization in all its richness, complexity, and dynamism" (*Evangelii Nuntiandi*, no. 17).

It is this ensemble of personal and collective experiences that underlies the reading of the scriptures that I shall here propose. A "subjective viewpoint," I shall be told. But can a text be read apart from all subjectivity? The worst subjectivity would be the hypocrisy of pretending to be neutral and objective. Genuine objectivity consists in entering genuinely into dialogue with the text, in honestly listening to it, and in a willingness to be deeply disturbed by this hearing. A study on mission in the Bible must not be an attempt to justify a personal approach or the positions of Vatican II or liberation theology or any other theology. It must be listening. It must seek only light. No one can claim to have perfectly attained to this degree of disinterest. One can only make the attempt. The proof of the authenticity of one's dialogue with the Word of God lies in the ability of that dialogue to achieve a better penetration of the truth of God, self, and others.

•

I have spoken of a journey. There is an interesting vocabulary problem that illustrates the hazards of this journey. I was a "missionary." I had left for the "missions." May we continue to use this language? In searching the Bible for a clarification of the nature of "mission," are we not, perhaps, asking false questions and simply invoking this text to shore up our crumbling illusions?

History has charged the word "mission" with ambiguity. Perhaps we may think of this ambiguity as caricatured in the popular image of the bearded "missionary," eloquent and colorful, his rifle on his shoulder and his crucifix in his belt, striding forth to bring the benefits of civilization to savage tribes and the true faith to the pagans. We all know that image to be false. And yet such is the power of archetypes that they continue to function in the depths of our linguistic consciousness long after they have been outstripped by fact. There are milieus in which the word "missionary" calls forth an instant smile, ironic or tender, depending on the cultural context. Elsewhere, it is worse, as in Israel or India, where the word "missionary" is so intimately associated with a savage, arrogant proselytism that its use has become altogether taboo. The fact that the association in question is illegitimate in the current context does not affect the linguistic reality. Paul VI unintentionally aroused a hostile reaction when he declared, in Bombay, that his journey to India was a "missionary" journey. Doubtless he meant that he had come not as a statesman, but as a priest. Still the very word was enough to raise hackles. John Paul II styled his own trip a "pilgrimage." There was more than a more judicious, more diplomatic choice of words here. The change in vocabulary reflected a raised consciousness of mission. Here was a new awareness of a mission in the image of Jesus' own mission: a humble, serving mission, which consisted not only in speaking, but in listening, as well.

Will these historical ambiguities and this new raised consciousness condemn the word "mission"? Need we forego the use of a word because it is ambiguous? The entire field of human expression would be obliterated by such an intransigent criticism of language. Love, father, mother, country, native land, freedom, youth, democracy, progress—the list of "ambiguous" words is endless. Even the humble words of daily life—the "wine" that rejoices the human heart but that is the target of campaigns against drunk driving, or "bread" with its good scent of the earth but that dieticians tell us is too rich in starch—are fraught with ambiguity. But need we therefore cease speaking of bread and wine, or mother and father—or mission?

Furthermore, the word "mission" can boast a respectable biblical pedigree. "Mission" means "sending." This is the idea expressed by the Greek verbs *pempein*, to "send" (used 79 times in the New Testament) and *apostellein*, to "send forth" (used 137 times, counting the 6 occurrences of *exapostellein* in the sense of sending). The "missionary," the one sent, is the *apostolos* (79 times), and the apostle's task is the *apostole* (4 times). An alternative to the words "mission" and "missionary" could therefore be "apostolate" and "apostle." But, even apart from the absence of any evident advantage of shifting from a Latin root to a Greek one, the various concrete connotations of the vocabulary of the "apostolate" would scarcely seem calculated to shed new light on the discussion: the apostle can be a missionary, yes, but "Apostle" is also the proper title ascribed to the Twelve; and "apostolate" has lost its reference to the notion of sending and delegation more than has the word "mission."

We shall abide by current usage, then. But we shall be on the alert to enrich and correct it. Thus, this study will bear on the theme of mission: on God's sending forth of messengers, first and foremost the Son of God and the people of God, to make known and to implement the divine salvific plan. This study will seek to situate this theme of mission in the context of the divine plan for human beings as manifested to us in the Bible. We may hope that this return to the Bible will help extricate our theme from the dross of distortions and ambiguities that has surrounded it and thus contributes to a recovery of the clarity and brilliance it had when the Risen One said to his disciples:

> As the Father has sent me,
> so I send you (John 20:21).

# PART ONE

# THE OLD TESTAMENT

To enter into a dialogue with the Bible, we must know how to listen to it, and listen to it in its entirety. We must not impatiently seize upon what is of special interest to ourselves. We must know how to share the concerns the Bible itself addresses and not simply impose our own questions from the outset. As Christians reading the Bible on the subject of mission, how we should love to begin with Jesus' missionary mandate, "Go, make disciples of all nations..." (Matt. 28:19)! But we must calm our impatience. We must begin at the beginning. We must take account of the Old Testament, in spite of its apparently limited missionary perspectives. We may actually discover new perspectives there.

# I

# A Preliminary Question

*If we would listen to the Bible, we must begin with the Old Testament.
But how early? Exodus? Abraham? Creation? The terms of our question
will predetermine the answer, since that answer will be found only within
the limited framework of our series of questions.*

## VARIOUS POINTS OF DEPARTURE

For example, if we have the notion that mission consists in going out to
the pagans to lead them to the true faith or convert them to the true God,
we shall find that, apart from rare exceptions (such as the Book of Jonah),
the Old Testament knows nothing of mission.

On the other hand, if we understand the concept of mission as coexten-
sive with that of universalism, then we shall find a missionary teaching
sketched in scores of Old Testament texts, notably in Isaiah with its image
of the gathering of the nations at Jerusalem in the messianic age. And we
shall find this eschatological, centripetal universalism-in-outline brought to
complete expression in the New Testament.

Or if mission is the pilgrimage of a liberated people, we shall find its
starting point in the Book of Exodus. For there it is that God leads Israel
out of captivity in Egypt, delivering them from the "place of slavery" (Exod.
13:3,14). Here we shall find the sociopolitical aspects of mission.

But ought we not rather to go back to Abraham, and the divine call to
"go forth" (Gen. 12:1)? Abraham's experience is also an exodus: like the
people of Israel under Moses, Abraham himself "goes forth," rejecting an
idolatrous culture (cf. Josh. 24:2) and traveling to a new land where he will
form a new nation (Gen. 12:1-4). Like Moses, Abraham can be looked
upon as a prototype of mission.[1] Does Abraham not bear the divine benediction to all nations (Gen. 12:3)?[2] But Abraham's experience is more
individual and more inward than that of the people of the Exodus, at least
as described in the biblical traditions, which seem to wish to stress the
patriarch's *kenosis* of faith. He who has been promised a land extending to

3

all the azimuths (Gen. 13:14-17) does not actually possess so much as the little plot of ground he needs to bury his wife, and he must engage in Levantine haggling to have a cave with a few trees around it (Gen. 23). The one to whom God has proclaimed that he will become a great people has an infertile wife, and when his child is born miraculously, he receives the order to sacrifice him. The history of Abraham actually unfolds contrariwise to the themes of the conquest that follow upon the Exodus and the sojourn in the desert. While the Exodus proceeds from the land of slavery to the wealth of Canaan and from the low estate of a gang of refugees to the dignity of a people, Abraham journeys from the wealth of Ur to the poverty of a vagrant in Canaan and from a home among his Amorite people to the solitude of a refugee. Abraham is to be despoiled. His story is as mystical as it is geographical: the great stages of his nomadism are punctuated with a recurrent dialogue with a God who will not have done with frustrating him and hurling him once more against the unknown. As Stephen (Acts 7:2-8), Paul (Rom 4:18-21), and the Letter to the Hebrews justly note, he is on a journey of darksome faith. We might say that, from the very outset, the Bible is concerned to put us on our guard against too triumphalistic a conception of the divine promises. The people promised to Abraham is not defined by a flood of milk and honey alone. It is defined by a faith, as well.

Let us note that, as we pass from Moses to Abraham as prototypes of mission, we are following the actual order of the redaction of the biblical texts, which begins with the foundational experience of the Exodus and then gradually integrates earlier patriarchal traditions. This movement from the Exodus to the ancestral sagas also corresponds to a spiritual itinerary, a deepening of Israel's faith. But then the biblical traditions make another theological leap. They go back to creation. In situating its historical perspectives on the Exodus and the patriarchs in the framework of the origins of the human being and the world, the Yahwist faith and hope assume the universal dimensions of a divine plan that embraces all humanity and all creation. This "soteriological conception of creation," as Gerhard von Rad calls it, has the twofold effect of bestowing on salvation history its universal dimensions and giving creation a historical thrust. Creation becomes the commencement of the grand adventure that hurled everything and everyone toward a future that, while in constant danger, is constantly renewed by God's promises. The human being will be fulfilled as the image of God by assuming responsibility for the earth and for history (Gen. 1:26-28). Is not this creative adventure also a definition of mission, understood in the larger sense? All that contributes to the improvement of the world, to its ennoblement, all that renders it more beautiful, more just, more worthy of the image of God — the arts, technology, science, justice, and peace — belongs to mission understood in the broad sense as participation in creation.

Finally, at the very heart of these broadened perspectives, which ultimately open out upon creation, we come to God — God perceived in a preexistent transcendence and emerging in an essential kenosis to leap into the hazards of a world entrusted to human liberty. This perspective is vigorously expressed in the first verse of the Bible: "In the beginning God . . ." (Gen. 1:1). In the beginning of salvation history, which is to unfold by way of Israel—before the Exodus, before the call of Abraham, and before the creation of the world—there is God. The sapiential literature will focus on this mystery of a fundamental mission already residing in God and will name Wisdom as the archetype of all divine action and mission (Prov. 8:22-36; Sir. 24:3-22). The Johannine Prologue will develop this theme. The Word who gives eternal life (John 5:24), who sets the world free (8:31-32), and who triumphs over death (John 8:51-52), the Word entrusted to the apostolic harvesters (John 17:17-19, 20:21), originally issued from the eternity of God. In the last analysis, it is this eternal reality of the Word in God that constitutes the force and ultimate content of mission. The words of the gospel proclaimed to the nations are but the echo of the Word pronounced by God from all eternity. By citing the Word that was in the presence of God in the beginning, who indeed was Godself (John 1:1), John's Prologue couples the themes of Trinity and mission: the gospel is divine reality. Rooted in the trinitarian eternity of God, mission acquires a profound theological dimension, prolonging the mission of the Son in the bosom of the Father (John 1:16-18, 20:21). But reciprocally, God is presented as Verbum, as communication (1:1), as light and life (1:4), as grace that saves and truth that liberates (1:14,17):

> In Jesus we see God as a missionary God, a God who busies himself with the salvation of his creatures, a God who, in all liberty, creates with them a relationship of love. . . . When we speak of Jesus Christ, we speak of the eternal mission of God. We understand our own mission in the light of the mission of Jesus Christ, who was sent by the Father in the power of the Spirit.[3]

## MUST WE CHOOSE?

It would be an easy matter to sketch the various types of missiology determined by these various points of departure, and in turn determining them.

If we began with the New Testament and the Pauline model, we would prioritize the itinerant mission in the style of St. Francis Xavier and the modern missions.

But Paul himself harks back to Abraham to establish his universalism on the grace of God. The latter goes before all human activity, even missionary activity. On this basis, we could develop a missionary theory that would accentuate faith as free gift, thus defying any triumphalistic activism or practical Pelagianism that would depend more on advertising propaganda than on the intrinsic dynamism of the Word. From another viewpoint: in our own day, concern for a mission that will enter into dialogue with Israel and Islam is a concern that must evoke the memory of Abraham, father of both Isaac and Ishmael.

The theology of liberation, for its part, regards the Exodus as the foundational account of a mission calculated to mobilize the people in a struggle against all oppression, so that they may embark on their journey to freedom. The Pastoral Constitution *Gaudium et Spes: The Church in the Modern World*, from Vatican Council II, frequently posits a relationship between the mission of the church and the first creation (nos., 12, 34, 49, 57): the role of the church is to guide the world in the creative movement launched by God at the beginning of time.

Finally, missionary monasticism follows the Johannine movement, recalling that, before being pronounced by the human voices of evangelization, the Word first lived in the heart of God, and that therefore this is where mission, too, should sink its roots. This is the meaning that Pére Monchanin, in particular, wished his presence in India, that "land of the Trinity," to have.

But we need not compare the respective merits of these various points of view and choose among them. The call to the nations, the Exodus, creation, and the Verbum in God are all biblical themes, and the types of mission attaching to these themes all bear the mark of the Spirit. St. Paul and St. John are both in the New Testament. St. Francis Xavier and St. Theresa of the Child Jesus do not contradict each other. Monchanin and the theologians of liberation do not appeal to different Gods. *Gaudium et Spes* and *Ad Gentes* emanate from the same Council and the same divine Spirit.

Rather than being antithetical, all of these various approaches are complementary. The trinitarian horizons suggested in the Johannine Prologue are surely sublime. Taken in isolation, however, they could be adrift in abstraction and dogmatism, if not gnosticism. It is good that the reading of the Exodus recalls the context of struggle and socioeconomic alienation in which the history of the Verbum is inscribed. Even John was concerned to underscore the descent of the Verbum into flesh, into the conflicts of light and darkness, and, still more concretely, into the quarrels between Jews and Samaritans, into the tensions between an "enlightened" elite and the world of blind beggars (John 9), into the problems of Temple mercantilism—in a word, into the reality of a world that is prey to conflicts and injustice and under the thumb of evil (John 17:14-18). At the same time, lest the struggle for the freedom to which the Exodus calls us becomes bitter, malicious aggressiveness, we must also hear the call to interiority that resounds in the deed of Abraham, and find serenity in such faith.

At all events, one must surely keep in mind the various ways of reading the Bible, and thereby avoid, if at all possible, an unconscious reduction of mission to a single type. Readers with blinders on, who prioritize one text over others, besides dangerously impoverishing the biblical message, will readily incline to exclusivism and fanaticism. We know the forms of this exclusivism, old and new: only those who go to far-off lands represent authentic mission; or only those committed to such and such a political option, or who contribute to techniques of development, or only those who dialogue with non-Christians, or only those who adopt a monastic lifestyle, and so on, represent real mission.

The danger lurking in any of these positions is in the "only" they contain. The Bible is not reducible to John or Paul or Exodus or Genesis. On the contrary, the correlation of all of these currents of thought, which are inspired by the same Spirit, lends them mutual illumination and balance.

This initial reflection on the point of departure of a biblical theology of mission should place us on our guard against any monopolistic conception of such a theology. Mission can no more be a mere accessory, a side-chapel of the big church, than can the Christian life of which it is an expression. Like the Christian life itself, mission is *koinonia*, the communion of a plurality and variety of gifts in the Spirit.

# Twin Poles of Israel's Mission

## ELECTION

*Lest we distort the meaning of the biblical texts by unconsciously forcing them into the mold of our own mental schemata, we must begin a study of these texts not with a preconceived notion of mission, but with the faith of Israel. Let us not be too hasty, then, to ask ourselves "what the Old Testament says about mission." Instead, let us first of all consider the bipolarity of Old Testament thinking with regard to election. That thinking is determined by the meaning of the election. Israel knows itself to be a chosen people. What makes it a people is the fact that it belongs to God in a special way. It is the people of God. This is what distinguishes it from other nations. Surely we shall find numerous texts addressing the nations and inviting them to turn to the Lord. But this will be mainly an invitation to share in the privileges of Israel. The universalistic texts of the Old Testament cannot be studied in isolation. Any attempt to separate them from the more general context of the election will only distort them. Thus, we must begin with an examination of the theme of election — even if, at first glance, it seems to run counter to that of universal mission.*

### ELECTION

The texts expressing Israel's consciousness of its status as the chosen people of God are numerous. God has chosen Israel as his "special possession" (Exod. 19:5; Deut. 7:6, 14:2, 26:18; Ps. 135:4; Mal. 3:17).

> When the Most High assigned the nations their
>     heritage,
>         when he parceled out the descendants of Adam,
> He set up the boundaries of the peoples
>     after the number of the sons of God;

While the LORD's own portion was Jacob,
His hereditary share was Israel (Deut. 32:8-9).

The allegory of the foundling in Ezekiel 16 is another way of expressing this love of election:

Then I passed by and saw you. . . . I said to you: Live. . . . I swore an oath to you and entered into a covenant with you; you became mine . . . (Ezek. 16:6-8).

Israel is the bride of God's election. This is the image that will frame the entire prophecy of Hosea, to return as well in Isaiah 50:1, 54:4-7, 62:4-5, etc. Elsewhere, perhaps even earlier, it is the image of a "son" that expresses this special bond between Israel and "its" God:

When Israel was a child I loved him,
out of Egypt I called my son
(Hos. 11:1; cf. Exod. 4:22; Isa. 1:2; Jer. 3:19).

Israel is also regarded as the Lord's vine (Hos. 10:1; Isa. 5:1-6; Ezek. 15:1-8, 17:6-10; Ps. 80:9-17), sheepfold (Ps. 23, 80:2, 95:7; Jer. 23:1-6; Ezek. 34:11-31; Mic. 7:14-15), servant (Isa. 41:8, 44:1), chosen one (Deut. 7:6, Isa. 41:8-9), and beloved (Hos. 2:25; Isa. 42:1).

None of these images do anything more than illustrate the basic theme of the covenant: "I will take you as my own people, and you shall have me as your God" (Exod. 6:7; cf. Lev. 26:12; Jer. 11:4, 24:7; Ezek. 11:20, 14:11, 36:28, 37:27).

This conviction is constitutive of Israel's faith. It will extend into the New Testament itself. When Paul mentions the Jewish people, he will continue to assert, "Theirs were the adoption, the glory, the covenants, the law-giving, the worship, and the promises" (Rom. 9:4). And he will add, "God's gifts and his call are irrevocable" (Rom. 11:29).

### PARTICULARISM?

In moments of crisis, this consciousness of election returned, to become even more intense. It strengthened bonds, but it also produced a rigidity. One of the harshest examples of this "stiffening" is the collective, obligatory repudiation of foreign wives after the return from exile in the time of Ezra (10:2–8). Those "guilty" of having taken foreign wives did as the priest commanded (v. 16). They repudiated their own wives and children, and each sacrificed a ram as a "guilt-offering" (v. 19).

In the same context, and in the same spirit, Ezekiel proposes to ensure the purity of a new Temple by building solid walls all around it, with pilasters with splayed windows, triple doors, and triple guard cells, so as to be able to control the entrances and make sure the Temple would be "kept pure of strangers and the impious."[1]

These attitudes constitute responses to situations of crisis in which it was crucial to strengthen the bonds of a people that had so recently been "scattered in every direction, dispersed among the nations" (cf. Ezek. 12:14-15). They were only a remnant now, "a few to have escaped the sword, famine, and pestilence" (cf. Ezek. 12:16). Having witnessed a horrible disaster of this kind sustained by the Jewish people in our own century, we are perhaps in a better position to understand these defense reactions and to show more sympathy than did the exegetes of the past with their epithets of particularism and exclusivism. Now we better understand Israel's desire to gather once more into one after the terrible holocaust of the destruction of Jerusalem in 587 B.C. and the scattering constituted by the Exile in Babylon. One must have suffered a great deal oneself to have the right to pass judgment on this reflex attitude of survival. And of course, anyone who had indeed suffered that much would no longer dare play the judge.

In any case, these extreme situations do not furnish us with a suitable point of departure for a reconstruction of Israel's attitude toward the nations. As for the term "particularism," so often employed in this context, this expression is altogether inadequate to account for Old Testament thinking here. This term would be inapplicable even to the rabbinical period during which the New Testament was redacted. We hear of the harshness of a Shammai, fending off postulants with his staff. Or we are reminded of the prayer, attributed to a rabbi, "I thank Thee, Lord, for not having created me a woman or a proselyte." But one must take into consideration the specifically Jewish tone of rabbinical sayings and stories and not take verbal sorties for dogmatic declarations.[2] For that matter, if, on this point as on so many others, Shammai tended to rigorism, his contemporary, Hillel, was more hospitable, and undertook to provide a proselyte with an adequate catechesis during the time the latter could manage to stand on one foot: Was the whole law not summed up in the single commandment of love?[3] This, too, comes to us from Palestinian Judaism, which has such a reputation of being reserved with foreigners. As for Hellenistic Judaism, there is an entire literature of propaganda and apologetics, including even an appropriation of the Greek classics, which were suspected of having plagiarized Moses.[4]

Israel defined itself by an acute awareness of its election, yes. But we should be picking quarrels and employing faulty methodology were we to single out certain extreme texts and attempt to burden them with the imputation of a "particularistic" theology. Israel knew that the Covenant had not reduced Yahweh to a local god. It may be that, at an early stage, the Israelites had not clearly perceived the universality of their God.[5] But this was only a lack of cosmological imagination, an inability to conceive the world in its totality. It was not a theological limitation imposed by the divine authority itself. Even if there are other *elohim*, the Israelites cried, there is none like Yahweh; and "wherever the human being and nature are to be found, there too is found the domain of Yahweh."[6]

Even the tenth-century Yahwist document projected the mighty deeds of the God of the Exodus back to human and cosmic origins. By reaching back beyond Moses and Abraham to the time "when the LORD God made the earth and the heavens" (Gen. 2:4), that text was deliberately opening all of its considerations with the attribution of a universal scope to the entire history of the chosen people, and to the promises made to the patriarchs.

Here Claus Westermann introduces a distinction between the God who saves through historical interventions and the God who bestows benediction in creation and the course of nature. The former aspect pertains to the linear time of punctual interventions—the time of the entire history of salvation and judgment. The latter aspect pertains to the cyclical time of the continuity and recurrence of seasons and days. The former is manifested in Israel's election, and in the forward journey of that people; the latter appears in the cycles of nature. The one belongs rather to the history of a people and the vagaries of that history; the other pertains to the domain of the family and daily life. God saves his people, but blesses Abraham. God saves his people in battle, but blesses the fruit of womb and soil (Deut. 7:13-16).[7] This distinction is surely enlightening. It correctly expresses the twin poles of election in history and of universalism, in the perspectives that characterize the whole of the Old Testament.[8] The very fact that the God who saves is also the God who blesses demonstrates that "the God of Israel does not limit his endeavor to this people alone, but is Lord of universal history, and of the entire cosmos."[9]

> Thus the Old Testament manifests a universalism that attributes to the saving God of Israel all that can occur from age to age . . . that universalism in which all things are situated in God's sight.[10]

To assert the power of Yahweh over Pharaoh of Egypt was itself a universalism of sorts. Egypt's affairs, like Israel's, pertain to the province of God. The expression, "God of Israel," does not signify that God's sway is restricted to his people alone. The God who has chosen Israel remains the great King who holds in his hand the chasms of the world and the peaks of the mountains (Ps. 95:4), and who lords it over all peoples (Ps. 99:2), exercising his sway over all the world and all who dwell therein (Ps. 98:7), the rivers, the mountains, the islands, and all the households of the earth (Ps. 96).

It is significant that nearly all of the prophetical collections contain a series of oracles upon foreign peoples. This is not a late development. The oracles upon the nations are found in the oldest of the prophets, Amos (1:3-2:3), and thereupon in Isaiah chapters 13-23, Jeremiah 25:14-38, chapters 46-51, Ezekiel chapters 25-32, and Zephaniah 2:4-15. Not all of these texts necessarily belong to the historical ministry of the prophets to whom they are attributed. But neither do exegetes dismiss them *en bloc* as later glosses. They would appear at times to annoy commentators, who tend to rush over them, content with a remark or two regarding their authenticity and their geographical and historical context. Actually, these texts have a scope analogous to that of the hymns to the universal kingship of Yahweh. Ammon and Moab, Edom and Arabia, Damascus and Lebanon, Tyre and Sidon, Egypt and Nubia (or Ethiopia—"Kush"), the islands, Cyprus and Yavan or Greece, in a word, all of Asia, Africa, and Europe as seen from Jerusalem, each and all are in the hand of Yahweh.

True, this universalism often seems aggressive. We should be tempted to speak of a menacing universalism, with precious little "missionary" cast! Here again, we must take account of the situations of extreme tension that furnish the matrix of these oracles. Besides, the threats addressed to the nations are no more terrible than those directed to Israel and Judah. The prophet is denouncing a situation of sin and is no more indulgent of the faults of the people of God than of those of the nations. With Amos, the transgressions of the nations only serve as the backdrop for an even more striking presentation of the crimes of Israel. The prophet equips his oracle with an exordium in the classic style of the oracles of malediction, roundly condemning Damascus, Gaza, Tyre, and so on (Amos 1:3-2:4)— but then his actual intent surfaces, when quite a longer curse falls upon the house of Israel (Amos 2:6-16). This unexpected sting in the text is tantamount to a reversal of the entire orientation of the execration. Or again: in the ceremony of the cursing of enemies as practiced, for example, in Egypt, the priest, at the beginning of a military campaign, regularly hurled an anathema against the foreign armies, with a view to safeguarding his own king and troops. In the mouth of the prophet Amos, however, the anathema falls back on the heads of the people of God, so hypocritically assembled in the sanctuary before the battle (cf. Amos 4:4-5, 5:21-27).

For that matter, we must not pay overmuch heed to the occasionally rather hastily composed headings that appear in certain editions of the Bible or in the commentaries. The prophetic texts *upon* the nations are not necessarily oracles *against* the nations.[11] Granted, these particular texts express both the resentment of the oppressed and the arrogance of the combatant; but other passages evince a beautiful openness of mind and heart. This is the case with, for example, certain oracles of the collection contained in Isaiah chapters 13-23. This particular example does raise certain problems of authenticity. We may accept the judgment of the *Traduction Oecumenique de la Bible*: whatever be the case with any alterations or later editions, the whole is "still inspired by Isaian fragments and motifs."[12] The passage on Moab is particularly impressive. Moab, Judah's hereditary enemy, has been devastated by an invasion of the Ammonites (or Assyrians, or some desert tribe). Isaiah, that "man of quality," as Richard Simon called him, well placed at court, knows the situation, and gives a detailed description of the route taken by the invaders (Isa. 15:1-6). The invasion is driving before it an afflicted mass of helpless refugees, who circumvent the Dead Sea and reach the frontiers of Judah. The refugees send a delegation requesting asylum (Isa. 16:1-4). What is to be done? The prophet is consulted (Isa. 16:3). He responds generously:

> Let your shadow be like the night,
> To hide the outcasts,
> to conceal the fugitives.
> Let the outcasts of Moab live with you,
> be their shelter from the destroyer (Isa. 16:3-4).[13]

How reminiscent of our contemporary political debate on the influx of "foreigners"! Nor has the prophetic response lost any of its currency in its appeal for compassion:

> Therefore I weep with Jazer. . . .
> I water you with tears,
> Heshbon and Elealeh. . . .
> Therefore for Moab
> my breast moans like a lyre . . . (Isa. 16:9-11).

In Isaiah 21:13-15, the Arabs of the desert will receive the same advice: in the face of war and misery, the same prophetic spirit is addressed to all peoples.

Indeed, when Isaiah speaks of the Egyptians or the Sudanese, he does so in detail (Isa. chaps. 18-19). He seems to be altogether cognizant of the geography of Egypt, with its landscapes of canals, reeds, and papyrus plants (19:5-7). He knows the human landscape, as well, the petty trades practiced along the Nile, and the political situation (vv. 8-14). His eye has delighted in the contemplation of Sudanese ambassadors, handsome men of ebony, tall and slender (18:2).

This humanistic interest on the part of the prophet is worthy of our attention. While the texts of execration see nothing in foreigners but adversaries to be crushed, and the apocalyptic literature will reduce them to terrifying symbols (a lion, a bear, a leopard, a ten-horned monster in Daniel 7, for example), Isaiah, like God, remains calm and impassible (18:4). His faith delivers him from his atavistic xenophobia. Even if a stranger comes as an enemy, even if the covenant strangers propose represents a danger, the strangers themselves are still human beings, and the prophet is capable of regarding them human being to human being. The universality of the divine might is the guarantee of humanism.

In a polytheistic context, the nations were incarnations of celestial or chthonian powers. Asshur was a god as well as a people. Behind Babylon lurked Marduk, and behind Ammon, the Baal Ammon, a monster terrible and ravenous. Faith in the God of the universe demythologizes this view of things. Asshur and Damascus, Egypt and Kush, Edom and Ammon, are human beings, not terrifying powers. They, too, are in the hand of God! They, too, enter into the long history that reaches back to the God of creation; the priestly tradition will delight in reconstituting long genealogies integrating all known peoples into a common ancestry (Gen. 5:10).

> The Egyptians are men, not God,
>    their horses are flesh, not spirit (Isa. 31:3).

Faith in the power of Yahweh delivers the believer from a blinding fear of the stranger. If this is not yet love of neighbor, at least it is respect for others. The foreigner may be "mad" (Isa. 19:13), "cruel" (19:4, 10:24), "prideful" (16:6), and the servant of ruin (19:5-6) and death (14:3-21); but he has a human face. This is not yet the universalism of universal conversion.[14] But it is already a universalism of human interest, founded on faith in the universal God.

While characterized by a sense of election, Israel's thinking is not, for all that, "particularistic," and still less, "exclusivistic." On the contrary, faith in the omnipotence of the one God entails the corollary of a universal view of things, and of the divine plan for things. God lords it over the nations. Delivered from fear by this faith, Israel adopts toward the nations an attitude of universal humanistic interest.

Thus, the sense of election to which the texts of the Old Testament bear witness is joined with a universalism potentially capable of embracing all that is human.[15] The God of the historical election of Israel is also the God of cosmic benedictions. The people of Israel, who know themselves to be the chosen of God, also see themselves placed amidst nations and a world that are submitted to the governance of that same God. We distort perspectives when we amputate the Old Testament teaching of the election from these extensions. Election does not cut Israel off from the nations. It situates that people in a relationship with them. The following chapter will attempt to specify this relationship.

# 3

# Twin Poles of Israel's Mission

## THE NATIONS

*The Old Testament's "universalistic dynamism" appears in the fact that, from the moment of Israel's first contact with the nations, the chosen people instinctively comprehend that their faith, their God, their election concern the nations, too. Let us review certain texts in which this dynamism is particularly manifest.*

### PSALMS OF THE REIGN, AND PSALMS OF ZION

#### PSALMS OF THE REIGN

The conviction that the sovereignty and call of God extend to the nations finds expression particularly in the "psalms of the Reign." The principal characteristic of this category of psalms (Pss. 47, 93, 97, 98, 99) is precisely that they praise God in a context of the universal divine sovereignty and invite the nations to join in this act of praise:

> Give to the LORD, you families of nations,
> give to the LORD glory and praise;
> give to the LORD the glory due his name!
> (Ps. 96:7-8)

> Sing joyfully to the LORD, all you lands. . . .
> With trumpets and the sound of the horn
> sing joyfully before the King, the LORD!
> (Ps. 98:4-6; cf. Pss. 47[1]; 117; 138:4-6; 148:11-12)

These psalms are beautiful prayers and universal in their scope. All peoples, the kings and princes of the whole world, are invited to join with

Israel in the profession of the Yahwist faith. Two observations, however, will help us grasp the more specific meaning of these texts.

1. The concrete setting of these psalms is that of the Temple at Jerusalem and the worship offered there. True, the invitation to praise the Lord is addressed to all nations; but it is framed in a context of the Temple celebrations. Indeed, Psalm 96 adds:

> Bring gifts, and enter his courts;
>   worship the LORD in holy attire.
> Tremble before him, all the earth (Ps. 96:8-9).

Or Psalm 99:

> The LORD in Zion is great,
>   he is high above all the peoples.
> Let them praise your great and awesome name;
>   holy is he! (Ps. 99:2-3).

In Psalm 98, all the earth is called to acclaim the Lord, with harp, trumpets and horn. That is, the world is invited to associate itself with the *teru'a*, the ritual acclamation that was celebrated in the Temple. If the nations praise the Lord and profess his name, it is not that faith in the true God has been carried to the ends of the earth; rather, the ends of the earth have been summoned to the Temple of the God of Israel.

2. Indeed, it would be naive to conclude from these psalms that their authors envisaged a concrete scenario in which the kings and princes of the whole world would stream to the Temple. These acclamations only assert the universal sovereignty of God; they do not suggest the actual conversion of the nations. The latter are invited to acknowledge that the Lord is great, in the same way as Pharaoh is called upon to do so at the time of the Exodus, or the Babylonians in the time of Ezekiel. "The Lord has made his salvation known: in the sight of the nations he has revealed his justice" (Ps. 98:2): the nations must needs recognize that they have found their master. They are no more "converted" than "the heavens . . . the earth . . . the sea . . . the plains . . . all the trees of the forest . . . the rivers . . . the mountains," which are likewise called upon to join in the ritual acclamation (Pss. 96:11-12, 98:8-9), or the very gods summoned to cry, "Glory!" in the Temple of Yahweh (Ps. 29:1-2, 9).

The psalms of the Reign are indeed universalistic prayer, then, but not in the sense of a call to conversion addressed to the peoples of the world in the framework of a dissemination of faith in the true God. The universalism of these psalms is a cultic one, focused on the Temple. The cult of Zion includes the world and the very universe in its perspectives when it proclaims the sovereignty of Yahweh.

Thus, these psalms do not necessarily represent a late expression of

Israel's faith. They have often been regarded as postexilic, and commentators have thought they had found in them the influence of a Second Isaiah. But there is no question, as yet, of bearing light to the nations, of rendering salvation present to the very ends of the earth (cf. Isa. 49:6-7).[2] In a context of the psalter and of Israel's worship, the psalms of the Reign correspond to the first chapters of Genesis in the cadre of the Yahwist and the historical traditions of the chosen people: like the faith of Israel in the account of origins, worship, too, in the psalms of the universal Reign, comes to involve a consciousness of vaster horizons. The universalism of these psalms is a universalism in the line of the cosmic blessing of which Westermann writes.[3] A new awareness of the remainder of the world, the remainder of the universe, comes to be integrated into Temple worship and bestows on that worship a universal dimension. This sort of universalism may well belong to a relatively early stage; in any case, it continues to function in terms of the faith of Zion, which becomes the center of the entire world.

### THE PSALMS OF ZION

While the psalms of the Reign are addressed to all nations, or the whole earth, the psalms of Zion (Pss. 46, 48, 76, 84, 87, 122, 24, 68, 132) sing of Zion and its Temple. The universalism of the psalms of the Reign has been centered entirely on Jerusalem and the Holy Place; now the "Zionism" of the psalms of the Temple opens wide to the nations.

Thus, Psalm 68, after describing the cortege of singers, musicians, and timbrel-playing maidens (vv. 25-27), followed by the princes of Benjamin, Judah, Zebulun, and Naphtali (vv. 27-28), goes on to see Egypt arrive with rich stuffs, and Nubia rushing toward God with full hands and the cry: "You kingdoms of the earth, sing to God, chant praise to the LORD" (Ps. 68:33).

Elsewhere, in a mysterious insertion, the furthermost reaches of Saphon are dubbed "mount Zion" (Ps. 48:3). In Ugaritic mythology, Saphon was the mountain of the North, where the assemblies of the gods were held. Thus, Zion requisitions the worship of all the holy places of the earth! The Temple of Jerusalem becomes the sanctuary of the entire universe, where all peoples gather. Psalm 87 gives a detailed description of this pilgrimage of all the peoples of the earth to Jerusalem to acknowledge Zion as their Temple, the place of their rebirth:

> His foundation upon the holy mountains
> the LORD loves. . . .
> I tell of Egypt [? — "Rahab"] and Babylon
>     among those that know the LORD;
> Of Philistia, Tyre, Ethiopia [or Nubia]:
>     "This man was born there."

And of Zion they shall say:
"One and all were born in her. ..."
And all shall sing, in their festive dance:
"My home is within you" (Ps. 87:1, 4, 5, 7).

Thus, the psalms of Zion and the psalms of the Reign of God represent, in complementarity, the two poles of God's plan: Zion and the nations. The former group emerges from Zion, center of salvation history and symbol of the election; the latter expresses faith in God's authority over all nations. It is all the more interesting to note that, from opposite points of departure, the two series of psalms converge. The call addressed to the nations by the psalms of the Reign invites those peoples to assemble in Zion, and praise of God's chosen dwelling rises up in a context of the nations streaming there. This is a typical example of the interlocking of the two viewpoints. There is no talk of election without a surmise of its extension to all peoples. And when the nations are thought of, it is in a perspective of their gathering in Jerusalem, around Zion. Far from "particularism" and then "universalism" being in simple juxtaposition, we recognize that in one and the same act of faith, Israel knows that it is chosen — and sees the nations as partners in this election.

## SECOND ISAIAH

The universalism of the psalms of the Reign and the Canticles of Zion is probably fairly old. It is not exactly the universalism of a conversion to faith in Yahweh. It is a cultic universalism, calling for acknowledgment of the universal sway of the God of Zion. The experience of the Babylonian Exile will one day occasion a different, more profound outlook on the nations. For the first time, the chosen people will find itself a minority in a milieu of foreigners, worshipers of other gods. Here, various attitudes will be conceivable. The chosen people might allow themselves to be assimilated, like their cousins of the Northern Kingdom after the Assyrian conquest of 722 B.C., entailing the bankruptcy of the Yahwist faith. To undertake the missionary conquest of these peoples was unthinkable in the context of a religion experienced as the appurtenance of a nation, much less a nation vanquished and captured. Then will they shut themselves up in a ghetto? The temptation must have been there, and it is possible that the captives yielded to it to some extent. Ezekiel's suspicions and warnings could not have shielded them from it. But not even Ezekiel could ignore the surrounding nations. The crimes of Israel had dishonored the divine name in the sight of the peoples (Ezek. 20:9, 36:20). The salvation of the chosen people would avenge the honor of the Name: "The nations shall know that I am the LORD ... when in their sight I prove my holiness through you" (Ezek. 36:23). Ezekiel goes no further. He does not suggest that, before acknowledging the Lord, the nations will be converted. His viewpoint remains that of the holiness of God, rather than of any faith on the part of pagans.

A more generous attitude will make itself evident some years later, on the part of the Prophet of Consolation in the second part of the Book of Isaiah (Isa. chaps. 40-55). His message reaches out beyond Israel to the "coastlands" (Isa. 41:1), to the "ends of the earth," where the people of sea, desert, and mountain are invited to take up the new song addressed to the Lord (42:10-12). Here again, as in the psalms of the Reign, the new worship takes on cosmic dimensions: skies and abysses, mountains and forests burst forth in cries of joy (Isa. 44:23). But here, a framework of worship is overreached. Here, the whole history of the nations is inserted into the perspective of the Creator's universal sway. All is in the hand of God. Cyrus himself, the conquering pagan from Persia, is the Shepherd, the Anointed/Messiah, charged with accomplishing the designs of God (Isa. 44:28, 45:1). From this point forward, all human beings are called upon to acknowledge that the God of Israel is the only God, and that there is no other (45:14).

As for the Servant, who incarnates Israel's mission in his person, he is the "light for the nations" (42:6):

> It is too little . . . for you to be my servant, to raise
> up the tribes of Jacob. . . .
> I will make you a light to the nations,
> that my salvation may reach to the ends of the
> earth (Isa. 49:6).

This is universalism of salvation. Now salvation transcends the case of Jacob to embrace the entire world. All nations walk in the light of God's glory. Thus, the Servant will be a "covenant of the people" and "a light for the nations" (Isa. 42:6, 49:6), as he has been the covenant of the chosen people.

Does this mean that "the author of the Servant Songs is the founder of mission"?[4] Does it mean that, "with Second Isaiah . . . Israel's world mission becomes the corollary of its election"?[5] These assertions are acceptable only with certain reservations. The Servant will not become a missionary going forth to preach the true religion and the true God to the coastlands.[6] The focus of these texts is still on Israel. The good news they bear is the deliverance of Israel and Judah (Isa. 40:9). In tender detail, the prophet cites the flock, the sheep, the lambs that the Shepherd will gather into his fold, and, when necessary, bear up in his arms; but he is still speaking of Israel (Isa. 40:10). If the nations and the whole universe sing a hymn to Yahweh, it is because Yahweh has redeemed Jacob and manifested the divine splendor in Israel (44:23). Cyrus is the messiah of God, yes, but only because he has had Jerusalem rebuilt (44:28). The Servant is the light of the nations, yes, not by becoming Yahweh's propagandist beyond the seas, but by manifesting the divine power that has delivered his people (42:7, 49:8-11). It is at the sight of the miracle of the liberation of the exiled people that kings will rise, princes fall prostrate (49:7), and peoples confess themselves vanquished and acknowledge the Lord (45:14-16).

Are we back with a particularism, then? And must we therefore write off Second Isaiah for purposes of a contemplation of mission? This would be a distortion and a failure to take account of the most explicitly universalistic book of the Old Testament. The Servant, the Light of Nations, is a missionary figure. But it would be just as problematic to wish to see in that figure a prototype of St. Paul and the itinerant missionaries. Second Isaiah evokes a different image of mission from this. In this book, mission is not a campaign to convert the pagans. It consists rather in testimony rendered "in the sight of all the nations" (Isa. 52:10) by the mighty arm of God stretched forth in behalf of his people and assuring their salvation (Isa. 52:10): "You are my witnesses, says the LORD, my servants whom I have chosen. . . . I am God" (43:10, 12; cf. 55:4-5). The "light of the nations" is not a teaching transmitted by human missionaries. It is the power of God manifested to the entire world through Israel.

It has two specific characteristics, then. First, it is *divine activity*, directly: it is God who manifests his glory in the sight of the nations, by saving his people. Second, it is activity addressed *primarily to the people of Israel*, and to other peoples only through them. The mission to the nations is surely very explicit in Second Isaiah; but it can be conceived only through the life and salvation of the chosen people. The reference to election is every bit as emphatic as the call to the nations. The primacy of the divine activity and the central position of Israel in a universalistic perspective: these are the fundamental traits of mission in Second Isaiah.

## GATHERING OF THE PEOPLES

These same traits will also be those of the beautiful texts that conjure up the eschatological assemblage of the peoples around the Lord.

The most celebrated of such texts is perhaps that of Isaiah 60. Basking in the glory of God, Jerusalem radiates that glory everywhere. In the darkness that covers the world, Zion is a beacon attracting the peoples.

> See, darkness covers the earth,
>     and thick clouds cover the peoples;
> But upon you the LORD shines,
>     and over you appears his glory.
> Nations shall walk by your light,
>     and kings by your shining radiance. . . .
> Caravans of camels shall fill you,
>     dromedaries from Midian and Ephah;
> All from Sheba shall come

bearing gold and frankincense,
and proclaiming the praises of the LORD
(Isa. 60:2-3, 6).

The text then dwells with delight on a description of the long offertory procession of camels from Midian, of gold and incense from Sheba, of sheep from Kedar, of rams from Nebaioth, of the wealth of Tarshish from beyond the seas, of trees from Lebanon (verses 6-13).

It is difficult to sort out the symbolic language of these texts from the concrete political and material expectations they evoke. On the one hand, the list of offerings suggests the customary tribute of conquered nations. Israel, so recently crushed by the Exile, now becomes the capital of the empire of the world, and the whole world pays it the tribute due a conqueror: "You shall suck the milk of nations, and be nursed at royal breasts" (Isa. 60:16).

On the other hand, all of the language is that of worship. The gifts are offerings destined for the altar or for the rebuilding of the Temple. The walls shining with gold instead of bronze, silver instead of iron, and iron instead of stone (v. 17) bear the names "Salvation," and "Praise" (v. 18). And all of this splendor is but a reflection of the divine glory:

No longer shall the sun
  be your light by day,
Nor the brightness of the moon
  shine upon you at night;
The LORD shall be your light forever,
  your God shall be your glory.
No longer shall your sun go down,
  or your moon withdraw,
For the LORD will be your light forever
(Isa. 60:19-20).

These frankly universalistic perspectives also remain unambiguously centered on Israel. It is from Zion that God's light shines on the darkened world, and it is to Jerusalem that the peoples stream.

This text is postexilic and cites the hope of a restoration. But the older oracle of Isaiah 2:2-5 (cf. Mic. 4:1-3) cited the same expectation. The mountain of God, raised above all other mountains, becomes the center of a worldwide pilgrimage:

Many peoples shall come and say:
"Come, let us climb the LORD's mountain,
to the house of the God of Jacob,
That he may instruct us in his ways,
and we may walk in his paths."

For from Zion shall go forth instruction,
and the word of the Lord from Jerusalem (Isa. 2:3).

If this text is authentically Isaian, it is striking to note that its scope is even more explicitly spiritual than Isaiah 60.[7] There is no question of tribute or gift, of gold, flocks, or incense. The Temple represents "instruction," and Jerusalem is the place of residence of the word of God. The gathering of the nations means, not the victory of one people over others, but universal peace, the victory of all: "One nation shall not raise the sword against another, nor shall they train for war again" (Mic. 4:3).

This is one of the most glorious texts in the entire Bible. It illustrates the religious (instruction and the Word of God) as well as the political (universal peace) aspects of the mission of Israel. It is also one of the texts that most clearly expresses the central role of Israel in this dream of universal conversion and universal peace. Conversion to Yahweh is, altogether concretely, a turning to Jerusalem.

Other texts are to be found in the same vein, such as Isaiah 25:6-8, which invites all peoples to the banquet prepared on Mount Zion, or again, Zechariah 2:15, which sees "many nations join[ing] themselves to the Lord," but, if we may believe the Septuagint, this means that they "dwell in thy [Zion's] midst." This, once more, is the viewpoint of Zechariah 8:20-22:

There shall yet come peoples . . . and the inhabitants of one city shall approach those of another, and say: "Come! let us go." . . . "I too will go to seek the LORD." Many peoples and strong nations shall come to seek the LORD of hosts in Jerusalem . . . (Zech. 8:20-22).

In the next verse, persons of every tongue "take hold of every Jew by the edge of his garment" (v. 23): herein is safety and salvation, for God is with the Jews.

So it is once more in Tobit 13:10-18, and in the postexilic additions to the prophetical texts upon the nations: foreigners are joined to the host of Jacob (Isa. 14:1); the nations stream to Jerusalem (Jer. 3:17, 16:19-21), seeking the glory of Israel (Isa. 11:10). The Kushites bring a present to the Lord (Isa. 18:7). And, as in Zephaniah 3:10, from beyond the rivers of Nubia, worshipers come bearing offerings. This is still the viewpoint of a universalism that remains altogether centralized. The perspective is not that of a word dispatched to the nations, but of a word that, emanating from Zion, fetches the nations to Israel, to seek God at Jerusalem.

## A DECENTRALIZED UNIVERSALISM?

Shall we find, anywhere in the Old Testament, at least a few pages detached from a Zionist centralism? Yes, a few. But one must keep a sharp eye out.

A decentralized universalism does seem to appear in a postexilic addition to the oracles on Egypt in Isaiah 19:19-22—an elegant text, rightly qualified by André Feuillet as the "religious zenith of the Old Testament."[8]

"On that day there shall be an altar to the LORD in the land of Egypt" (Isa. 19:19). Does this mean that Egypt will be converted to Yahwism, as Feuillet holds? Or does it only mean that the Israelites established in Egypt (at Elephantine and Leontopolis) will have full liberty to practice their worship there, as Duhm holds? The question is still an open one. Feuillet adduces very strong arguments. In any hypothesis, the worship of Yahweh is clearly decentralized here, and the Deuteronomic prescriptions regarding the singular nature of the sanctuary are omitted. Even if the Egyptian worship is to be understood as worship offered by Israelites, it is accessible to others:

> The LORD shall make himself known to Egypt, and the Egyptians shall know the LORD in that day: they shall offer sacrifices and oblations, and fulfill the vows they make to the LORD (Isa. 19:21).

A common faith in God will unite Egypt and Assyria and put an end to the age-old wars of these great rival peoples. This reconciliation will take place in the worship of the same God: "On that day the Egyptians will adore with the Assyrians" (Isa. 19:23).

Thus we find a broad universalism. But we cannot call it a completely decentralized one. While "there shall be a highway from Egypt to Assyria" (v. 23), we must not forget that Palestine lies midway between them. While Egypt becomes the people of God, and Assyria the work of his hands, Israel remains his special inheritance (v. 25).

Will not this central position of Jerusalem, still underlying the visions of the future of Isaiah 19, completely disappear in the celebrated oracle of Malachi?

> For from the rising of the sun, even to its setting,
>     my name is great among the nations;
> And everywhere they bring sacrifice to my name,
>     and a pure offering ... (Mal. 1:11).

What priests are here, and what sacrifices? Are they Jewish priests of the Diaspora (Duhm)? But it would have been passing strange for a prophet otherwise so jealous of the dignity of the Jerusalem Temple to exalt the more or less schismatic sanctuaries of Elephantine or elsewhere. Many think that the prophet is speaking of an eschatological worship in spirit and truth (Gelin, Jacob, Chary, Jerusalem Bible). But there is nothing in the context to indicate a reference to the future. "The contrast bears not on times, but on places."[9] In order to understand this verse, we must avoid isolating it from its context. The verse does not constitute a free-floating oracle. It is an oratorical exaggeration, part of a diatribe against the permissiveness and carelessness of the priests of Jerusalem.[10] A. Lods is basically correct, erring on the side of exaggeration himself, when he qualifies this verse as "paradoxical whimsy."[11] The solemn passage is scarcely "whimsical," any more than is the character of the prophet himself. But the latter does wish to contrast the nobility of foreign worship with the negligence infecting the worship at Jerusalem, and he is toweringly indignant. It is not out of the question that he was thinking, for example, of the Zoroastrian fire worship, so noble and so unostentatious, still celebrated today by the Parsees of India. Theodore of Mopsuestia thought he was, a millennium-and-a-half ago.[12] This does not make Malachi a "syncretist." Perhaps he is exaggerating his indignation, his rhetoric, and his idealized foreign worship. All missionaries have done so, amidst non-Christians, to stimulate the zeal of their neophytes—"Look at the pagans! They behave better than you do!"—but they would have been very surprised to see or hear themselves dubbed "syncretists" on the basis of this pious hyperbole. For that matter, why should respect for foreigners and foreign religious practices necessarily be "syncretism"? Let us simply say that Malachi places the surrounding world and its religions in a new light. Withal, the passage does not conclude with verse 11. The movement of the text is calculated to revive priestly zeal at Jerusalem. As with the oracle of Isaiah 19 on Egypt and Assyria, Malachi's openness to the nations remains focused on Jerusalem and its Temple.

The same polemical background must be taken into account if we are to grasp the meaning of the Book of Jonah. The universalism of the Book of Jonah is outstanding. It has even been supposed that it was written to protest the reactionary spirit of Ezra and Nehemiah. All of Jonah's subterfuges are without avail: he must preach to the citizens of Nineveh. The great pagan city is converted. The prophet resents the divine bounty. But God says:

> Should I not be concerned over Nineveh, the great city, in which there are more than a hundred and twenty thousand persons who cannot distinguish their right hand from their left, not to mention the many cattle? (Jonah 4:11)

Let us not forget this verse with which the book concludes, and which is scarcely flattering to the Assyrians. They do not know their right from their left! And the pity accorded them by God is the same as for their beasts! In its last note on the book, the Jerusalem Bible speaks of a "sweet, kindly irony." Irony it surely is. The entire book, of a profoundly comical cast throughout, is ironical. The hero is a kind of prophetic Falstaff, an antihero, a coward and a grumbler, who confronts one tragicomic situation after another and ends his adventures whimpering under a vegetable bush! Irony this surely is; but "sweet," or "kindly"? The Jerusalem Bible is rather overdainty here. Surely it would have been more accurate to speak of a scathing irony. We are dealing with something like a sulky universal pessimism. Seen from the human side, there is nothing here but weakness, and ridiculous weakness at that. The prophet is a crybaby and the Ninevites cattle. Nothing remains but God's love. Thus this comedy, casting all human pridefulness to earth, finally brings us face to face with the only thing that abides: God and the divine tenderness.

The universality of God's love, in the face of the universality of human misery, abides. Nothing else. This is a frequent theme in the Bible. It is the meaning of the Book of Job, which also has its comical side, with its succession of high-flown orators, each more inept than his predecessor, all of them leaving poor Job helpless on his dunghill, alone with his misery, alone facing God. All reason, and all human friendship, have failed. But Job has met God. "My eye has seen you" (Job 42:5), he says, and that is enough. Meanwhile, let us note that Job is a saintly pagan, of the land of Uz, in Edom. Job's problem is a universal problem, and the divine response, as well, has universal validity. Here indeed is a decentralized universalism, in the sapiential tradition.

The meaning of the Book of Qoheleth is close to that of Job: all is vanity (Ecclcs. 1:2). The human condition is pursuit of empty air (cf. Eccles. 1:6). Only the fear of God has any lasting value in the universal debacle: "Fear God and keep his commandments, for this is man's all" (Eccles. 12:13).

This last verse is not an "appendix."[13] It expresses what remains when all aspects of human existence have been cruelly stripped away by an abrasive reflection whose equal is to be found only in Buddhism.

This is likewise what the prophet had said when contemplating the accumulated ruins of the Exile:

> All mankind is grass,
>> and all their glory like the flower of the field.
> The grass withers, the flower wilts,
>> when the breath of the LORD blows upon it.
> [So, then, the people is the grass.]
> Though the grass withers and the flower wilts,
>> the word of our God stands forever (Isa 40:6-8).

This, when all is said and done, will be St. Paul's theme in the Letter to the Romans. After having placed Jews and Gentiles on the same level (Rom. 1–2), as has Jonah and so many of the prophets, Paul will conclude—somewhat after the fashion of Jonah, but in a more dramatic style: "Jews and Greeks alike ... are under the domination of sin. ... All men have sinned and are deprived of the glory of God" (Rom. 3:9,23). Further on, he will be more precise: "God has shut up all men in disobedience to have mercy on all." Let us note the context of this last reference. It is from Romans 11:32, in the section where the apostle unveils his missionary strategy. Standing as a background to the universality of his missionary strategy is the universality of human bankruptcy and of divine love. At this profound level, Old and New Testaments meet. Not that the Old Testament has already presented missionaries with models. At the most, Jonah might be a candidate; but in that case, what a comical model, that antihero!

The universalism of the Old Testament comes in a number of different guises, then, ranging from a humanistic universalism in the sapiential line to the universality of Yahweh's triumph; from a universality of conversion to a universality of salvation; from the universality of the Creator's blessing to the universality of the sinful human condition. These various guises are taken up in various currents of thought: wisdom, Covenant, God the Creator, or the one God.

Thus, the theme of universality is not a specific development of a single branch of Israel's faith, standing in some splendid isolation of its own. Various currents of Old Testament thought, various Old Testament themes, spontaneously tend in this direction. Universalism is an integral dimension of the Old Testament as a whole.

But we must not attempt to divorce this universalism from the seemingly opposed, but actually complementary, theme of election. Regardless of the level at which we consider God's plan in the Old Testament, we perceive the twin poles of election and mission, separation from the world and a sending to the world, to constitute the systolic and diastolic rhythm of a divine call. Abraham leaves Ur (Gen. 11:31, 12:4) with the promise that he will become, on the one hand, a special people (12:2), but on the other, a blessing for all communities of the earth (12:3). Moses leads his people apart into the Desert, but already, in the person of Jethro, "Moses' father-in-law, the priest of Midian" (Exod. 18:1), at the sight of the marvelous works of God, the nations bless the Lord, and acknowledge that "the LORD is a deity great beyond any other" (Exod. 18:11). Through the witness of this deliverance, Pharaoh himself comes to know that Yahweh is God (Exod. 7:17, 9:29, 10:2, 14:4,18). God's call is addressed to the world, but it begins with Israel and invites the nations to join with the people of the election. This is perfectly expressed in the missionary paean of Isaiah 2:2-5: the word "goes forth" from Zion, and the multitude of peoples "comes" to the mountain of the Lord.

This double polarity of the choice of a people and openness to the nations is in the image of a God who is simultaneously the Holy, the Utterly Other, infinitely removed from human contingencies, the God of love, the Father and the Bridegroom, entering into solidarity with his own, and drawing near them in creation, the Covenant, and all the history that follows (Deut. 4:32-39).

It is in this double polarity of distance and proximity, withdrawal and approach, that we must understand the position of the Old Testament vis-à-vis the nations—the dialectical rapport between what have been called particularism and universalism. Just as election is not exclusivism, so neither is universalism reducible to the dissemination of a disincarnate belief. Universalism is the invitation addressed to all peoples to join with the people of the divine adoption. Old Testament universalism and election are incomprehensible in disjunction. The universalism of the divine plan springs from a matrix of the election of the chosen people; but this election finally acquires all of its dimensions only in universalism. Universalism is not an ideological abstraction. It is an invitation, addressed to the whole world, to sit at the banquet of the Covenant, to become heirs of the promises made to the Fathers, to Abraham, and to his seed forever.

As we move on to the New Testament in Part 2, we shall attempt to discern the extent to which these perspectives continue to prevail when Abraham's progeny comes to be defined by faith instead of ethnic origin. But it is not too early to draw certain conclusions and identify certain trains of thought.

# 4

# Some Conclusions and
# Some Questions

*By way of terminating our rapid examination of the Old Testament, let us sketch certain conclusions, and take note of certain questions that we shall have as we pass to a study of the New Testament.*

## A BASIC HERMENEUTIC PROBLEM: DEVELOPMENT OR PLURALISM?

Christian exegetes frequently employ the notion of "development" in their interpretation of the data of the Old Testament. The concept is a valid one and dates back to the theme of the economy of the divine plan as we have it not only in the Fathers, but even in Ephesians 1:10, 3:2,9.[1] As for universalism, there is no doubt that the Old Testament evinces a progressive awareness of the universal scope of God's salvific activity and plan. For example, we need only compare, in numerous passages, the original text of the prophecies with their postexilic alterations (e.g. Isa. 18:7, 19:16-24; Zeph. 3:9). At the same time, this notion of development calls for many qualifications.

### PLURALISM

First of all, it would be naive to conjure up the image of a linear, homogeneous development that would automatically relegate all particularist texts to an earlier era and all universalist texts to a more recent one, specifically, to a postexilic period. There is no reason to suppose, in an a priori fashion, that all of the psalms of the universal Reign of Yahweh were necessarily late. There is also a very old sapiential universalism, dating from the Yahwist document itself. Nevertheless, there are late returns to particularism in Ezekiel, Ezra, and Zechariah.

The development in question actually occurred in several directions at once. There was no such thing as a single universalism with a progressive development. Rather there was an ebb and flow of various currents. There was a sapiential universalism or cosmic blessing, a universalism of the divine power exercised in judgment upon and subjugation of the nations, a universalism of justice avenging the opprobrium of the exile and causing the glory of God to flash forth in the eyes of the peoples, a universalism of the assembly of the whole world in a new Zion, a universalism of sin that placed Jews and Gentiles on the same footing, and, to be sure, a universalism of the divine love and salvation, as well, as all women and men gather in the great and gladsome festival of the last banquet. It would be risky in the extreme to seek to range all of these views end to end along a single evolutive line. They comprise a list of tendencies, and the only thing they have in common is faith in God as the universal Lord of all the earth.

### VIRTUAL CONJURING AWAY OF THE OLD TESTAMENT

The danger of a unilinear evolutive perspective is that it ultimately guarantees a practical conjuring away of the Old Testament. If the New Testament is fulfillment, and the Old but imperfection, then surely the imperfect gropings of the latter (being sheer preparation) will disappear in the face of the perfection of its ultimate fulfillment. At the dawning light, one snuffs one's candles. But if this was the case, why has Christian tradition so jealously preserved the Old Testament and condemned all forms of gnosis that rejected the scriptures of the Old Covenant? True, Christian practice has not always matched its preaching. A practical negligence of the Old Testament is doubtless the consequence of the evolutive perspective in which the Old Testament is regarded as mere roadbuilding of some sort. The relationship between the Old and New Testaments has frequently been the object of dispute among theologians, ancient and contemporary. We shall return to it in this chapter precisely in the context of the problem posed by the sociopolitical content of the life and mission of Israel.

### SINGLE POINT OF ARRIVAL?

Another shortcoming of the unilinear evolutive schema is that it necessarily supposes a single point of arrival, to be determined by unconsciously projecting upon the Old Testament either the Christian missionary type in general, or, more precisely, the modern (and passé) missiological model. Mission is reduced to the explicit proclamation of the gospel to the pagans. Therefore, one assigns priority to certain rare Old Testament texts that might be understood in this fashion, and all the rest—the entire history of the people of God—becomes groping in the dark, a preliminary stage, the manifestation of an imperfect sense of mission. Were we to regard things from this viewpoint, we should indeed have reason to doubt the existence of a sense of mission in Israel.[2] But why should Israel, living in

the specific circumstances of its own history and environment, have culti-
vated the type of "missions" maintained by Western Christian churches in
modern times? May we take it upon ourselves to define mission from what
we perceive with our own eyes—and perceive very ill—and then force it
on the Procrustean bed of that definition?

On what grounds might we set up an a priori criterion in function of
which the bulk of the Old Testament would be declared forfeit? In actual
fact, we are still attempting—and let us hope that we shall be doing so until
the end of time—to understand mission. Even a casual acquaintance
with the progress of the theology of mission before and after Vatican
Council II, or the series of documents published by the World Council of
Churches—if we think, for example, of the discussions that paved the way
for and accompanied the 1974 Synod on Evangelization, or the rich theological debate currently in progress on the relationship between mission
and development, human promotion and liberation, or the non-Christian
religions—must bring us to admit that it would take a great deal of pre-
sumption, or a great deal of ignorance, to pretend to know just what mission
"is."

This sort of impoverished view of the text of scripture has led a certain
American manual of the biblical theology of mission[3] to sum it all up in a
diagram labeling the Old Testament "Come!" and the New, more generously, "Go!" Actually, the mission of Israel in the Old Testament is a
response to the double summons, "Come!" and, "Go!" Come join the
assemblage of the People and the peoples. Go, resume your journey, again
and again, since what defines you as a people is that you seek a God who
will always escape your images, your structures, your views, and your grasp,
a God who will always be beyond you. Mission in the Old Testament is the
mustering of a people, but this people is a people *in via*, a people caught
up in an Exodus, a people ever and again set *en route* by its history and its
God.

## GATHERING OF A PEOPLE: COME!

### MISSION OF A PEOPLE

Mission is a response to a divine call addressed to a people. As such, it
is not restricted to the initiative of a few powerful personalities. True, the
initiative of mission is often exercised by prophets of a powerfully molded
individual character. But even if the prophet must at times confront his
people, he does so in the name of what gives this people their identity. The
role of the prophet is to revive the awareness that Israel should maintain
its charge of mission. Israel is "a kingdom of priests, a holy nation" (Exod.
19:6), a people formed by God to make known his glory (Isa. 43:21).

## FORMATION OF A PEOPLE

God's call culminates in the formation of a people. It is more than a call to the service of the true God. Its intent is to integrate human beings into the people of this God. Here, too, one can think of Pascal: Not the God of philosophers and scholars, but the God of Abraham, Isaac, and Jacob! Not the God of a truth that can be "learned" or reached in isolation, but a God bound to a human family and encountered only within this family. The goal of the mission of Israel is to create a community—to arouse not only a faith, but a shared faith.

### A PEOPLE IN FESTIVAL

This faith is shared in celebration and festival. The call addressed to the nations invites them to Zion, to the mount of the Temple and its celebrations. "Come," says God to the peoples. But the text often says: "Come, let us sing joyfully to the LORD. . . . Let us greet him with thanksgiving; let us joyfully sing psalms to him" (Ps. 95:1-2; cf. 96:1, 66:1-2).

The people assembled by God's call are a people who pray, sing, and celebrate. They are a people of festival. The Letter to the Hebrews has summed up this atmosphere of jubilation very strikingly: "You have drawn near to Mount Zion and the city of the living God, the heavenly Jerusalem, to myriads of angels in festal gathering" (Heb. 12:22).

The new element introduced by this New Testament composition is that the earthly Zion has become the heavenly. But the festal atmosphere prolongs the memory of the old Zion. The New Testament will broaden perspectives, yes, but it will continue to focus on a community that "gives thanks," that "exults," that gives itself to "jubilation," that "praises," that "celebrates," that "blesses." These words punctuate the letters of Paul, the writings of Luke, and the Book of Revelation, just as they echo through the Old Testament Psalms.

### WITH ALL THE CONCRETION OF THE LIFE OF A PEOPLE

As the expression of the life of a people, the mission of Israel has all the density of the life of a people. Shared by the entire people, mission is experienced at all levels of the life of that people. It is the mission of the patriarchs, those immigrant ancestors, as it is of Moses the lawgiver, Joshua the warrior, the judges who liberated, the kings who organized, the prophets, the priests, and the sages. Nothing of the fabric of a people's life, none of the aspects of that life, whether social and political, or religious in the strict sense, is stranger to this mission.

Will this still hold true in the New Testament? Here again we encounter the hermeneutic problem of the relationship between the Old and New

Testaments—a basic question to which Christian reflection has constantly returned since the time of St. Paul, and which it has never perfectly elucidated. According to the Christian view of history, the New Testament bestows "plenitude" on the Old Testament, "fulfills" it, "reveals" it, and the Old Testament emerges from this process of fulfillment subsumed but transformed. The Letter to the Hebrews is particularly jealous of this process of transference. The ancient sacrifices have lost their value, the sacred writer insists, as has the Levitical priesthood. But the faith of the patriarchs abides as the prototype of the new faith. (Heb. chaps. 7, 8, 11). How is it that the Old Testament sacrifices are passé, out of date, while the faith of the Old Testament retains all its validity? Where are we to "draw the line" between the transcended and the abiding?

We have the answer in the Sermon on the Mount: "Do not think that I have come to abolish the law and the prophets. I have come, not to abolish them, but to fulfill them" (Matt. 5:17). The examples then given illustrate what it means to "fulfill" the law: it means to radicalize and interiorize it. But this entails an important consequence, which St. Paul will explain (Gal. 5:23-25; Rom. 8:2), and which Jeremiah has already foreseen (Jer. 31:31-34): a law thus interiorized and "written upon hearts" is no longer a law. It is the "law" of the Spirit of life (Rom. 8:2), of the spirit that is distinguished from the letter, from the law written on tablets of stone (2 Cor. 3:3-6), the Spirit that delivers (2 Cor. 3:17).

The new economy is "spiritualized, then." It is a covenant according to the Spirit (Jer. 32:38-40; Heb. 8:7-12, 10:15-17; 2 Cor. 3:3); its worship is a worship according to the Spirit (John 4:23-24), and its ministry a ministry according to the Spirit (2 Cor. 3:6-8). The new life is a life according to the Spirit (Rom. 8:2-11; 2 Cor. 3:17), since it is the Spirit who has invested Jesus himself with the new life and power of the Resurrection (Rom. 1:4, 8:11; 1 Cor. 15:45).

It is the Spirit, then, granted, who constitutes the novelty of the new era in which all is "spiritualized." But let us not mistake the meaning of this "spiritualization." It is not that the New Testament is characterized by some manner of "etherealization." This mistake has been made often enough, even theoretically, and even more often in practice. But the Spirit of the Bible is not a Platonic spirit. This Spirit is no "spiritual principle," but the Power of Godself, animating and transforming all reality, material as well as "spiritual." A reduction of the New Testament to "spiritual realities"—to a realm from which all socioeconomic components of human life have been eliminated—is a complete misinterpretation, and one which has not always been avoided. "Spirituality" becomes evasion and individualism.

Mission is not exempt from this misunderstanding when it is defined as "purely spiritual"—when a watertight bulkhead is erected between mission and development, mission and human promotion, mission and liberation, mission and the sharing of human aspirations and struggles—as if the New Testament had placed barriers between faith and charity or the Word had not become flesh or Jesus had not proclaimed the gospel in words and deeds in the concrete context of first-century Palestine.

There is no need to adopt "materialist readings of the Bible" to accept these evidences. The fact remains that the socio-political and economic dimensions of Christian life are often more implicit than explicit in the New Testament. Neither the gospels nor the letters present any "Christian" economic or sociological programs. Only incidentally do the questions they pose ever seek to articulate in a concrete way the practical consequences of "life in the Spirit." And even at that, they often do so in purely pragmatic fashion, without any attempt at a systematic presentation. Thus, in 1 Corinthians 6:1 Paul reproaches the Christians of Corinth for resorting to pagan tribunals to settle differences that might arise among them. But one or two years later, writing to the Romans, he recommends they be submissive to the power of magistrates: after all, "there is no authority except from God" (Rom. 13:1-7). There is nothing in the New Testament to correspond to the bold undertaking of the codes of the Pentateuch in translating the Covenant into terms of the concrete problems of social relationships and division of land, resources, and tasks on the scale of the total life of a people. The reason for this "haziness" in the New Testament is partly theological: the gospel is not law but Good News, with all the eschatological impact this implies. But there is also a historical, contingent reason: while the Old Testament extends over a period of more than a thousand years and is addressed to an organized people with problems of interior and exterior policy to resolve, the New Testament, from Jesus to Paul and John, covers less than a century and concerns a small, outnumbered and scattered group of persons. On the scale of the Roman Empire, Christians made up a tiny, insignificant group; on the centuries-long scale of the history of peoples, the age of the New Testament is more like a bolt of eschatological lightning than the project of a new society. The New Testament represents only a very limited experience of human reality or practical implications of its message. Paradoxically, no New Testament writing (apart from the Book of Revelation) has taken serious account, on the basis of its Christian reflection, of the realities of war, invasions, famines, corrupt and oppressive rulers, the politicization of religion, international commercial relations, or natural calamities—all of which weave the warp and woof of the life of peoples. But (out of an unconscious fear of addressing these problems?) the Book of Revelation has been left to the scholars and the sects.

The reticence of the New Testament in the area of practical policy must not deceive us. The fact that the New Testament did not have time to pose explicit questions about a life in community does not mean that no such questions arose. They arose indeed. Jesus had to confront Herod, that fox (Luke 13:32), Pilate, and the authorities of the Temple. Paul had to deal with the case of a fugitive slave. Luke had to face the problem of a mixed community of rich and poor. It would have taken a much more protracted experience to develop a practice and coherent system of solutions—entailing, by the way, the risk of returning to the Law and forgetting that the Christian message is first and foremost Good News.

In sum: On the one hand we have the "fulfillment" of the New Testament, but without the advantage of long experience. On the other, we have an Old Testament that is "unfulfilled," imperfect, but rich in a centuries-old dialogue with the God of the Covenant and the complex realities of human history. The two Testaments are complementary, then. It is not simply that the New Testament fulfills the Old. The Old Testament gives the New its historical and human dimensions. The Old Testament retains its primacy as revealer of the concretion of the Covenant, even of the New Covenant, and of the mission the Covenant entails. The Old Testament helps us perceive the life of a people as the vehicle of mission. It is not by chance that the theology of liberation returns to the themes of the Exodus, the land, and social justice. One cannot fault it on this point. A "spiritual" conception of the New Testament, of Christian existence, and of mission actually derives from a practical exclusion of the Old Testament, which once upon a time merited the anathemas hurled against the "insane doctrine of the Manichaeans, who have said that the God of the New Testament is not the God of the Old."[4]

The Old Testament is a story of wars and exiles, migrations and occupations, divisions of land and laws governing properties, social relations and conflicts, kings and judges, the agony of drought and famine, the joy of harvests, extortion and appeals for justice, asses, camels, oxen, goats, and sheep, bushels and bins full or empty. Why not? This is what our lives are made of, and Jesus himself will make use of this material, drawn from everyday life, in his parables. It will ever be thus, as long as the world shall last.

Rich in this long history, the Old Testament retains priority in the framework of an integral biblical revelation. Nor therefore is it an "old" Testament in the sense of one to be replaced. Incorporated into the New, and illumined by this new context, it too becomes a "new" Testament, bestowing on its "New" counterpart the historical and human density that the latter would have lacked.

To be sure, we must not remain prisoners of the ethnic limitations of the old economy. We must not, for example, return to Caesaro-Papism in the name of the books of Kings. In Christ Jesus there is no longer Jew or Greek, and the Old Testament itself inaugurated the transcendence of such limitations. But neither may we thrust the Old Testament aside and thereby eviscerate the biblical message of its human concretion.

Mission in the New Testament, then, cannot be basically different from that of Israel on this point. The people who are the vehicle of this mission are now a people according to the Spirit and no longer according to the flesh, a people characterized by faith and no longer by ethnic origin. But they remain a people with a community engagement in a history. An investigation of the New Testament will explain this fundamental truth more precisely. It will not contradict it.

### PERMANENCE OF ISRAEL'S ROLE?

Does the central position of the people of Israel in the divine plan as it appears in the Old Testament still have validity? We have just insisted that the vehicle of mission is ever a people. Must we then say that it is this particular people, the people of Israel as so defined ethnically and geographically? Does the world's salvation pass by way of the destiny of Israel according to the flesh? The problem of the meaning of Israel in the Christian economy already arrested the attention of Paul and Luke. We must return to it and profit by their reflection.

## A PEOPLE *IN VIA:* GO!

### TOWARD NEW HORIZONS

The people thus gathered has not been called together to install itself in the material security of a safe situation and the spiritual comfort of a custom-made God all its own. This people was summoned together that it might embark on a journey. Its history began with Abraham's departure, and "the patriarch, as resident alien, was to be the *typos* in which the people of Israel would see a reflection of its own nature."[5] This history continued with the Exodus, another foundational myth of Israel's consciousness.

One of the basic themes of biblical thought is that of the Promised Land. But:

> [This theme] functions in terms of two subthemes. One of these is that of the Land, where the people are installed and live in *shalom* — in peace and security. The other is that of the Promise — the not-yet-attained, toward which one journeys, journeying in hope. Land and exile, rest and the road, holy city and desert, temple and mobile tabernacle, peace and trial, salvation but only in hope, possession but only in the darkness of faith: we could multiply the various expressions of this fundamental binomial. Thus the biblical human being is at one and the same time the citizen of a Kingdom, and a stranger, en route to elsewhere.[6]

Ever and again the Spirit sets the history of this people in motion, to encounter new obstacles and meet with new adventures. Its horizon cannot be bounded by deep-delved furrows or cities with solid foundations. Nothing would be more unbiblical than a smug satisfaction in goods possessed in security. Biblical Israel sees its thirst for peace endlessly confronted with the exciting, perilous encounter with the God who creates what is new. The theme of novelty will be one of the great themes of the mission of the prophets: new covenant, new creation, new Jerusalem, new people, new life. It is as if their Holy, Utterly Other God wished to call his people unceasingly to follow him, and thereby to find him in the unexpected and the unknown.

## TOWARD OTHER PEOPLES

A particular aspect of this call to emerge from self is openness to the foreigner. The God who is Other invites his people to encounter others. He does so in the law he gives them: "God loves the foreigner. ... Love the foreigner, for, in the land of Egypt, you were foreigners" (Deut. 10:18-19).

> In a powerful abridgment, Deuteronomy makes of the foreigner a central theme of the Bible. The foreigner serves as revealer of the divine Love ("God loves the foreigner"). He is the touchstone of genuine biblical justice ("You shall love the foreigner"), and this because he constitutes a reminder of the fundamental trait of the history of Israel ("You were foreigners"). The foreigner is situated at the focal point of the theodicy, the ethic, and the history of the people of God.[7]

God likewise summons his people to an encounter with others in the history in which he inserts that people. God chooses Israel from among the nations. The promised land is not a country retreat; it is the metropolis of the peoples (Ps. 87). This rapport with other nations is not always an irenic affair. The risk involved in this face-to-face encounter with others is hostile confrontation, and it cannot be denied that Israel sometimes succumbed to the temptation to hostility. But as we have seen, this people also demonstrated receptivity and openness. In either case, the people of the Bible find it impossible to sit with their eyes closed, like the Buddha, absorbed in the interiority of their profound being. Election does not render the chosen people blessed (or afflicted) introverts. Openness to others remains the hallmark of the people of the Holy, Utterly Other God.

We have seen the various relationships that Israel struck with other peoples. But the massive fact is that, from its birth in the land of Canaan of an Amorite father and a Hittite mother (Ezek. 16:3), the people of Abraham found itself face to face with the nations and had to understand its election in the living context of this symbiosis. "Then shall they know that I am the LORD, when I disperse them among the nations and scatter them over foreign lands," said Ezekiel (Ezek. 12:15). A product of the Exile, Ezekiel had learned by personal experience that the encounter with the stranger creates a connaturality with the God of all "exodi."

## THE GOD WHO COMES

But the final consideration of our reflection on the Old Testament must be that in all of this, what is at stake is God. The people that carry mission to the world are the people of God. It is the word of God that has gathered them, that calls them, and that continues to challenge them, encourage them, and thrust them forward ever and again. The activity of every prophet, like the dynamism of this whole prophetic people, flows from the word that has been entrusted to them "to plant" (Jer. 1:9-10). It is fundamentally God, then, who is the real agent of Israel's mission. It is God who makes his glory to shine among the nations (Ps. 98:2). It is his word that subsists throughout the defeats of human weakness (Isa. 40:7-8). It is God who sends forth the prophets, even the most inadequate and recalcitrant of prophets, like Jonah. The word that dwells in Zion and that "emerges" thence (Isa. 2:3) is the Word of God—a vivid image of the Word as a missioner "departing," the ultimate missioner. God himself is the light attracting the nations (Isa. 60:19-20). God himself approaches Zion as the latter faces the nations, and like a shepherd, carries his lambs (Isa. 40:10-11). In the last analysis, before being a sending of prophets, the Servant, and messengers, mission is the beginning of a journey by God himself, who becomes Emmanuel, the God-with-us of the entire world. Mission is the coming of the Lord who is Sovereign of the universe, and it is the invitation to the peoples to celebrate this advent:

> Give to the LORD, you families of nations,
>> give to the LORD glory and praise;
>> give to the LORD the glory due his name! . . .
> Say among the nations: The LORD is king . . . .
>
> Let the plains be joyful and all that is in them . . .
>
> before the Lord, for he comes;
>> for he comes to rule the earth.
> He shall rule the world with justice
>> and the peoples with his constancy
>>> (Ps. 96:7,8,10,12-13).

# PART TWO

# THE GOOD NEWS OF JESUS

Our study of the Old Testament has afforded us a glimpse of certain guiding principles. It has also enabled us to ask ourselves some questions.

Is not Israel's way of seeing things completely reversed by the novelty of the Christ event?

Has not Old Testament universalism been centripetal, while that of the gospel is an explosion outward to the world? Does not Jesus say, "Go into the whole world and proclaim the good news to all creation" (Mark 16:15)? Has not the eschatological expectation of the final assemblage been replaced by an active campaign of evangelization—"Go, therefore, and make disciples of all the nations" (Matt. 28:19)? Is faith not to replace the law, and accordingly, will not the constitution of a people be replaced by the call of the gospel?

Will the perspectives opened by the Old Testament not disappear in the economy of the New? This is the question that we must now ask ourselves, as we examine what the gospels tell us, first about the thought and practice of Jesus, then about the impact of the Resurrection on mission.

# 5

# "The Gospel of Jesus Christ"

*"Here begins the gospel of Jesus Christ, the Son of God" (Mark 1:1). This exordium is not a banal tautology, as if Mark were saying, "This is the start of the book I am going to write about Jesus Christ." Neither in Mark nor elsewhere in the New Testament, does the word "gospel" have the meaning it acquired after the composition of the books about Jesus: that of precisely such a book. Throughout the New Testament, "gospel" retains its etymological meaning: Good News. Then does Mark mean that the pericope on John the Baptist, which follows immediately, constitutes the prologue to the Good News? Many commentators think so, and they appeal to the parallel in one of Peter's discourses in Acts: "This is the message [God] has sent . . . the good news . . . beginning in Galilee with the baptism John preached . . ." (Acts 10:36-37). But other exegetes see in Mark 1:1 the title of the entire account, and not only of the section on the Baptist.*

> *It is the history of Jesus, from his baptism by John to his death and resurrection, that forms the beginning and the foundation of the Gospel. . . . Manifestly, Mark is asserting here that the proclamation of Jesus Christ in primitive Christianity—what missionary language will abbreviate as* evangelion—*comes down, historically as well as actually, from Jesus of Nazareth himself, who came to Galilee as a messenger of the gospel of God (1:14) and called for faith in this gospel (1:15). From Jesus' gospel, Mark is telling us, the Gospel of Jesus Christ emerged: the message of his life, death, and resurrection.*[1]

*If this is the meaning of the title Mark gave his account, then this account was intended to show Jesus as the prototype (archē) of mission. This is likewise the meaning of Acts 10:36-37. The message, the word, that is to grow through the "acts," the deeds, of the apostles (Acts 6:7, 12:24, 19:20) begins with Jesus. The history of Jesus is the beginning of the history of that word. The Letter to the Hebrews will say it more concisely and more explicitly: Jesus is the Apostle who has given us our profession of faith (Heb. 3:1). He is the Apostle par excellence, the* archēgos, *of our faith, as the letter will say elsewhere (Heb. 12:2). We might translate: founder* (archē) *and guide* (ēgos) *of the proclamation of the gospel.*

*Thus the writings of the New Testament converge to make Jesus the point of departure of Christian mission. But in what way is he this commencement, and what sort of mission does he propose to us by his actions and his words?*

## PRELIMINARY QUESTIONS

From the moment that we begin to speak of Jesus of Nazareth, we touch on a problem that cannot be avoided. Is it possible, through the gospel texts, to reach the Jesus of history and to grasp the image of Jesus the missionary? The problem is not a new one, and we have no intention of addressing it *in globo*. We shall content ourselves here with a sketch of certain reflections on the manner in which the problem presents itself from the viewpoint concerning us.

### PRESUPPOSITIONS OF A READING

First, we must be on our guard against an unconscious process that is generated in the very practice of reading the gospel texts—as indeed in reading any text. The reading of a text is always made through a predetermined grid. One finds only what one seeks. The history of Christian iconography shows that this was particularly true of the gospels. That iconography, like its corresponding biblical reading, saw Jesus as the *Pantokratōr* in the Byzantine style, or as a mystic after the manner of the Neoplatonists, or as a model of the religious life. More recently, he has been the romantic dreamer of the Galilean shores, or a generous master inculcating a nebulous morality of freedom and love. Tolstoy and Gandhi saw Jesus as the hero of nonviolence. Revolutionary Christians find in him the prototype of their subversive practice. No generation, no ideology has failed to recreate Christ in its own image and likeness. True, the fullness of Christ is too rich ever to be exhausted. But this does not give us the right to make Christ into some "god who will be our leader" in the sense of Exodus 32:1, whose only role would be to justify our existing practices. With regard to mission, we must not impose on Jesus our conception and current practices and demand that he correspond to them. Indeed, we shall presently see that the gospel data resist this treatment.

### TENDENCIES OF GOSPEL TRADITION AND REDACTION

An integral study of the missiology of the gospels would take up a detailed analysis of the perspectives proper to each of the evangelists, and then go beyond these perspectives to the sources utilized by the evangelists and the traditions underlying these sources. Only a series of monographs subjecting successive aspects of the text to a detailed examination will adequately perform this task.[2]

These studies would reveal a pluralism of viewpoints, as we shall see below in the case of the accounts of the sending of the Twelve by the Risen One.[3] Similarly in Mark 6:8-9, Jesus sends his disciples forth to mission equipped with a heavy cudgel and a solid pair of shoes, while in the parallel in Matthew 10:10 (cf. Luke 9:3, 10:4) he forbids stick and sandals alike. In the disciples' mission to Galilee, Mark presents a preview of the universal mission undertaken by the Hellenistic churches. One does not set out for Antioch, Corinth, Rome, and the far West without a minimum of good management. This is apostolic common sense. But it is also a different conception of mission from that of the Galilean mission. The latter was of the charismatic itinerant type. Mark's mission is more like the city-based Pauline kind, which did not hesitate to employ means of transportation or to request necessary funds (cf. Phil. 4:10-20, 2 Cor. 11:8-9, Rom. 15:24).[4]

In fact, when we superimpose on the gospel texts the data furnished by Acts and the apostolic letters, we discover a variety of missionary practices and perspectives that could not have failed to influence the manner in which Jesus' own gospel ministry would be understood. Does this fact completely obliterate the actual traits of the historical Jesus of Nazareth? Will it actually be impossible to recover the image of Jesus the evangelist? Scripture scholars have returned to a more balanced appraisal of the value and limitations of historical testimony in this area. We no longer look to ancient historians and gospels for a photographic image of the materiality of the words and deeds they report. But neither do we conclude to the impossibility of historical knowledge.[5] On the particular question of interest to us, we should have to be very presumptuous to reject as null and void the conviction of Mark, and of the churches that developed the traditions of the fourfold gospel, that Jesus was the "beginning of the gospel"; nor, today, would even the most radical criticism blithely attempt to cast doubt on that fundamental datum so important to the three Synoptics: "Jesus appeared in Galilee proclaiming the good news of God" (Mark 1:14; cf. Matt. 4:12,17; Luke 4:14,18; see also John 1:43,51). Let us retain the two points enunciated by these two brief phrases: (1) Jesus presents himself as the messenger of the Good News; and (2) he does so in Galilee. We shall construct our study around these two points.

## MESSENGER OF THE GOOD NEWS

### PRESENTATION OF THE MESSENGER

Jesus appeared in Galilee proclaiming the good news of God: "This is the time of fulfillment. The reign of God is at hand! Reform your lives and believe in the gospel!" (Mark 1:14-15).

This is Mark's "summary" of an entire slice of Jesus' ministry. In it, the evangelist admirably expresses what was new and astounding about Jesus' arrival on the Galilean scene. That novelty is precisely expressed by the phrase, "proclaiming the good news."

Second Isaiah had announced the coming of the one who would proclaim salvation:

> Go up onto a high mountain,
> Zion, herald of glad tidings;
> Cry out at the top of your voice,
> Jerusalem, herald of good news!
> Fear not to cry out
> and say to the cities of Judah:
> Here is your God!
> Here comes with power
> the Lord GOD . . . (Isa. 40:9-10).

In the Greek Bible, "herald of glad tidings" is translated, *"ho euangelizomenos"* — literally, evangelizer. The original Hebrew doubtless meant that Zion (Jerusalem) was called to carry the Good News to the cities of Judah.[6] The transposition made by the Greek version shows that the latter envisaged an individual messenger, the "evangelizer" of eschatological salvation.

So also in Isaiah 61: "The Spirit of the Lord God is upon me; for he has consecrated me with his anointing; he has sent me to bear the Good News to the poor . . . to proclaim liberation to the captives" (Isa. 61:1, Sept.).

Here, even the Hebrew original has an individual messenger. Let us also note the convergence of the themes of the Good News and the Messiah. ("He has consecrated me with his anointing" is equivalent to: "He has made me the Anointed [Messiah].")[7] The evangelizer of eschatological salvation is a "messianic" figure.

And this is the implication of Mark's exordium. In an atmosphere of the eschatological expectancy that had been revived by the preaching of the prophet John, another personage arrives on the scene, whose message is no longer warning, expostulation, or promise, as with the old prophets, but good news, or rather *the* Good News — no longer a preparation for the eschatological coming of God, but precisely the proclamation of that event in progress. In Mark, the suddenness of this manifestation by the evangelist has all the more impact in the absence of a preparatory infancy account. The apparition of the Baptist is described in a few deft strokes. Jesus is presented without any description at all. Nothing is said of his family, his appearance, or his origins, save that he is of Nazareth. Mark's presentation of Jesus recalls the evangelist's intent. There is no describing Jesus. He is wholly and entirely absorbed and subsumed by his role of messenger of the Good News.

In the other synoptic source common to Matthew and Luke, the very form of the Beatitudes suggests the coming of the evangelizer announced in Isaiah 61:1. In proclaiming the poor fortunate or blessed, Jesus assumes the role of the Anointed One, the Messiah sent to proclaim the Good News to the poor.[8] He neither disputes nor tests nor reprimands; he proclaims eschatological joy. Here is a new language, a language corresponding to the new role assigned by God to his Servant and Son.

It is the image of the evangelizer, once more, that Luke presents in the pericope on the inauguration of Jesus' ministry in the synagogue of Nazareth. Coming to the city "where he had been reared" – his native area, then – Jesus pronounces his first discourse, and his theme is that of the evangelizing Messiah of Isaiah 61:1. He reads the text aloud and comments on it, saying, "Today this Scripture passage is fulfilled in your hearing" (Luke 4:18-21; here, v. 21). The redactional element is doubtless more pronounced in Luke than in the synoptic texts of Mark and Matthew, but Luke remains faithful to the fundamental datum of the gospel tradition that sees Jesus fundamentally as the messenger of the Good News in the light of Isaiah 61:1.

### LIFESTYLE OF THE MESSENGER

In the context of Isaiah 61:1, the title of evangelizer is accompanied by that of envoy, of one "sent." ("He has sent me . . . .") Particularly frequent in John, this title is not absent from the synoptic tradition (Matt. 10:40 and par., 15:24, 21:37 and par.; Luke 4:18). Luke 4:43, especially, links the themes of evangelizer and missionary envoy: "To other towns I must *announce the good news* of the reign of God, because that is why *I was sent*" (Luke 4:43).

The parallel in Mark 1:38 suggests a mysterious emergence, or coming forth: "Let us move on to the neighboring villages so that I may proclaim the good news there also. That is what I have come [*exēlthon*, come out, emerged] to do" (Mark 1:38). Our French translations say, "it is for that that I have come forth," (*sorti*). We should be transcending the framework of Mark's christology should we wish to interpret this logion in Johannine fashion and conjure up a trinitarian emergence or issuing of the Son from the bosom of the Father (cf. John 8:42, 13:3, 16:27,28,30, 17:8). But it is perhaps too trivial an explanation of the *Traduction Oecumenique de la Bible* to add, in a note: "Sorti de Capharnau" – " – come forth from Capernaum."

The perspectives are far more immense. Jesus' "emergence" suggests the whole style of his ministry and implies the beginning of the journey upon which he is thrust by the urgency of a proclamation of the gospel. Under the impulse of the Spirit that has consecrated him to proclaim the Good News, Jesus finds it impossible to remain rooted to one spot. He must "move on," like the Word of God that could not but "go forth" from Zion in Isaiah 2:3. Whether or not this logion is from Jesus' own lips, in any event it evokes the memory he has left behind – the image of someone on the move, on the road, the bearer of the Good Tidings, himself carried forward by this Word, "sent," "missioned" by the Spirit as the herald of new times.

Availing themselves of the instrumentality of a more scientific sociological analysis, exegetes have attempted to determine the type of activity performed by Jesus of Nazareth. Was Jesus essentially a carpenter, regularly devoted to his manual task who only occasionally, when so moved by the Spirit, forsook his workbench to go forth to proclaim the Word of God? Or instead, was he one of the sociological type of itinerant charismatics, vagabonds of God, and wonder-workers living on the margins of society, wandering wherever the Spirit might list? Or again, is he not often called master or teacher, so that we ought to picture him in a more formal posture, surrounded by disciples and forming them by word and example? Or he was also regarded as a prophet; but the prophets of the Old Testament readily interfered in political matters; thus, we have been called upon to see Jesus as a religious agitator, a zealot, a subversive.

The debate is not without its value. The truth of the Incarnation will never be a truth apart from sociological realities and schemata. The sociological discussion brings out various aspects of Jesus' message and conduct. But the very variety of the images proposed by the New Testament demonstrates the difficulty of compressing the personality of Jesus into a rigid classification. "You have a greater than Jonah here," he said. Jesus is more than a sociological case.

Regardless of the sociological model we select as our perceptual grid, we must always take account of the unique quality of the eschatological messenger. All of the gospel traditions agree that this is basic. Even if Jesus was a carpenter or an itinerant charismatic, he was an altogether special carpenter or charismatic, as he went about carrying the unique message of the Reign of God. A teacher he surely was. But this teacher was unable to restrict himself to his little group of disciples, surrounded by their attention and respect. He must "emerge," go to the crowd, to the uninitiated, to the poor and the little, even to sinners; thus, he ventured beyond the familiar circles of his personal religious life. He used prophetic accents and did prophetic deeds. He roused hearts, and the Reign he proclaimed unsettled the established order. Indeed it was the death of him. He did so, however, not out of some pessimistic, restless humanism, but out of the serene certitude that God was on his way to establish his Reign. And indeed, amidst the various models that have been proposed for capturing the sociological image of Jesus, we discern a "type" consisting of a single individual: that of messenger of the Good News, who proclaimed the eschatological salvation brought by God and his Reign.

### THE GOSPEL IN DEEDS

We find the prophecy of Isaiah 61:1 recalled in another text, one common to Matthew 11:2-6 and Luke 7:18-23. In response to an inquiry from the imprisoned Baptist, who had sent to ask whether Jesus was really the one to come, Jesus refers the messengers to what they can "see and hear." There they will find the fulfillment of a chain of Isaian prophecies concluding with Isaiah 61:1: glad tidings to be proclaimed to the lowly. In other words, Jesus' activity in behalf of the poor is proof that he is the evangelizer foretold by Isaiah.

Jesus' option for the poor is verified in what his witnesses can "hear," for example, in the Beatitudes proclaimed to the poor, and in Jesus' attitude toward the poor, the blind, the lame, lepers, the impure, sinners, in a word, all of those left out of account by Palestinian society. Jesus proclaims the Good News to the poor not only in words, but in deeds, as well.

Luke draws our attention to the cures and exorcisms that Jesus performs at this moment, because he ascribes a special value to Jesus' miracles as a pragmatic proclamation of the good news of salvation (Luke 7:21). And indeed, Jesus' miracles are the gospel in act. The cures Jesus works are part of God's campaign of liberation from the alienation of disease and death. The exorcisms demonstrate that the Reign of God has arrived (Matt. 12:25-27; Luke 11:17-22; cf. Mark 3:24-27). These deeds of (divine) power (*dunameis*), as the Synoptics call them, constitute more than a simple apologetical confirmation of the validity of the Master's teaching. They are not a mere attempt to prepare people's minds to receive the Good News. They have as much evangelical value as the Sermon on the Mount, the Beatitudes, or the parables. Like symbolic actions of a prophet, the miracles performed on behalf of the lowly of Galilee speak the messianic Good News to the poor.

But in ascribing such great importance to the miracles, Luke narrows his perspective. Matthew, and the original source of the logion, did not envisage miracles alone. The good news that one "sees" is constituted also by the ensemble of Jesus' attitudes. Like the Old Testament prophets, Jesus proclaims his message by symbolic deeds as much as by word. Thus his entry into Jerusalem seated upon an ass and the purification of the Temple, his meals taken with tax collectors and the welcome he offers sinners, have the value of evangelical signs. All of these are statements of the good tidings of God's eschatological intervention in behalf of the poor, just as authentically as any words that may have issued from the Master's mouth.

This basic attitude on Jesus' part was likewise enunciated by the "emergence" that, once again, characterized his evangelical activity. In Jesus, the Word of God had "emerged" from the Temple to journey to Galilee, on the periphery of the Promised Land, there to encounter not sages and scholars, but the weak and the humble (Matt. 11:25; Luke 10:21). What so many prophets and righteous would have wished to see and hear but could not, was now manifested to the marginal population of far-off Galilee (Matt. 13:16-17; Luke 10:23-24).

Here we can only underscore the subversive aspect of the "emergence" inherent in Jesus' evangelical practice. As we hear in Jesus' response to the envoys of the Baptist, this sort of gospel is a "stumbling block" (Matt. 11:6, Luke 7:23). The Good News of a Reign of God in behalf of the poor is tantamount to a reversal of the scale of values of Palestinian theocratic society. As Fernando Belo has shown in a book that, while at times annoyingly dogmatic, is nonetheless often enlightening, Jesus overthrew all of the codes that channeled the currents of thought and life of the society of his time.[9] He overturned the geographical code in situating the center of gravity of his activity not in Judea but in Galilee, not at the Temple or in the synagogues but in fishing boats or town streets. He shattered the religious code by causing the divine activity to appear not in the framework of sacrifices and festivals, but in the misery and the life of the poor. He upset the social code when he chose sinners, the common people (*àm háaretz*, the people of the earth, in the contemptuous parlance of the rabbis of the time) instead of the religious elite. In other words, Jesus' evangelical practice, like his words, proposed a total "conversion," an absolute reversal of the scale of values of contemporary society.

This was why Jesus had to die. His death, too, had the value of gospel, of good news. Jesus' silence before his accusers proclaims the superiority of the divine might over earthly sovereignties. His courage testifies to the freedom of the Son of God in the face of all oppressions. His life tells of the triumph of life when one is prepared to lose all in the unstinting gift of the Servant (Mark 8:35-38 and par., 10:43-45 and par.). What Paul called the "message of the cross" (1 Cor. 1:18) was the most electrifying constituent of the proclamation of the Good News. The cross was the ultimate parable of the call and impact of the gospel.

## IN GALILEE: A LIMITED MISSION FIELD

However, Jesus' activity as the eschatological messenger of the Good News was performed in a very limited field. The same texts that suggest the "pressure" of the Spirit thrusting Jesus to "emerge" and proclaim the gospel, at once fall back into more humble perspectives. "Jesus appeared in Galilee" (Mark 1:14). Galilee was the obscure border province that had played no role in the history of Israel since the time of Isaiah (8:23-9:1). Nor, at least according to the Synoptics, will he leave it before the last days of his life.

In Matthew the contrast is particularly striking. The account of the temptation in the desert had led Jesus up the cosmic mountain, where he beheld all the kingdoms of the earth (Matt. 4:8), to triumph over Satan there — Satan the Master of the universe. Jesus' triumph in the desert over the empire of evil anticipated the universal power "given to me both in heaven and on earth," given to the Risen Lord (Matt. 28:18). The inauguration and the conclusion of Jesus' ministry form a powerful "inclusion," then, providing the activity of the Christ with a universal framework. But the actual ministry thus gloriously framed is much less impressive. Immediately after its lofty exordium, the account subsides, the scene retracts: "Jesus withdrew into Galilee" (Matt. 4:12). The contrast between our introduction to Jesus in terms of a cosmic, universal reference and the limited theater of his activities borders on the comical.

Mark establishes an analogous contrast, if in a different manner. We have already noted the missionary tone the second evangelist gives his account, with his solemn declaration, by way of a foreword (Mark 1:38-39), that Jesus is impelled to "go elsewhere," to "depart"—terms calculated to suggest a missionary dynamism. But then this dynamism appears to be brought up short. The grand departure ends so drably: "Let us go elsewhere . . . to the neighboring towns." The Greek word here (kōmopoleis: cities of the countryside) conjures up the lowly horizon of the little country towns where Jesus' activity is to be confined. What can be the meaning of this contrast between a mission of cosmic dimensions and an activity so narrowly circumscribed?

## THEOLOGICAL FRAMEWORK OF JESUS' MINISTRY: THE JOURNEYS

Mark has sought to erase the contrast by portraying a ministry of more sweeping proportions. At the beginning of his ministry, and in contrast with Matthew's account, Mark's Jesus does not "withdraw" into Galilee, he "goes" there (Mark 1:14), to inaugurate his evangelical campaign (1:15-16). From Capernaum he will move out to "neighboring towns," he will "go elsewhere," in a movement of emergence, of "departure" (1:38-39). In Mark 5, Jesus is in Decapolis, hence in pagan territory, as we may deduce from the presence of a herd of swine (5:1-20). A short while later he is in the territory of Tyre (7:24), where he performs a miracle in favor of a pagan (7:26) by exorcising a young Lebanese. Thereupon chapter 7 describes a broad, sweeping route "from Tyre via Sidon toward the Sea of Galilee, across the territory of the Decapolis" (7:31), where Jesus will once more perform a miracle (7:33-35).

It would be difficult indeed to map the complicated itinerary that could have taken Jesus from Tyre to the Sea of Galilee by way of Sidon and Decapolis. Maps that attempt to chart Jesus' journeys can do so only by tracing broad, very improbable spirals. One sees no reason why Jesus would have made such a detour. The gospel tradition records no evangelical discourse over the course of it. Such a trajectory is all the more curious in view of the fact that Jesus did not intend to extend his ministry to non-Jews (Mark 7:27) and wished to remain incognito (7:24).[10] Some commentators have therefore concluded that this journey through pagan territory is an invention of Mark's, and that Jesus never actually set foot on pagan soil.[11] Doubtless this is an exaggeration. Jesus would certainly not have had to go very far to have left the confines of Israel. Syro-Phoenicia was very close to Galilee. It extended as far south as the approaches of Maritime

Caesarea, along the bay of Akko and Carmel. The Syro-Phoenician frontier passed within a very few miles of one of the possible sites of Cana. Jesus could have crossed this border, then, without making a "journey," still less a "missionary journey." If we accept the data furnished by the text, he did so not to propagate the faith but to conceal himself for a time, until the excitement that he had aroused should die down (cf. Mark 7:24,36).

This is again the case with the journey to the "villages around Caesarea Philippi" (Mark 8:27). A visitor to the romantic site of the sources of the Jordan, which issue from a grotto in ancient Banyas, will perhaps spontaneously attempt to imagine Jesus' reaction to this site of natural beauty peopled with devotees of the god Pan. But the gospel text does not say precisely that Jesus went to Caesarea. It speaks only of the "neighborhood of Caesarea" (Matt. 16:13), or again, perhaps more precisely, the "villages around" Caesarea Philippi (8:27)—villages belonging to the administrative region of that city. It is not in Caesarea, then, but on the road to Caesarea, that Peter makes his profession. Here once more, under close scrutiny, Jesus' long journey abroad slips from the exegete's fingers.

The conclusion, then, would be that, on occasion, whether toward Decapolis to the east, Syro-Phoenicia to the west, or the upper Jordan to the north, Jesus occasionally did forsake the confines of Herod's kingdom. His attitude toward the Holy Land was the same as toward the Temple: he respected each, but he was not their slave. He was free, and when need be, did not hesitate to transgress traditional boundaries. On the other hand, these trips into foreign territory were never very extensive. Mark singles out a few sojourns across the border and promotes them to "journeys," presenting a somewhat Paulinized image of Jesus' ministry. Written in an ecclesial context of commitment to a mission to the nations, the Second Gospel sees Jesus' activity through the lens precisely of this kind of itinerant mission. But the rare citations of Jesus' actual journeys float about in the framework of a mission to the pagans that is really too large for them.

*Luke*, as well, has projected the journey theme onto Jesus' ministry, and does so to the point that it actually becomes the guiding thread of his composition. From 4:14 to 9:50 Jesus is in Galilee. From 9:51 to 19:28—ten chapters—he is en route to Jerusalem. Jesus' journey to Jerusalem, which forms the background of his ministry in Luke, is rich in meaning.[12] One aspect of this meaning is the itinerant accent it lends to the Master's work. We might even wonder whether, in the general parallel established by Luke between his gospel and Acts, Jesus' journey in the second part of the gospel is perhaps the counterpart of Peter's journey to Caesarea (Acts 10:1-11:18), and, even more so, of Paul's journey to Rome and "the ends of the earth" (cf. Acts 1:8). The parallelism is even more striking in light of the fact that, as with Jesus, the voyages of Peter and of Paul culminate in the "passion" of an arrest and imprisonment (Acts 12:21-28).

Samaria plays an important role in the framework of this "journey." Luke is the only one of the Synoptics to mention this sojourn in Samaria

(Luke 9:52, 17:11) or to assign any role to the Samaritans (10:33, 17:16). The meaning he bestows on Samaria and the Samaritans is revealed by the outline of Acts sketched in Acts 1:8 and by the Samaritan section of Acts (Acts chaps. 7-8, 9:31). Samaria serves as a transition between Judea and the nations. Jesus' sojourn in Samaria anticipates and represents the emergence of the young church from an authentic Jewish milieu, thus constituting a stepping-stone to the "ends of the earth" and a sign of universalism.

John will assign Jesus' Samaritan sojourn an analogous signification, making the faith of the Samaritans a sign that Jesus is truly the "Savior of the world" (John 4:42).

For Matthew, the symbol of universalism was "heathen Galilee" (Matt. 4:15), an expression borrowed from Isaiah 8:23, which recalled how long the north of the country, after the Assyrian invasions, had remained pagan before being reconverted at swordpoint by Aristobulus in 104 B.C. "Heathen Galilee," of course, was a very pejorative expression. After the reconquest by Aristobulus, Galilee had been repopulated by Judaean colonists from the south and would distinguish itself by its intense religious life, eventually to become a celebrated center of rabbinical studies.[13] But Matthew must find symbolic support for his universalistic theme. The symbolic values he attributes to Samaria or Galilee are instructive. While the gospel tradition had known missionary journeys of Jesus into pagan territory, these would not have interpreted trips to Galilee or Samaria as symbol of universalism. It would have been enough simply to underscore Jesus' apostolate among the Gentiles.

These reconstructions of Jesus' ministry in the form of "journeys" are interesting. They are based on a few actual trips by Jesus into non-Jewish territory, and they have the merit of setting in relief the missionary thrust implied by a proclamation of the Good News. Through the Resurrection and under the impulse of the Spirit, the gospel proclamation must reach all nations, and the evangelists, enlightened by the experience of their churches, and in a very correct view of faith, were at pains to trace this missionary dynamism back to the activity of Jesus himself.

Nevertheless, the fact remains that this missionary thrust was largely only implicit in the ministry of Jesus the Galilean. The inconsistency between the theological framework of the gospel accounts and the concrete historical data they contain is revealing. It shows what the Hellenistic and Judaeo-Hellenistic missionary churches looked for in the Master's example. They naturally tended to find in Jesus the beginnings of the options and stategies of which Paul would give a clearer example. However, they were too faithful to received tradition simply to invent a story out of whole cloth. Jesus was not Paul; the facts were ill suited to the reconstruction to which the understanding of the missionary churches tended. In its way, this inconsistency is a guarantee of the historical authenticity of the accounts. The primitive churches did not write the gospels simply to suit their fancy. The gospels have sufficiently shown that Jesus the Galilean preached in a limited geographical area. We therefore pose the question of the *meaning* of this anomalous small-scale geographical backdrop.

## GEOGRAPHICAL SETTING OF JESUS' MINISTRY: GALILEE

The geographical framework of Galilee is a very limited one. To see this little territory on the map, one would be tempted to say that Jesus' ministry was itself very limited. As a field of missionary activity, Galilee is incomparably less impressive than the Mediterranean world where St. Paul would develop his own ministry.

The Galilean kingdom of Herod Antipas did not even reach the Mediterranean on the west, and on the east it ended on the eastern shore of the Sea of Tiberias (the Sea of Galilee). Thus it stretched a scant twenty-five miles from east to west, and a mere thirty from Nain in the South to the heights of Safed in the North. Within this district, Jesus' ministry was largely confined to a squat little "evangelical triangle" with a four-mile base and a two-mile height, circumscribed by Tabgha on the western bank of the lake, Bethsaida on the east, and Chorazin to the north. Its center was Capernaum, a "modest village," having "neither theater nor baths," with houses built of untrimmed basalt stone and roofed with coated branchery.[14]

The two cities of the lake shore were actually Taricheae and Tiberias. According to Josephus, Taricheae numbered 40,000 inhabitants, and counted 230 fishing boats. It is mentioned only indirectly in the gospels — under its Aramaic name, Magdala, as the city of a certain Mary, one of Jesus' disciples.[15] Tiberias, for its part, was a new city, recently built (A.D. 17-22) by Herod. When Jesus came into the towns to the north of the lake, Tiberias, a few kilometers to the south, was a beehive of activity. It was the residence of the king and his court, and its elaborate spas were frequented by the high society of the Syrian world. True, as Herod's city, Tiberias was avoided by religious Jews, who swore it had been built on a cemetery. But Jesus, as we know, was uninhibited by ritual scruples, and had he wished to meet the crowds and go to the pagans, he could find them in Tiberias, just a walk away. In fact, however, Tiberias is mentioned only three times in the gospels, and then only by way of a geographical reference (John 6:1,23, 21:1). Jesus never visited the city.

Nor shall we see Jesus at Sephoris, the administrative capital of Galilee, a short distance to the northwest of Nazareth. From his childhood village Jesus would have been able to see this neighboring city and may well have had dealings with it as a woodworker.[16] The other Galilean villages of any importance were Jotapata and Gischala, two fortified towns which would make their name as strongholds of the Galilean resistance at the time of the A.D. 66 revolt against the Romans. But these names are unknown to the gospels, just as is Ptolemais (Akko, Saint John of Acre), the Mediterranean port that was, for that matter, beyond the confines of Herod's Galilean kingdom. These cities are known to us especially through Josephus, and from his historical and political viewpoint. But one has the impression that Jesus avoided these cities. It has been justly observed that, to compare the places mentioned in the gospels with the ones Josephus mentions, one might as well be looking at two almost entirely different maps.[17] Jesus' world is the world of Capernaum, Bethsaida, Nazareth, and Cana, the homes of humble people. The people he met were the fisher from the lake shore, the small artisan, the farmer, or at the outside, the tax collector who exploited them. Jesus was a stranger to the world of the royal court and politics which Josephus was to frequent, the world of business that wove its webs at Sephoris, Ptolemais, Tiberias, or Maritime Caesarea. Jesus' attitude contrasts with that of Paul, with his carefully planned strategy of attack on the great urban centers of the Greek world: Antioch, Iconium, Thessalonica, Athens, Corinth, Ephesus, Colossus, Rome, and more. Paul is like a missionary Alexander the Great. Jesus is but the carpenter of Nazareth, a person of the little towns of the lake shore.

Let us summarize these missionary "journeys" of Jesus:

1. Jesus did travel to proclaim the gospel: for this purpose he adopted to a certain extent the style of the itinerant charismatic preacher.

2. But he limited his ministry almost entirely to Galilee. He was known to have broached the confines of Samaria, according to Luke and John, and, especially according to John, exercised a Judean ministry in Jerusalem and its environs. But he addressed the bulk of his ministry to that part of Galilee that surrounded the lake.

3. While still within the orbit of the Jewish world, the Galilean ministry represented, vis-à-vis that world, a frontier ministry. Even if Matthew forces things a bit with his "heathen Galilee," the fact remains that Galilee was not the seat of the Temple, the priesthood, the Sanhedrin, or the Davidic expectations. A Galilean activity was all the more peripheral in that it touched especially the humble folk, the common people, the àm háaretz, the "people of the land," this "lot, that knows nothing about the law" (John 7:49). By proclaiming his gospel in Galilee and to those who lived on the margins of Judaism, Jesus was turning his back on the focus of the life and the expectancies of official Judaism. As Mark 1:38 puts it, Jesus said he must "move on." But his moving on was more sociological and religious than geographical.

4. In particular, Jesus undertook no systematic campaign in foreign territory. He did not completely exclude non-Jews, however, and when they presented themselves, he was willing to acknowledge the divine sign constituted by their faith. The initiative came not from him, however, but from the One who had placed this faith in their hearts.

Thus, Jesus cannot be presented as a model of the missionary to the nations. It would scarcely be unrealistic to say that, when it came to apostolic boldness and the breadth of territory, Jesus was inferior to Paul as a missionary. The outrageous character of such an assertion demonstrates by its very absurdity that the problem must be seen from another perspective.

The notion that Jesus was a kind of a small-scale Paul cannot represent the final state of affairs. Paul himself would have been afflicted—or infuriated—to hear of such a thing. How, then, are we to interpret this arresting circumstance?

## A PARTICULARISTIC DISCOURSE?

Jesus' words correspond to his practice. A universal mission is mentioned only twice in his words—in a parenthetical remark in the eschatological discourse ("But the good news must first be proclaimed to all the Gentiles," Mark 13:10; = Matt. 24:14), and in Jesus' response on the occasion of the anointing at Bethany ("Wherever the good news is proclaimed throughout the world, what she has done will be told in her memory," Mark 14:9; = Matt. 26:13). These two texts are redacted in identical fashion. Furthermore, they are not found in the parallel text in Luke, to whom, nevertheless, such universalistic declarations would surely have been of great interest (Luke 21:13; cf. 7:40-50). And finally, in Mark 13:10, especially, the parenthetical remark fails to fit the context. For these reasons, the commentators see an addition by Mark to his source.[18] Adolf von Harnack's remark, then, is still valid: the command of universal mission was placed by the church on the lips of the Risen One, and not in the mouth of the prophet of Nazareth.[19]

In just the opposite direction, we have Jesus' stern warning against the proselytism of the Pharisees, who "travel over sea and land to make a single convert, but once he is converted . . . make a devil of him twice as wicked as [them]selves" (Matt. 23:15). We must not attempt to extract too much from this logion, however. It must be situated in its context of a diatribe invested with a certain amount of rhetoric. Furthermore, as the point of the text is found at the end of the text, a sound literary analysis will reveal that Jesus is focusing not so much on the energy devoted to making a disciple, as on the final outcome, the making of that disciple into a "devil."[20] What is condemned is the kind of proselytism that would create adepts without eliciting their conversion. This being said, the fact remains that Jesus does not make common cause with those who cross oceans. We wager that Paul would not have expressed himself in this manner.

But other texts seem squarely to reject a mission to the pagans, at least during Jesus' lifetime. In Matthew 15:24 Jesus states expressly: "My mission is only to the lost sheep of the house of Israel." In Matthew 10:5-6, in the missionary discourse, Jesus enjoins the same on his disciples: "Do not visit pagan territory and do not enter a Samaritan town. Go instead after the lost sheep of the house of Israel." The former text defines Jesus' own attitude; the latter imposes that attitude on his disciples. These texts are to be found only in Matthew; they are absent from the parallels of Mark 6:7-9 and Luke 9:2-5. They may be a creation of the Judaeo-Christianity of Matthean churches less open to the mission to the pagans than was Hellenistic Christianity.[21] On the other hand, as Joachim Jeremias observes, it is doubtful that such a shocking statement would have been invented by a church "that, with the pre-Pauline era, had begun a missionary activity among the pagans (Acts 11:20ff.)"[22] and whose gospel concluded with the dispatch to "all the nations" (Matt 28:19).[23]

In any hypothesis, the restrictions of Matthew 10:5-6 and 15:24 surely correspond to Jesus' own practice. Even if they are to be attributed to a Judaeo-Christianity, being the expression of a scant enthusiasm on the part of the Palestinian churches for the mission to the pagans, the limitation is only an extension of Jesus' own attitude. Not that Jesus rejected the pagans. He admired their faith and worked an occasional miracle on their behalf. But he did not do so on his own initiative. He submitted to the evidence of this faith when it was forced upon him; but he did not of his own accord propose the gospel abroad. His evangelical campaign plan did not extend to "pagan territory." He addressed only the lost sheep of the house of Israel.

The same restriction is found in another passage of the missionary discourse, in Matthew 10:23: "You will not have covered the towns of Israel before the Son of Man comes."[24] No missionary injunctions are in question here, and there can be no suspicion that this text reflects Judaeo-Christian prescriptions. For that matter, the logion is too arresting to have easily been the creation of a postpaschal church. The horizon it implies continues to be limited to Israel. It is the same Israelite backdrop as suggested by the very number of the Twelve, recalling the twelve tribes and twelve patriarchs.

The horizon of Jesus' prepaschal mission, then, is still like the one we have seen to be that of the Old Testament. For the gospel tradition, Jesus' ministry remains centered on Israel. Jesus has come to gather the lost sheep of the house of Israel. Non-Israelites are not excluded, but they have no priority. The outlook is a prolongation of the Old Testament perspective: Israel's central position, and the prioritization of the formation of a people. We see how mistaken it would be to attempt to erect a contrast between a "Christian" attitude of outreach to the nations with a "Jewish" attitude of leading those nations to Israel. In this scenario, Jesus would have made a poor Christian! The beginning of the gospel, as Mark terms it — the foundational act of Christian mission — was in complete harmony with the attitude of Judaism. It is not on this point that the old and the new economies are to be distinguished.

## ESCHATOLOGICAL GATHERING OF THE PEOPLES

Are we to say, then, that Jesus has failed to transcend the particularism of the Old Law? And must we see in Paul, rather than in Jesus, the real founder of Christian mission?

But we have already noted that Israel's consciousness of its election did not entail a "particularism." So too will it have been for Jesus. While he envisaged his ministry only within the restricted framework of his people, he did not, for all that, exclude the nations. On the contrary, a number of Jesus' declarations in the gospels very explicitly suggest the final assemblage of the peoples.

From the outset of his ministry—at least according to Luke, in the discourse at Nazareth—Jesus is perfectly clear: Elijah, sent to the pagan widow of Zarephath, and Elisha, sent to the Syrian Naaman, prefigure the salvation that, rejected by Israel, will be welcomed by the nations (Luke 4:25-27). True, this text is proper to the Third Gospel: Luke has reworked the material he has found in Mark 6:1-6 in his own fashion, so as to be able to place at the exordium of his work the great universalistic themes that will dominate that work. Jesus' programmatic discourse in Luke 4 bears a very close resemblance to Paul's epilogal discourse in Acts 28:25-28, and the aim of the latter composition was doubtless to link Jesus' time and the time of the church in one and the same perspective.

But this Lucan text is not isolated. A number of logia cite the eschatological gathering of the peoples.

### GATHERING OF THE PEOPLES FOR JUDGMENT

The notion of "gathering" is important in biblical theology. For example, we read:

> At the judgment, the citizens of Nineveh will rise with the present generation and be the ones to condemn it. At the preaching of Jonah they reformed their lives; but you have a greater than Jonah here. At the judgment, the queen of the South will rise with the present generation and be the one to condemn it. She came from the farthest corner of the earth to listen to the wisdom of Solomon; but you have a greater than Solomon here (Matt. 12:41-42).

In the parallel text of Luke 11:31-32, only two differences appear: Luke reverses the order of the verses, and, in the second verse here, replaces "this generation" with "the men of this generation." These are minor differences. The solidity of the tradition suggests a very old logion that had made a strong impression. It is prophetical invective in the authentic style. It reproaches Israel for its hardened heart. It likewise represents the Old Testament theme of the universality of sin and judgment. The Book of Jonah had illustrated this universalistic theme.[25] Indeed, our logion refers explicitly to that book. But here the judgment is eschatological: it is on the day of judgment that the nations will gather with Israel at the grand assizes of the universe, there to rise as witnesses for the prosecution.

Matthew 25:32 describes the same eschatological tribunal at which "all the nations will be assembled." Here, the separation between the sheep and the goats will be effected not in terms of ethnicity, but on the criterion of charity toward the "least."

We find this same perspective of universal judgment in the mission discourse: "I assure you, it will go easier for the region of Sodom and Gomorrah on the day of judgment than it will for that town" (Matt. 10:15; cf. Luke 10:12).

The same words are found in Matthew 11:24, where they have been preceded, in verse 22, by an identical declaration apropos of Tyre and Sidon (cf. Luke 10:14). Doubtless we are dealing with a free-floating logion which could be employed in various contexts. It reversed the classic oracles of the prophetic tradition against Tyre and Sidon (Isa. 23:1-18; Ezek. 26-28; Joel 4:4-8; Amos 1:9-10; Zech. 9:1-4). Even those paragons of iniquity, Sodom and Gomorrah (Gen. chaps. 18-19; Isa. 1:9, 3:9, 13:19; Jer. 23:14, 49:18, 50:40; Lam. 4:6; Zeph. 2:9; Ezek. 16:48-56) deserve as much, and more, of the divine mercy than does Israel.

## UNIVERSAL INVITATION TO THE BANQUET

The same eschatological universalism appears, in more engaging fashion, in the image of the banquet. In Matthew 8, seeing the faith of the centurion, Jesus conjures up the vision of the eschatological feast, to which all women and men would be called:

Mark what I say! Many will come from the east and the west and will find a place at the banquet in the kingdom of God with Abraham, Isaac, and Jacob, while the natural heirs of the kingdom will be driven out into the dark (Matt. 8:11-12).[26]

By inserting this logion in the context of the episode of the centurion, and attaching it to Jesus' cry of admiration for the faith of this pagan, Matthew underscores the importance of faith:

Thanks to the logion, . . . the story of the centurion ceases to be the account of an exceptional case. . . . This pagan becomes the prototype of "many" another pagan who will sit at the banquet of salvation. . . . The episode thus acquires a general sense that would explain the situation before which Christians found themselves at the close of the apostolic age.[27]

In Luke, the logion is inserted "in a series of disparate fragments relating more or less to the theme of the requirements to fulfill in order to be saved" (Luke 13:22-30).[28] Thus the logion becomes a threat against perpetrators of injustice (cf. v. 27).

With Matthew and Luke interpreting the logion along the lines of their respective theologies, we find, transcending their redaction, a level of the text in which it represents first of all a warning to presumptuous Jews (as in Luke 14:16-24 and Matt. 22:2-10), and at the same time, in counterpoint, a promise to other beneficiaries, to pagans who will come from everywhere.

> [This message is] not actually basically new. It simply confirms what was accepted among the Jews regarding the eschatological assembly of the nations. At the very most, we may observe that it is no longer Jerusalem, or Mount Zion, that is presented as the goal of the pilgrimage of the pagan peoples, but the Reign of God: thus, the Holy City seems no longer to constitute the center of the new world.[29]

This level of meaning, underlying the redactions of Matthew and Luke, fits in well with what the evangelists tell us of Jesus' missionary practice.

> Its well-founded authenticity allows us to form a correct idea of the manner in which, in the course of his public ministry, Jesus spoke to his Jewish audiences of the salvation of the pagans.[30]

He proclaimed the incorporation of the pagans "as an eschatological act of the power of God—the last great revelation of God's grace."[31]

### OTHER UNIVERSALISTIC THEMES

This same eschatological universalism is suggested by other themes in the gospels. The *Son of Man* incarnates the call addressed to "nations and peoples of every language" (Dan. 7:14). The *Son of David* is called to rule over even the most hostile of peoples (Ps. 110:2). The *Servant* will be the light of nations (Isa. 49:6). Jesus will demonstrate the meaning of these titles in his entry into Jerusalem, in the figure, foretold by Zechariah, of a "king . . . a just savior . . . meek, and riding on an ass, on a colt, the foal of an ass . . . and he shall proclaim peace to the nations" (Zech. 9:9-10).[32]

Jesus' last sign of the universalism of his mission is that of his blood "poured out in behalf of many" (Matt 26:28; Mark 14:24). The reference to "many" is not found in 1 Corinthians 11:25 and Luke 22:20. This omission is curious on the part of Luke and Paul, the two most explicitly universalistic authors of the New Testament. If the case had been just the reverse—with the word "many" present in Luke and Paul, and absent from Matthew and Mark—we might have suspected its interpolation in function of the demands of the theology of the former pair. No such surmise is possible with Matthew and Mark. The word "many," *polloi*, is a Semitism translating *rabbim*, the "many" whom the Suffering Servant was to rescue:

> Through his suffering, my servant shall justify many,
> and their guilt he shall bear. . . .
> Because he surrendered himself to death . . .

And he shall take away the sins of many,
and win pardon for their offenses (Isa. 53:11-12).

In the context of both the Servant poems and the life of Jesus, sinners in need of forgiveness are first of all the Israelites. But the astonishment occasioned by his expiatory death is shared by "many nations," as well (Isa. 52:15).

> The formula, "for many," is an open one. While it speaks in the first place of Israel, . . . to whom the gift of reconciliation is offered . . . by Jesus' death, it does not thereby exclude the multitude of the peoples of the world of which Matt. 8:11 speaks.[33]

According to the gospel tradition, then, Jesus' universalism, like that of the Old Testament, is eschatological and is centered on Israel. On this point, Jesus' discourse and practice alike are situated quite in the line of the Old Testament prophets.

## THE GATHERING BEGINS

However, Jesus' ministry presents a new element, and one of capital importance. The pressing tone of the appeals he addresses to human beings indicates a messianic urgency. Eschatology is no longer relegated to a distant consummation of the world and described in more or less mythical fashion. Suddenly the hour is at hand. It is to this important specificity of Christian eschatology that we now turn our attention.

With Jesus, a realized eschatology commences. The Reign of God is at hand (Mark 1:15). We pray for its coming (Matt. 6:10); at the same time, faith perceives it already at work, in signs, like the miracles (Matt. 11:4-5), the exorcisms (Matt. 12:25-28), the choosing of the Twelve (Matt 10:1-7), or the proclamation of the Good News to the poor (Matt. 5:3-11; Luke 6:20-22). Though it is still in seed, the seed has now been sown, and the promise of the harvest is sure (Mark 4:3-8 and par., 4:26-29). Already "the fields are shining for harvest!" (John 4:35). The laborers have now been summoned, and Jesus himself sets about gathering the firstfruits of the nations.

### HARVEST AND LABORERS

It is in a context of this theme of the harvest that we must understand Jesus' declaration concerning the laborers: "The harvest is good but laborers are scarce. Beg the harvest master to send out laborers to gather his harvest" (Matt. 9:37-38).

This statement, cited as a prologue to the mission discourse, contains a wealth of meaning. It is cited in exactly the same terms in Luke 10:2. This perfect parallelism indicates an important logion, one so striking that it had marked the collective memory of the primitive church. It even has its correspondent in the Johannine tradition (John 4:35-38).[34] Its semitic, parabolic style is altogether in Jesus' manner. The originality of its thought is also a gauge of its authenticity: an Old Testament theme is taken up, but the outlook is reversed—continuity and breach, in Jesus' typical style.

The image of the harvest, both in the Bible (Amos 8:2; Isa. 27:12; Jer. 51:2,33; Joel 4:13-14) and in the intertestamentary literature (2 Baruch 70:2-71; 4 Ezra 4:28-39, 9:17,31-37), is frequently employed to evoke the gathering of the peoples in the context of a scenario of the last judgment. In these texts, the harvest theme presents three characteristics, which Jesus will modify:

1. The harvest is eschatological: in Amos 8:2, "ripe fruit" signifies the end of days.

2. It is a harvest of judgment and slaughter:

> Apply the sickle,
>    for the harvest is ripe;
> Come and tread,
>    for the wine press is full . . .
>    great is their malice.
> Crowd upon crowd
>    in the valley of decision . . . (Joel 4:13-14).

3. Especially in the intertestamentary era, the harvest is entrusted to angels—another way of expressing its apocalyptic character. The participation of angels in the judgment is a frequent theme of the apocryphal writings, especially the Book of Enoch (1 Enoch 53:1, 54:6, 55:3, 56:1-4, 62:11-12, 63:1, 100:4-5; see also the Assumption of Moses 10:2). Several New Testament texts take up this motif, borrowing the image of the harvest (Matt. 13:39-41, Mark 13:27, Rev. 14:14-16).[35]

The originality and precise meaning of Matthew 9:37-38 appear by contrast:

1. The eschatological harvest is transferred to the present: "The harvest is. . . ."

2. It is a harvest of joy and grace, as is seen throughout the gospels (Matt. 13:8,23,30; John 4:35-38).

3. Because it is transferred from apocalyptic eschatology to the concrete reality of the present, it is entrusted to human beings, to "laborers" (cf. John 4:38; Matt. 20:1, 21:34).

These remarks help us understand the scope of the logion concerning the laborers of the harvest. It is not, as it is so often misinterpreted to be, an invitation to prayer for an abundance of apostolic laborers—for "vocations," as we say. It is a prayer for the coming of the end, to ask God to bring the eschatological harvest to maturity in our own days, to transfer it from the remote apocalyptic future to the present era and the concrete framework of human activity. It echoes another eschatological prayer taught by Jesus to his disciples: "Your kingdom come. . . . Subject us not to the trial but deliver us from the evil one" (Matt. 6:10,13), a prayer to be developed by an anaphora of the early church:

> Remember, O Lord, your Church. Deliver it from all evil, and perfect it in your love. And gather it from the four winds into the Reign that you have prepared for it. . . . May your grace come, and this world pass. . . . Maranatha! (*Didache* 10:5-6)

The prayer in which we are invited to join focuses not on a multiplicity of human laborers, then, but on the fact of the intervention of these laborers. It is a prayer for the immediate commencement of the eschatological harvest of the nations, and this in the concrete framework of human mediations and exchanges. It is a "missionary" prayer, and it reveals Jesus' radical originality vis-à-vis the expectations of Judaism: the harvest of the end time is already ripe and is entering human history; human harvesters, especially Jesus and his disciples with him, are called to associate themselves with it.

We must express an important reservation concerning Joachim Jeremias's exposition of Jesus' eschatological universalism in his enlightening study *Jesus and the Pagans*. The German exegete has propounded Jesus' eschatological universalism in admirable fashion; but we must not forget that it is an eschatology already on the way to realization—already becoming, here and now, a realized eschatology. The eschatological gathering of the nations begins in the very ministry of Jesus.[36]

## JESUS AND THE PAGANS

Jesus himself undertakes to gather the first ripe ears. He himself welcomes representatives of the nations, such as the Canaanite woman, the centurion, and perhaps the possessed man of Gerasa, and bestows on them a participation in the benefits of the Reign.

Let us note that Jesus does not take the initiative. God alone will give the signal for the harvest of the nations; the sign that the harvest is ripe is given in the faith of the pagans. "Woman, you have great faith!" says Jesus to the Canaanite, as if he is taken aback (Matt. 15:28).[37] The key to the Reign is faith and conversion (Mark 1:15)—no longer mere ethnic origin (cf. Matt. 3:8). Where faith appears, the Reign is present. This is the principle in virtue of which Paul, in the Letters to the Galatians and the Romans, can incorporate the uncircumcised into the descendancy of Abraham (Gal. chaps. 3-4). Just as Jesus, following the prophets, perceived a universalism of sin in which Bethsaida and Chorazin sink to the level of Tyre and Sidon, as Capernaum had sunk lower than Sidon (Matt. 11:21-

24), he also foresaw a universality of faith that would gather up all of the erstwhile rejected, whether of Rome, of Syro-Phoenicia, or of Galilee.

This is what we find in the introduction to the Sermon on the Mount:

> His reputation traveled the length of Syria. They carried to him all [the] afflicted. ... The great crowds that followed him came from Galilee, the Ten Cities, Jerusalem and Judea, and from across the Jordan (Matt. 4:24-25).

It is in this context that, ascending the mount, not to withdraw, but to be seated as the new Moses on the new Sinai, Jesus opens his lips to address this mass of humanity, all humanity, and proclaim the joy of the Reign to all the poor of the world. The universality of human distress issues in a universality of faith, or poverty of heart, which in turn calls for a universality of the divine gift. Once more we find the great lines of thought that Paul will develop in the Letter to the Romans:

> We have already brought the charge against Jews and Greeks alike that they are under the domination of sin. ... All men have sinned and are deprived of the glory of God. All men are now undeservedly justified by the gift of God, through the redemption wrought in Christ Jesus. ... By what law, the law of works? Not at all! By the law of faith. ... It is the same God who justifies the circumcised and the uncircumcised on the basis of faith (Rom. 3:9,23-24,27,30).

This is what Paul calls the "justice of God which works through faith in Jesus Christ for all who believe" (Rom 3:22). This, for Paul, is the principle of the universalism of salvation. Confronting his opponents in Galatia, Paul rightly insists that he has invented nothing (Gal. 1:11-12), that this has already been "the gospel of Christ" (Gal. 1:7).

Such indeed had been the principle that had led Jesus to transcend the wall of separation between the nations and the Jews.

## THE GOSPEL: THE POWER OF GOD

A sense of election and a sense of universalism are mutually reinforcing. The dynamics of these twin dimensions of the divine economy in the Old Testament are prolonged in the practice and words of Jesus. It was precisely in his having been sent to the lost sheep of the house of Israel that Jesus was universalistic. But was his universalism not too passive? Did it not consist in simply awaiting the eschatological action of the divine might, on the chance that it might be anticipated in rare cases in which this divine grace would force his hand? Even with Israel, as we have seen, Jesus has no interest in methodically mapping out his terrain and attacking it strategically. Still less does he go running to the diaspora—which, however widely scattered through the world, was also Israel (cf. John 7:35).

It will not be enough to respond that he did not have the time — that his ministry was too brief, of three years' duration at the very most, perhaps only a few months' if we credit the Synoptics. Nowhere do Jesus' words suggest the kind of universal mission that, for example, Paul will expound to the Romans (Rom. 15:19-29). The fact remains that, while his activity is of the briefest, Jesus is the Founder of the Christian faith, and Paul and the peoples after him will acknowledge him as the source of all their apostolic dynamism. "What, then, is the source of this power?" was the question that was asked even during his lifetime (cf. Mark 6:2-3 and par.). Whence this radiancy? After all, it does not emanate from a deliberate effort to convince the peoples of the world, or from a specific strategy of carrying a message to the ends of the earth. What is the meaning of this seeming passivity?

### TO PROCLAIM

The answer can be summed up in a single word — a word that occurs frequently in the gospel tradition, especially in Mark, to describe Jesus' activity. It is the verb *kērussein*, to "announce," to "proclaim."

This Greek word denotes the activity of the *kērux*, the municipal or royal "herald" whose role consisted in communicating information of common interest. Used 33 times in the Old Testament, it is only rarely applied to the preaching of the prophets.[38] A notable exception is to be found precisely in Isaiah:

> The spirit of the Lord GOD is upon me,
>   because the LORD has anointed me;
> He has sent me to bring glad tidings (*euaggelisasthai*)
>   to the lowly. ...
> To proclaim (*kēruxai*) liberty to the captives ...
>                           (Isa. 61:1).[39]

In the New Testament, the verb *kērussein* becomes the standard designation for Jesus' basic activity (9 times in Matthew, 14 in Mark, 9 in Luke). To be sure, the New Testament uses other words to describe the communication of the Christian message, as well: teach, inform, explain, preach, interpret, testify, profess, convince, prophesy, hand on.[40] Some of these terms are used to describe the ministry of Jesus himself. But proclamation constitutes the basic form of Jesus' language: scripture derives his "teaching," his "exhortations" and his "warnings," his "interpretations," from the Good News he proclaims. For example, the invective against the rich in Luke 6:24-26 is only the other side of the coin of the proclamation of the Good News to the poor in the verses immediately preceding. The parables are only a dramatic presentation of this same Good News, with its paradoxes and demands.

The use of the verb *kērussein* is not restricted to descriptions of Jesus' activity. By the time Mark employed it, it had doubtless already become a technical term in the Christian vocabulary. The gospels also apply it to the preaching of the Baptist (Mark 1:4,6); the Twelve are sent forth to proclaim (*kērussein*, Mark 3:14, 6:12); even the leper who was cleansed began to "proclaim the whole matter" (Mark 1:45), as did the demoniac who had been healed (5:20) and the witnesses of a miracle that Jesus had performed (7:36). But they all only anticipate or extend the new style of announcement introduced by Jesus.

> It is easy to notice the unity of all these texts: to proclaim, or, more precisely, to proclaim the Gospel, or the required conversion, characterizes the time of salvation, and signals God's intervention among us, from John the Baptist all the way to the present.[41]

The difference between the oracles or warnings of the Old Testament prophets and the Christian "proclamation" is the novelty of the fulfillment of the kairos or fixed time (Mark 1:14), the novelty of Jesus Christ manifested in the basic structures of language itself.

In contradistinction to the other words used to describe the communication of the Christian message, and cited above, the verb *kērussein* presents the following characteristics:

1. It announces a deed, not a doctrine. A deed is proclaimed; a doctrine is taught. The deed in question will be one performed by another; the "herald," the proclaimer, is a messenger. The role of the herald is to make known the deed of someone other than the herald.

2. The deed in question will have just been performed, or will be just about to be performed. Herein resides the difference between proclamation and prophecy. The latter consists in promises or threats whose accomplishment is at least somewhat afar off and which is uttered primarily in an apocalyptical perspective. The herald's message, by contrast, bears upon the present or upon a future so imminent as to have an immediate influence on the present.

3. Finally, the designation of the activity of the "herald" as one of "proclaiming" implies only minimal personal interference on the part of the herald. This messenger is invested with no original, personal authority. The authority in question originates with the one who has just performed, or is just about to perform, the deed proclaimed. By contrast, "teaching," for example, presupposes an altogether personal investment on the part of the "teacher." Teachers must first fully assimilate the knowledge they are about to communicate and search for an effective way of overcoming the resistance, reticence, and immaturity of their disciples, if they are to hope to be able to transmit their knowledge to them. The very word "evangelize"

implies an ongoing activity of mediation: the key syllable of evangelize will often be the suffix "-ize" — stressing human activity to be performed vis-à-vis the gospel. Thus, for Luke, who is particularly fond of this verb (employing it 10 times in his Gospel, and 16 times in Acts), to "evangelize" is to accomplish the deed of Peter and of Paul, to show generosity, to take initiatives, to accept suffering, and to survive the trials that Acts is so concerned to describe. *Kērussein*, on the other hand, "to proclaim," is only to be a messenger, to disappear behind the message, in self-effacement, and to conceive no other authority or efficacity than those of the act one is reporting and of the accomplisher of this act.

Thus it was with Jesus. The books that report his coming to us are not called Acts of Jesus, but Gospels. For this alone had Jesus come: to report the Good News in the world. The rest was up to God.

## THE GOSPEL

Just so, the expected object of the verb *kērussein* is the noun "gospel." As Luke speaks so often of "evangelizing," Mark prefers the word *euaggelion*, "gospel" (8 times, counting Mark 16:15; 4 times in Matthew; never in Luke).

In the Greek Old Testament, the verb is employed more frequently than the noun, and the noun, in its rare occurrences, has only the profane meaning of good news relating to ordinary life.[42] It will be in the Hellenistic world, particularly in a context of emperor worship, that *euaggelia* will acquire a religious meaning, even denoting the sacrifices offered on the occasion of a military victory.[43]

It is likely enough, then, that Jesus himself preferred the verb to the noun, after the manner of Second Isaiah. But philological considerations do not tell the whole story. Whether or not the noun was used by Jesus, it faithfully reflects his theological "passivity."[44] As a complement to the verb *kērussein*, the word *euaggelion*, as used by Mark (1:14,15, 13:10, 14:9, 16:15), reduces the fact of Christ essentially to the good news of what God has accomplished. "Good News" and "proclaiming" are mutually complementary, and the complementarity is basic for a grasp of the fact that Jesus' fundamental activity consisted precisely in disappearing behind the message he carried. Jesus "evangelized" less than he was himself the gospel, the Good News. The most important thing in Jesus is not to be sought on the level of the human qualities he brought to his task, such as zeal, dynamism, or breadth of view to be placed in the service of the propagation of the gospel. Jesus' power and the secret of his evangelical "effectiveness" was his perfect identification with the message he proclaimed. The Gospel was not only proclaimed by Jesus: that Gospel was transparent to all his work. His miracles, exorcisms, symbolic deeds, the attitude he adopted toward the lowly, the way he mixed with sinners and tax collectors, the company in which he took his meals — all of this transmitted, in terms of concrete life, the Good News of a Reign of God accessible to the poor. His freedom from legalistic taboos and social pressures, the poverty of his lifestyle, his fearlessness in the face of the mighty of this world, the authority with which his words rang and his deeds shone, proclaimed the message of freedom and of victory over all powers, social, economic, political, or cosmic. Jesus announced the Good News not only by what he did and said, but by what he was. As John says (John 1:14), before saying the words of God, Jesus *was* the very Word of God.

## THE SON

This is likewise the meaning of the "Son of God" theme. John dwells on this theme. The Son and the Father are one (John 10:30). Jesus' teaching is not his own, but that of the Father, who has sent him (John 7:16; cf. 3:11-13, 12:44, 14:10), and his words are the words of this Father (3:31-36). His actions are the very actions of God (5:19-20), and his deeds are God's deed (5:17, 10:36-38, 14:10). One who knows Jesus knows the Father (8:19), and one who sees Jesus sees the Father (14:10). As Son of God totally identified with the Father, Jesus is the revealer of God (1:18).

But John is only giving clearer expression to what the Synoptics saw in Jesus. A logion reported by the tradition common to Matthew and Luke had said: "No one knows the Father but the Son—and anyone to whom the Son wishes to reveal him (Matt. 11:27; Luke 10:22). The image of Jesus presented by all the gospels is that of a transparency integral to the work of the Father, a filial identification with the plans, thought, and action of God, in words and deeds, in life and death. The most concrete, and perhaps the most meaningful expression of this filial identity occurs in the account of the Passion, when, in his agony, Jesus accepts the fusion of his will and his outlook on life with the will of the Father, even if this means death: "Let it be as you would have it, not as I" (Mark 14:36; Matt. 26:39). Luke has brought this Fiat of Jesus nearer the formulation of the great filial prayer, the Our Father: "Not my will but yours be done" (Luke 22:42).[45] Jesus has enunciated this prayer and has taught it to his disciples. Now he lives it and incarnates it to the bitter end. On Calvary, Jesus' words become his flesh and blood.

It is especially in death that Jesus manifests this total transparency to the word of God's salvation—a transparency to God's will to give new life through death, a transparency to God's love lived to the very surrender of his life, a transparency to the message proclaiming the great revolution of the Reign and the reversal of every human value, indeed of life itself, in death (Mark 8:34-35), a transparency to the mission of the Servant who has come not to be served but to serve and to give his life as a ransom for the multitude (Mark 10:45). The cross is the supreme parable of all that the gospel has signified. It is of the word of the cross that Paul utters (1 Cor. 1:18)—a word pronounced not in discourse, but in the absolute silence of Calvary. It is this Word that must echo throughout the world—not by dint of verbal eloquence, or by art of communication, nor indeed by virtue of any human zeal or devotion, but through the impact of its authenticity: in its weakness and foolishness, the Word echoed with all wisdom and divine power (1 Cor. 1:18-25).

As Jeremias says at the end of his book, Jesus did not Christianize the world; he died on the cross. It is in reliance on the truth and authenticity of this word of the cross that Paul and his like will traverse the world as universal messengers of the gospel. But it was first necessary for this word to be pronounced in all its purity. And it was necessary that the Word become flesh in a particular life, a message, an activity, an attitude toward life, power, and love, and finally, in a death that would recapitulate all of this and in a resurrection that would place on it all the seal of the divine approval. It is this authenticity of word and this glory of the Verbum (John 1:14), this filial transparency to the plan of the Father that is the foundation of mission.

# 6

# The Risen Christ

*The attitudes of Jesus of Nazareth reflected the same profound tendencies as the Old Testament: an accent on the election of Israel, and the eschatological character of the gathering of the nations. In mission as in so much else, Jesus of Nazareth was altogether "Jesus the Jew." When he proclaimed the novelty of the Good News, this word of God had first to be pronounced in a concrete human condition and among the chosen people. But through this people, the privileges of election were destined for all nations, and boundaries must fall. Christ's Resurrection razed the walls and obliterated borders (cf. Eph. 2:14). In his exaltation, Jesus of Nazareth became Christ the Lord of all.*

*Let us now consider the new scope bestowed on mission by the Resurrection. A certain particularity of the gospels will be our guide in this study: most, if not all, of the gospel accounts of the Resurrection conclude with an apparition of the Lord sending his disciples forth to mission. First we shall present an overview of these accounts of the sending, then we shall examine them more closely, especially those of Matthew and Mark.*

## OVERVIEW

The gospel accounts of the Resurrection present rather disparate narrative elements. All four gospels begin with the account of the empty tomb. Then they report different apparitions — different addressees (one or more women in Matt. 28:9-10; Mark 16:8-11; John 20:11-18; certain disciples in Luke 24:13-35 = Mark 16:12-13; John 20:24-29, 21; the Eleven in Matt. 28:16-20; Mark 16:14-18; Luke 24:36-49; John 20:19-33) and different locales (Jerusalem in Luke 24 and John 20; Galilee in Matthew 28 and John 21; and both places in Mark 16:9-20). However, the accounts converge in a single ending: the sending of the disciples forth on a mission to the world. It is the same with Acts 1:8. In the context of such a broad divergency in the choice of the other apparition accounts, this convergence in a conclusion is all the more striking, and so orderly that the texts in question can be arranged in a synopsis.

## CONVERGENCE

| Matthew 28:19-20 | Mark 16:15 | Luke 24:47-49 | John 20:21-23 |
|---|---|---|---|
| | | | As the Father has sent me, so I send you. |
| Go ... and make disciples of all the nations. | Go into the whole world and proclaim the good news to all creation. ... | Penance for the remission of sins is to be preached to all the nations. ... | If you forgive men's sins they are forgiven them. ... |
| Know that I am with you. ... | | See, I send down upon you the promise of my Father [the Holy Spirit]. | Receive the Holy Spirit. |

### a. Some Observations

Certain observations will clarify the data of this synopsis.

1. The parallel from Mark is taken from the "longer ending" — verses 9-20, whose absence from quite a number of manuscripts poses a problem to which we shall return later in this chapter. In this preliminary overview, however, we shall include these verses, first of all because they exist, and second because their formulation is scarcely foreign to Mark's theology ("proclaim the good news").[1]

2. According to the exegetes, John 21 is a later addition in the Fourth Gospel. Before this material was appended, this gospel had ended with chapter 20, with verses 30-31 constituting the conclusion of the Johannine account. In the original framework of the Gospel, then, the apparition to the disciples in John 20:19-23 is Jesus' last manifestation.[2]

3. As with the synoptic analysis generally, Matthew and Mark on the one side, and John and Luke on the other present more mutual contacts with each other than with either member of the other pair. Still, Luke has the verb "proclaim" in common with Mark, and with Matthew the formula "all the nations," as well as the promise: "Behold ..." ("Know ..." "See ..."). With John he shares the emphasis on forgiveness of sin and the gift of the Spirit. It is not easy to explain such precise similarities in a context of such evidently independent Resurrection accounts.[3] They only indicate a convergence still more worthy of attention.

### b. Significance

This convergence has an evident significance.

1. Christ's missionary mandate does not rest exclusively on the Matthean text that we hear cited so often, and too often in isolation.[4] All four gospels conclude their Resurrection account with a missionary dispatch.

2. Accordingly, in all four gospels, Jesus' Resurrection generates mission. Each gospel, and each in its own fashion, may underscore one or other aspect of the message of the Resurrection; but none found it possible to understand the Resurrection apart from mission. Indeed, this was Paul's viewpoint, as well (1 Cor. 9:1, 15:6-11; 2 Cor. 4:6-13; Gal. 1:15-16).

We know Rudolf Bultmann's dictum: Christ was raised in the kerygma of the church. This is not necessarily to deny the Resurrection. It can be understood as a vigorous assertion of the manner in which the Resurrection was perceived.

> Bultmann's formula can be retained: "Jesus was raised in the kerygma." It must not, however, be understood in an exclusive sense. Jesus' resurrection as such escapes history in the common meaning of the term: it has entered history not only by apparition, but by the preaching of the apostles, and faith in their word: "The risen one, in his apparitions, seizes upon the word of those who see him and whom he sends to proclaim this word." And it is in this word that he is manifested as Christ raised and glorified. The propagation of the gospel, striven for in the certitude of having received a mission, and the acceptance of the gospel understood as birth to a renewed life, are, on an equal basis with the apparitions, signs of Jesus' irruption after his death into history and human experience.[5]

3. Conversely, mission is unintelligible apart from the Resurrection. It is the expression of its impact—the actualization of the universal power imparted to the Risen One (Matthew), the implementation of the energy of the Spirit emanating from this Resurrection (Luke and John). One of the points emerging from our study thus far is that the mission to the nations would not simply have constituted an a priori evidence. Neither the perspectives of the Old Testament nor the practice and words of Jesus make it obvious that one must go out to the peoples of the world to lead them to faith and the worship of the one true God. If there was in fact an apostolic mission, then something else must have happened, something that had opened up new horizons. The four gospels and Paul all agree that it was the Resurrection, with Luke and John adding the gift of the Spirit consequent upon the Resurrection.

Even if none of the synoptic texts had come down to us, the missionary practice of the earliest times of the church could not be explained apart from a like command on the part of the Lord.[6]

To be sure, the disciples did not set out for mission Easter evening. A series of events and human factors would have to intervene to specify the import of the paschal message. But the missionary consciousness of the primitive church traced its origin to this experience of the Resurrection as the triumph of the word proclaimed by Jesus of Nazareth. Later, with mission already under way, the various gospel traditions will agree that the point of departure of this missionary thrust was the encounter with the Risen One.

4. Even the restrictive texts of Matthew 10:6 and 15:24, which we examined in the preceding chapter, must be understood in this context. It is possible that they were preserved by a Judaeo-Christian tradition that was hostile to the mission to the nations. But the final redaction of Matthew shows that it was universal mission that finally prevailed. The admittance of non-Jews aroused many tensions, sometimes violent ones, and we must not overlook the pluralism of missionary goals in the infant church. But the final concurrence of the evangelists shows that accord ultimately prevailed. Nor must we underestimate the significance of the quest for unity implied in the very formation of, first, the several gospels as we have them today, and finally, the New Testament canon.

### MISSION OF THE DISCIPLES AND JESUS' MISSION

#### a. Parallelism

The accounts of the missionary dispatch of the disciples by the Risen One call for a supplementary observation: in each of the four gospels, the apostolic commission is couched in terms of Jesus' own ministry.

1. In Matthew the apparition of the Risen One takes place in Galilee (Matt. 28:16), the starting point of Jesus' ministry (Matt. 4:12-16).There, on "the mountain," where he had always communicated any important message (Matt. 5:1, 14:23, 17:1), Jesus cites the "authority" that he has received, a power that has already characterized his preaching (7:29), his miracles (9:6,8), and all his activity (11:27). The envoys will be "disciples," therefore persons whom he has previously dispatched. The baptism that his disciples are to confer will recall the trinitarian manifestation on the occasion of his own baptism in the Jordan. Their teaching will restate "everything I have commanded you." Finally, the last phrase of the first gospel (Matt. 28:20) encapsulates the meaning of these mandates: in the apostolic mission, the Jesus of the gospel will remain present until the end of time. The Resurrection will extend, to all times and all nations, the salvific presence of Emmanuel (cf. 1:21-23).

2. Again, in Mark's longer ending, the missionary dispatch of Mark 16:15-20 restates, point by point, the résumé of Jesus' work as given in Mark 1:[7]

| *Mark 1* | *Mark 16* |
|---|---|
| 14: Jesus appeared in Galilee proclaiming the good news of God. . . . and proclaim the good news of God. . . . | 15: "Go into the whole world and proclaim the good news to all creation." |
| 15: "The reign of God is at hand! Reform your lives and believe in the gospel." | 16: "The one who believes and is baptized will be saved. . . ." |
| 23-28: (Exorcisms) | 17: "Signs like these . . . they will use my name to expel demons . . . |
| 29-34: (Cures) | 18: the sick upon whom they lay their hands will recover." |
| 38: "Let us move on . . . so that I can proclaim the good news there also." | 20: The Eleven went forth and preached everywhere. |

There are enough differences between the two texts to make it plain that the second is not simply a copy of the first. The matter goes deeper than that. At stake is a fundamental correspondence between the mission embraced by Jesus and the one entrusted by the Risen One to his own. The parallelism between Mark 1:38 and 16:20 reveals the meaning of this correspondence: the apostolic "departure" will continue to pursue the goal for which Jesus had "emerged." Each of the two missions sheds light on the other. Jesus' mission is conceived in parallel with the apostolic mission: Jesus' mission, too, after its fashion, had been a "departure," a "moving on." And the apostolic mission has no other content or motivation than Jesus' own "moving on" to proclaim the Good News.

3. We discover the same balance between beginning and end in Luke. According to Luke 24:47-49, the *Spirit* will impel the apostles witnesses to *proclaim* to the nations *"remission" (aphesis)* of sin, and bestow power upon them. But the same *Spirit* had come upon Jesus to anoint him as the Messiah charged with *proclaiming deliverance (aphesis)* to prisoners (Luke 4:18-19), and it is by this *power* of the Spirit that Jesus had commenced his task in Galilee (Luke 4:14; cf. 1:35). The parallel between the two missions is very precise. But neither are the differences neglected: the Spirit is upon Jesus, while only transmitted to the apostles; thus they are but "witnesses," while he is the Anointed, the Messiah. Between Jesus and those Jesus sends there is continuity, but not identity.

4. Finally, in John the bond between Jesus' mission and the apostolic mission is formulated explicitly: "As the Father has sent me, so I send you"

(John 20:21; cf. 17:17-19). As this gospel opened, the Baptist had presented Jesus' mission thus: "Look! There is the Lamb of God who takes away the sin of the world!" ... "I saw the Spirit descend ... and it came to rest on him" (John 1:29,32).

After the Resurrection, the Lamb himself ushers in the apostolic mission by inviting the Ten to *see* the marks of his sacrifice, and by giving, with the *Spirit*, the power to forgive *sins*. It may seem surprising that, at the conclusion of John's gospel, the purpose of mission is reduced to the forgiveness of sins (John 20:22). This is simply because these are the terms in which Jesus' own mission had been described, in John 1:29. "A vast Semitic 'inclusion' has been suggested here, not without reason. It would embrace the entire gospel, and define one of its major aspects."[8] As in the other gospels, the apostolic mission is only a resumption of Jesus' own cause.

### b. Significance

This rapprochement of the beginning and end of the four gospels—of the terms of Jesus' ministry and the apostolic mission—is rich in significance.

1. It reveals the *meaning of the Resurrection* in function of the earthly ministry of Jesus of Nazareth.

> Far from making of Jesus a new personage, [the Resurrection] reveals the Risen One to be precisely the person and teacher his disciples had always known. Not only is the Risen One the Crucified One (Mark 16:6), but he comes to prove to his own that the Resurrection, though it snatch him from death and usher him into the power and glory of God, ... does not strictly change anything in his relationship with his own, his original physiognomy, or the secret of his person.[9]

To put it in Johannine terms, one might say that the Resurrection is a judicial review of Jesus' trial. God reverses the guilty verdict, convicts the jury on all the same charges, and manifests the defendant's innocence and righteousness (cf. John 16:8-11, 8:46). In his Resurrection, Jesus' word is fulfilled: "Now has judgment come upon this world, now will this world's prince be driven out, and I—once I am lifted up from earth—will draw all men to myself" (John 12:31-32).

The Resurrection does justice to Jesus' message, activity, and basic options. It consecrates them and at the same time endows them with universal scope and definitive validity. Mission, consequently, is the gospel confirmed and universalized by the power of the Resurrection.

2. It also shows the *meaning of the gospel accounts in function of mission.* Everything the gospels say of Jesus would be no more than ancient history, a dead letter, had this account not been taken up by the gospel proclamation and thereby rendered present and actual for those who hear it. What the conclusion of each gospel says, in taking up once more the terms

of Jesus' ministry, is that what Jesus did and said is once more living word, to the ends of the earth, to the consummation of the ages. It is in the mission entrusted by the Risen One to his disciples that the gospel, in the banal sense of an account of Jesus, becomes gospel in the sense in which Paul and Mark understand "gospel": the power of God for the salvation of all who believe (cf. Rom. 1:16; Mark 1:15, 16:16).

3. Reciprocally, it follows that *mission has all the dimensions and scope of Jesus' own ministry*. Mission consists not only in proclaiming and teaching, but also in healing and liberating, praying and glorifying, becoming incarnate, living the filial condition of the Servant, and hence, it may be, dying.

## THE ACCOUNTS OF THE SENDING: VARIATIONS

While the gospel narratives all conclude with the accounts of the sending, they do so in different ways. Each evangelist reports the missionary command in function of that evangelist's particular orientation. Thus, the variations will reflect a variety of apostolic experiences. They will also reflect, by induced effect, different ways of conceiving the ministry of Christ: missiology follows christology, and vice versa. Lest we be too long in our present considerations, let us move more rapidly with the endings of Mark, Luke, and John, and then peruse Matthew and Mark 16:1-8 more closely, as their understanding poses special problems.

### MARK 16:14-20

In the longer ending of Mark, the order in which the gospel is to be proclaimed corresponds to the summary of Jesus' activity in Mark 1:14-15 and suggests a kerygmatic, itinerant form of evangelization—a rapid communication of the Good News in which the latter acts through the impact of the joy it arouses.[10]

### LUKE 24:44-49

In his account of the sending, Luke sees mission at once as proclamation (v. 47: "Penance for the remission of sins is to be preached . . .") and as witness (Luke 24:47; Acts 1:8). What this means is illustrated by Acts 2, which summarizes the grand lines of Christian mission. When the Spirit is given to the apostles (Acts 2:1-13), they emerge and speak, and three thousand persons join them (Acts 2:14-41). But there is more to it than this.[11] This new community rendered such witness—in its miraculous power, its unity, its sharing, its joy, and its praise—that "day by day the Lord added to their number those who were being saved" (Acts 2:47). To the power of the proclamation, described in the first part of Acts 2, is added the influence of community witness. In Acts 2 as in Luke 24:44-49, the action of the Spirit produces a dynamism of word and community alike.

## JOHN 20

In John, the mission entrusted to the Eleven by the Risen One (v. 21: "As the Father has sent me, so I send you") is described in terms of interiority—as a total experience of integral liberation and rediscovered peace (v. 26: "Peace be with you . . ."; v. 23: "If you forgive men's sins, they are forgiven them . . ."). The deed of the Spirit is to create—despite sin and its consequences of darkness, slavery, and death—saved, luminous, free, and living persons, reconciled with God, with others, and with themselves because they have been admitted to Love. The First Letter of John will give us a description of this new identity: sinners forgiven and saved, who have "passed from death to life . . . because we love . . ." (1 John 3:14).

## MARK 16:1-8 AND MISSION

### a. Problem of the Shorter Ending

The questions raised by Mark's ending are well known.[12] The final twelve verses are missing from the oldest manuscripts; and except for verses 15-16, and perhaps 17-18, as we have seen, they are not composed in Mark's style.[13] Furthermore, it would be surprising if Mark had brought his gospel to such an awkward conclusion. It would simply end with the observation that the witnesses fled, neglecting to carry out the commission with which they had been charged, because they were afraid!

It has been thought, then, that Mark had not had time to finish his book; or that, like Luke, he had projected a second volume, but had not had time to compose it; or again, that the end of the book has been lost in the copying process.

All of these conjectures enjoy some degree of probability. At best, however, they are mere hypotheses. It would be better to begin with the textual evidence and to seek to evaluate Mark 16:1-8 on its own merits. The hypotheses will have been of no help and will collapse under their own weight, were it to be found that, on the whole, the shorter ending constitutes an altogether suitable conclusion.

### b. Announcement of the Resurrection

Many a study has sought to reconstitute the original form of the empty tomb account.[14] Whatever the value of the solutions proposed, even in its current form the account is governed throughout by a unifying theme. But this theme is ill expressed by the usual title, "The Empty Tomb."

It is not the discovery of the empty tomb that terrifies the women. It is the encounter with a "young man . . . dressed in a white robe" (v. 5). In terms of conventional apocalyptical symbolism, this young man must be a heavenly messenger (*aggelos*), an angel. But if there is an angel, there is a message: and it is the message of the angel at the tomb that will actually be the first Easter proclamation, the primordial *praeconium paschale*.[15]

Let us observe the formulation of this proclamation. The angel does not say in Mark, as he says in Matthew, "He is not here. He has been raised ..." (Matt. 28:6), but vice versa: "He has been raised up; he is not here" (Mark 16:6). He does not start out with an empty tomb to be explained by a Resurrection. The point of the account is not the mystery of an empty tomb. The primary element is the announcement of the Resurrection. The empty tomb, which is mentioned for the first time only in verse 6, three-quarters of the way through the account, is only a consequence. The viewpoint is not apologetical, but kerygmatic. The account does not turn on the enigma of the disappearance of a corpse; it turns on the angelical proclamation of a divine message.

### c. The First Profession of Christian Faith

The angel's message is comparable to Gabriel's announcement to Mary in Luke 1:32-35. The annunciation to Mary sets forth a résumé of the Christian faith, and does so in the framework of an apocalypse.[16] Before following its course upon earth as human word, the Christian message first descended from on high as the divine Word. Luke, the historian of the increase of the Word, is also the theologian of the origin of the content and power of this Word in God.

This is also the meaning of the angelical announcement of the Resurrection in Mark 16:1-8. It closely follows the Christian professions of faith:

1. Jesus is the Nazarene. The designation is no longer a geographical one. *Nazarēnos*, "Nazarene," suggests *netzer*, the "shoot" that was to sprout from the stump of Jesse (Isa. 11:1) and alludes to the Davidic title (cf. Matt. 2:23). Jesus is the "new" David, the heir to the messianic promises, as in Luke 1:32.

2. He is also the One crucified-and-raised. Here are the two terms of the fundamental binomial of Christian faith (cf. 1 Cor. 1:23, 2:2, 15:3-4; Rom. 10:9; 1 Thes. 1:10; Acts 2:36; etc.).

Jesus, the Son of David, who died and was raised: such are the three terms of the angelical proclamation in Mark 16:6, and thus the terms that summarize the evangelical proclamation in Acts 4:10, 10:3-42, and 13:22-37. The gospel proclamation is made here for the first time, then, and it is made by a divine messenger. It is not mere human language. It is divine word, transmitted by angelical mediation. Before being promulgated by human beings and becoming missionary preaching, the Good News is from God and is invested with divine authority and power. As Mark says at the beginning of his book: it is the Gospel of God (1:14). As in the case of the Annunciation in Luke, an apocalypse founds mission.

### HUMAN WEAKNESS AND DIVINE MIGHT

What matter, then, that the emissaries fail to discharge their commission? It has been thought that their silence is to be explained by the messianic secret.[17] Actually, the women's silence prolongs that of the cross and tomb. Theirs is the silence of the radical deficiency of all human activity. Rarely will the divine work find any but timorous collaborators. But this will not mean the failure of God. The Good News of the Resurrection has resounded in the world in a great cry of triumph, and Jesus' promise to walk at the head of his assembled flock cannot but be realized (Mark 16:7; cf. 14:27-28). The very existence of the Gospel of Mark proves that the power of the Word of God cannot not be fettered by human weakness. The contrast between verses 6 and 8, between the triumphant accents of the angelical proclamation and the pusillanimity of its hearers, recalls the words of Isaiah:

> All mankind is grass,
>   and all their glory like the flower of the field.
> The grass withers, the flower wilts,
>   when the breath of the LORD blows upon it. . . .
> Though the grass withers and the flower wilts,
>   the word of our God stands forever (Isa. 40:6-8).

Thus, Mark 16:1-8 is not the "Empty Tomb Pericope," but the gospel proclamation issuing from the gaping mouth of that tomb with all the authority and power of the divine Word.[18] Mark has indeed completed the program he sketched out when he wrote: "Here begins the gospel of Jesus Christ . . ." (Mark 1:1).

It has been remarked that, in the shorter ending, "Mark effects in an indirect way what the other evangelists did in more direct fashion when they placed the missionary mandate on the lips of the Risen One."[19] The silence of the angel's hearers would be a way of questioning us: "And you— what will you do? Will you, too, remain silent? Or will you carry the message?" We are not mistaken if we detect a missionary point in Mark's shorter ending. But the point must be made explicit. The perspective here is less "missionary" than "evangelical." As in Mark's theology generally and in Jesus' practice, the important thing is not so much evangelization as it is the gospel. Antecedent to any consideration of human cooperation is the impact of the triumphal announcement addressed to the world: The crucified Nazarene has been raised! And it is with this cry that Mark concludes. From the tomb the basic gospel springs. In the silence of the cross, the tomb, and human beings, God, through the angel, trumpets the victory cry of the Resurrection, the cry that will now fill the world and gather the peoples.

### THE MISSION THAT MAKES DISCIPLES: MATT. 28:16-20

While Mark's shorter ending places such emphasis on the divine power of the gospel, Matthew's conclusion, by contrast, details the aspects of the human task to which the Risen One sends the disciples. Let us single out the major elements of that task.

### a. "Make Disciples . . ."

The mission on which Jesus sends the Twelve is a mission of teaching: "Make disciples . . ." (Matt. 28:19). This standpoint corresponds both to a Judaeo-Christian missionary experience in the rabbinical style, and, again in a Palestinian focus, to the christology of a Master who forms "disciples." The Matthean christology could be portrayed in the image of Jesus seated on the mount, surrounded by his disciples, and "beginning to teach" them, with dignity (Matt. 5:1-2)—beginning a long, carefully structured discourse calculated to present a synthesis of his doctrine (Matt. chaps. 5-7). The mission visualized in Matthew 28:19 follows the same model. "Making disciples" conjures up the image of a master initiating his disciples through an organized process in the rabbinical style, progressively communicating a teaching and a lifestyle corresponding to this "tradition." This kind of activity suggests more the instructor's podium than the "feet of those who announce good news" (Rom. 10:15). It was this kind of mission that Matthew had in mind when he cited the logion of the "scribe who is learned in the reign of God" and who "can bring forth . . . both the new and the old" (Matt. 13:52). This "learned" (literally, "made into a disciple"—*mathēteutheis*, the verb of Matt. 28:19) Christian scribe can in turn teach others (cf. 2 Tim. 2:2). He will surely relay the gospel of the Reign. But the image used does not represent him as racing to the ends of the earth. He is more like a steward seated amidst a treasure, taking a careful inventory of the wealth to be found in ancient tradition and in the Christ.

### b. "Baptize them. . . . Teach them to carry out. . . .

The missionary commandment thereupon specifies the ecclesial actions that are to comprise the Christian initiation: baptism and a Christian instruction calculated to lead to a practice: "to carry out . . ." We have come a long way from simple proclamation—from Mark's *kērussein*, which relies solely on the radical, instant impact of the Good News. In Matthew, "mission" denotes a long-term program: sacrament, continuous formation, an ethic in accordance with the new justice. The Judaic background of rabbinical instruction is evident. Likewise evinced is a long missionary experience, and the development of an ecclesial practice. Paul's protracted dispute with the church of Corinth and the directives he felt obliged to enjoin upon that church show that this development had begun very early.

Proclamation was not enough. Initiation and formation were required. An ecclesial framework was required. Paul himself had grasped this; all the more so had the Matthean churches, with their Judaic background as synagogues and their lengthier experience as churches.

### c. "Go[ing], therefore . . ."

It is in this context that we must understand the verb at the beginning of verse 19, which we are accustomed to see translated in the imperative:

"Go. ..." But in the Greek text we have only a participle: *poreuthentes*, "having gone," "having left," "having journeyed." When we translate this participle in the imperative, we falsify its import. We shift the emphasis of the sentence. "Make disciples" is the imperative and carries the principal emphasis. The commandment bears on the formation of disciples, not on departure. To be sure, one cannot make disciples of all the nations without going forth to the nations; but the accent is not on the going forth. "The principal, dominant assertion is that disciples are to be made."[20] The context, too, suggests this, as we have seen: the image is rather one of a teacher seated and imparting instruction than that of a messenger coursing to the farthest corner of the earth.

Exegetes have even wondered whether the participle *poreuthentes* actually has any contentual signification of its own at all. Might it not be a simple expletive? The Semitic language of the Bible is filled with such redundancies. ("He answered and said..." "He rose and went..." "He went and dwelt..." "She conceived and gave birth....") In the Matthean context, the participle *poreuthentes*, "going," or "having gone," "having left" may be "essentially an auxiliary having no denotative value."[21] Certain commentators have made a comparison between Matthew 28:18 and: "Do not visit pagan territory and do not enter a Samaritan town. Go instead after the lost sheep of the house of Israel" (Matt. 10:5-6). But the comparison becomes a contrast: in Matthew 10:5-6, the itinerary is precise, and the text specifies the destinations to be sought and avoided. This connotation is altogether absent from Matthew 28:18. Nor are we any better off with the parallel from Mark 16:15, which likewise specifies the route to be followed: "Go into the whole world...." Further, it is poor methodology to attempt to explain Matthew by Mark, since, the image of mission, whether it be that of Jesus or that of the disciples, is different in Mark and Matthew. It is curious to observe, with even the most competent translators, the insidious temptation to reduce mission to the sole schema of the romantic image of the missionary!

### d. "And know that I am with you...": The Missionary Mandate and the Presence of the Risen One

Another unconscious distortion occurs when verses 18-19 are isolated from their context. The point of the passage is then perceived as the activity of the disciples, which of course has already received a false accent from the use of the imperative, "Go." We then content ourselves with speaking of a missionary mandate, and classifying the passage in the literary genre of "apostolic commission." By making the disciples' activity the dominant note of the pericope, we automatically subordinate all else beside. The last verse of the Gospel of Matthew, in particular, becomes Christ's promise to be present till the end of time to assist in the apostolic endeavor.[22] The first part of the pericope, verses 16-17, is now reduced to a narrative framework, or residue of traditions on the Resurrection, poorly linked to the missionary command and of little significance.

But the structure of the pericope is much more cohesive than this. The passage must be taken as a whole and examined more closely.

Taken in its entirety, the pericope is in two parts: the first two verses (vv. 16-17) form the narrative element, and the last three (vv. 18-20) deliver the message. Or we might say that the first two verses bear on the disciples, on their actions and reactions, while the second part places Jesus at center stage, reducing his activity to his message.

A surprising aspect of this construction is the apparent lack of connection between the two sections. What Jesus says in the second part seems irrelevant to what the disciples have been doing before he speaks. They have been doing homage or doubting; but Jesus' words take no account of their attitude. He no more congratulates them on their faith (as he does in Matt. 16:17) than he reproaches them for their incredulity (as in Mark 16:14). Nor does he attempt to answer their doubts (as in Luke 24:38ff.). His message is on another plane altogether. He functions spontaneously. He does not respond to a concrete problem, but issues a declaration invested with absolute value. His response transcends particular circumstances. He is content with certifying his authority, and human frailty is no obstacle. The mission to the nations will rest not on human ability, but on the authority of the Risen One. The relationship of the two parts is one of contrast. In the face of the immense task assigned them in verses 19-20, the image of confusion and indecision portrayed by the Eleven is tragicomic. But the point is precisely that it is not human beings, but the authority of the Master and his continuing presence, that will take the nations in charge.

This analysis of the whole of the pericope is buttressed by an analysis of each of the two sections.

In the first part, it is human beings who act. Jesus is merely the object of their activity. They go to the mountain; they see Jesus; they do homage; they doubt.[23] The initiative is theirs, and Jesus is framed by this human activity of which he is the object. We are in the area of human initiative, then. Nor does this initiative lead far. It issues in indecision, divided between worship and doubt.

In the second part, Jesus takes the initiative: Jesus came forward and addressed them in these words:

Full authority has been given me both in heaven and on earth;
go[ing], therefore . . . make disciples of all the nations.
Baptize them. . . .
Teach them. . . .
And know that I am with you always, until the end of the world!

Jesus enters [appears on] the scene. He takes matters in hand. He had been only the object of the account; now he becomes its subject. From the eleven disciples, the initiative passes to Jesus. The disciples had come and had offered only a wavering faith. Jesus comes, and the irresistible might of his word prevails.

In this second part, contrariwise to the first, the action of the Eleven is framed by that of Jesus. It simply flows from the "authority" or power given to the Risen One. The "therefore" of verse 19 underscores this subordination: a declaration of seizure of power and enthronement overshadows the "apostolic commission." The christological aspect dominates the missiological.

These observations aid us in grasping the import of Christ's words: "I am with you always, until the end of the world." This declaration is not subordinated to the dispatch to mission, as if Jesus were promising to be present to "help the missionary work along." Verse 20b resumes the outlook of verse 18. The Messianic presence is not subordinate to mission; it dominates it. It constitutes the milieu in which mission is to be performed. In the parlance of structuralism, we might say: in function of the construction of verses 19-20, and contrariwise to verses 16-18, Jesus is the one acting, and the disciples are his assistants. Any interpretation that would reverse the proposition and make the disciples the principal agents and Jesus an auxiliary one would be to falsify the import of the text. The conclusion of the gospel of Matthew says not that Jesus abets mission, but that he performs it.

This is the premise of the construction not only of verses 19-20, but of the entire last chapter of the First Gospel. Verse 20 cannot be regarded as a postscript to the dispatch on mission. It is the point of the whole account of the Resurrection. From a point of departure in his Resurrection, Christ, who has conquered death and been installed as Lord of earth and heaven, will always be present with his universal "authority" and might.

This is likewise the interpretation called for by the Gospel of Matthew as a whole, in which this last verse sounds the final note. The introduction has proclaimed the coming of Emmanuel, God-with-us (Matt. 1:23). The corpus of the gospel has shown this power at work. The conclusion assures us that this presence abides and that the power of God-with-us is about to be exercised in definitive fashion. Mission is but the implementation of this presence and power.[24]

Finally, our interpretation is justified by the parallel with Luke and John, while helping to specify the Matthean viewpoint vis-à-vis these other two evangelists. The latter present a christology and missiology of the Spirit. Returning to the Father, Christ sends his Spirit (Luke 24:49; John 20:22; cf. John 14:17, 15:26-27). It is the Spirit who will bear witness and who will "bear," will carry, will support the witness of the disciples (cf. John 15:26-27). The Spirit does not come to "assist" the witness of the church; on the contrary, the witness of the church flows from the testimony of the Spirit: "He will bear witness on my behalf. You must bear witness as well" (John 15:26,27). In Luke, then, the gift of the Spirit determines the preaching of the gospel (Acts 2) and even the apostolic strategy (Acts 13:1-3, 16:6-10).

As has frequently been observed, the Acts of the Apostles are first and foremost the Acts of the Spirit. As for Christ, both Luke (Luke 24:51: "He left them ...") and John (John 14:3-5, 16:7) perceive him as somehow absent, in the nostalgic tone this separation might well be expected to involve (Acts 1:10-11; John 16:5, 19-20).

Matthew, like Paul, is more sensitive to the continuing presence of Christ in the age of the church. Not that he employs the Pauline theme of life "in Christ." But he knows that where two or three are joined in Christ's name, the latter is in their midst (Matt. 18:20), that whoever receives Christ's messenger receives him personally (Matt. 10:40-42), and that whatever is done for good or ill to the least of his siblings is done to him (25:40-45).

But neither Luke nor John nor Matthew envisage an independent missiology. For the gospels, mission is not an activity performed apropos of Jesus and with the latter's benevolent assistance. It is primarily an activity of Jesus himself (or of his Spirit). The christological or pneumatological aspect predominates over the missiological. Mark had made this point as concisely as it could be made: the gospel is the gospel of Jesus Christ (Mark 1:1). It is not only the gospel concerning Jesus, nor again only the gospel borne to us by Jesus; it is the gospel identified with the ongoing deed and constant presence of Jesus Christ.

According to Gunther Bornkamm, "Mt. 28:18ff. bears primarily on the life of the church itself, and not on the practice of mission."[25] This is true enough, provided the life of the church be understood not in the static sense of its organization, but in the dynamism that thrusts it toward the world. We should have to go even further and say that the conclusion of the Gospel of Matthew bears primarily on Christ, whose continuous presence prolongs, with all the universal authority acquired in and from the Resurrection, all that he has said and done, all that he incarnates, all that he has lived, struggled, and died for.

## CONCLUSION

I have dwelt more at length on Matthew's conclusion because this text is so often cited, altogether correctly, as one of the principal keys to an understanding of Christian mission. Thus, it is important to evaluate its actual scope. The reading often made of it is impoverished by an unconscious semi-Pelagianism — a tendency to prioritize human intervention and to relegate the power of God to secondary status.

Projecting upon this text an a priori conception of mission, we isolate verse 19, concealing both the immediate and the general context of that verse. Thus seizing upon this single text, we thereupon assign priority to the verb "go" and make of this fabricated imperative the dominant theme of both the sentence in which it occurs and the entire pericope. This series of fillips distorts the text, forcing it into the mold of an activist missiology bereft of all christological and ecclesiological support—founded, with precious little why or wherefore, on a simple "missionary commandment" of Christ. Thus isolated, mission becomes a specialized activity left to a few volunteers, to be recalled once a year on "Mission Sunday," when the homily will once again take up this text in the same truncated fashion, and eventually, by dint of sheer repetition, this interpretation will practically become the official one, a fitting hermeneutic for a demobilized church.

This distortion is a betrayal of the gospel. It is also, and just as genuinely, a betrayal of the experience of mission in the interiority of missioners' faith and the creative variety of their charity. Even on the external, physical level, it is a distortion of a life lived amidst the hazards of the thousand concrete circumstances into which the ever unforeseeable currents of history draw them.

There is a great deal of convergence among the accounts of Jesus' Resurrection. They all conclude with the triumphant cry of the word, and with the apostolic mission that echoes that word. Thus, they conclude in a celebration of the power of a gospel whose victory transcends the cross, and whose source is the vibrant power of the ministry that Jesus has already practiced, but that now has had all its limitations removed, to penetrate the nations and the ages.

However, this fundamental unity is refracted in a variety of ecclesial and social milieus and missionary experiences: irruption of the power of the gospel in the shorter ending of Mark, itinerant mission in the longer ending, teaching mission in Matthew, mission of community witness in Luke, transforming mission in John. The Resurrection accounts present an arresting series of samples of different forms of mission as practiced in the primitive church. From Mark's shorter ending, content to raise the victory cry of the Resurrection, to the detailed description of the stages of Christian initiation presented in Matthew, the conception of mission has come a great distance, covering a goodly part of the first Christian century.

Nor is this journey to be understood as a development or series of stages that would render earlier stages obsolete. Mark, while older than Matthew, is not supplanted by it in the canon. In the history of mission, Mark's way of saying things has remained valid, and the Spirit has continued to arouse, through the ages, missions of proclamation whose rapid, brilliant success has pointed up the irresistible power of the Gospel of God. Thus we have Paul, who wished to know only Christ and him crucified, we have Francis Xavier, covering Asia in mighty apostolic bounds as if driven by an eschatological fever. But not all are Pauls and Xaviers, nor would it be well if they were. Matthews are needed, as well, "masters" of formation. Along Luke's lines, a mission is needed that is rooted in the soil, inculturated, growing and enduring.

In mission, the "Jesus affair" goes on, and the four gospels converge on this basic truth. But the power of the gospel is manifested in very different ways, and even the conclusions of the gospel accounts present an image of this diversity.

The church that lives in the gospels is invited not only to testify to the power of the word that it has received, but also to deliver itself from all manner of sectarianism by accepting the variety of ways in which this power is manifested.

# 7

# Some Reflections on Jesus and His Mission

*A hermeneutic problem has arisen with regard to the transition from the Old Testament to the New. What effect will the novelty, the newness, of the gospel have on the Old Testament? Will the new efface all that is old, render it a negligible quantity? We confront the same problem when we come to Jesus' Resurrection: or rather, the problem of an Old and a New Testament reaches its climax in the Resurrection, the birth of a new person, the appearance of a "new creation," the dawn of a "new world." Will this novelty of Resurrection not cast out all that has come before, including the historical acts and deeds of Jesus of Nazareth? For example, does not Jesus' emphasis on the priority of the mission to Israel lose its meaning with the great universalistic commandment of the Risen One? Do not the miracles of healing eventuate in—as it were—a paltry material residue to be sublimated in sacrament? Is not the Reign of God "spiritualized" by the Resurrection? In two chapters we have examined the mission of Jesus on earth and the missionary echo of his Resurrection. Might we not simply do without the first, and pass directly to the second, since, once more, the latter comprises the clearest expressions of the "missionary command"? Just as we have posed the question of the validity of the Old Testament once the New Covenant has come, we must also ask ourselves what the Resurrection changes and what it maintains.*

1. The Resurrection has established Jesus as Lord and Christ (Acts 2:36). It has made him "Son of God in power" (Rom. 1:4), has revealed him as the triumphant sovereign of heaven and earth (Matt. 28:16), Son of God exalted to the Father's right hand and sender of the Spirit (Luke 24:49, John 16:7-11), new human being in whom the division between Jew and Gentile is abolished, the wall of separation razed, and hatred done to death (Eph. 2:14-17), the Lamb who has ransomed human beings "of every race and tongue, of every people and nation" (Rev. 5:9; cf. 7:4-17). Under a

variety of images, the same basic perception remains: in the Resurrection, the promises of God are fulfilled, and all the nations of the earth are called to judgment and salvation. The Resurrection bestows upon the Christ event *the complete extent of the divine power, and, therefore, universal scope*. In the Resurrection, boundaries collapse, and the nations fall into line behind Israel in the great procession of the saved.

2. With Jesus' Resurrection, the eschatological assembly of the nations, already envisaged by the Old Testament, presents two crucial modifications. First, it moves from the indeterminate eschatological future to the *present*. Next, it becomes a task God shares with human beings, thus shifting from the field of angelical interventions to that of the *human activity* of "laborers to gather his harvest" (Matt. 9:38). Indeed, the earthly Jesus had himself anticipated this novelty, selecting the Twelve and sending them forth to proclaim, as did he himself, the Good News of the Reign. It is at once the Resurrection and the Incarnation, then, that set mission in motion as a human activity calculated to evangelize the very ends of the earth.

3. Then are we to speak of a realized eschatology in the mission of Jesus and his disciples? Or are we dealing rather with an eschatology in the course of realization? In other words, will mission effect a historical realization of the gathering of nations? Or instead, like Jesus himself, must not the post-paschal mission merely posit signs—signs of the word, signs of an action and of attitudes that incarnate this word, the sign of a community of witnesses and disciples? Until the coming of the last days, the only eschatology will ever be an *eschatology in the course of realization*. As Paul will say to the Romans, night is ending and day is dawning (Rom. 13:12). But there is not as yet the great light that will eclipse sun and moon in the blinding glory of God (Rev. 21:23). Eschatology cannot be realized in history. What God has in store for those who believe ever transcends all that we can ever ask or imagine (Eph. 3:20). The eschatological fulfillment will ever remain the deed of God. If mission effected a realized eschatology, the latter would no longer be the grace of God, but human deed, and mission would lose its dimensions of faith and hope. The Kingdom is not of this world. The church is not the Reign. *The church is the sign and servant of the Reign.* The mission of the church, like Jesus' mission, is limited to the level of sign. If mission sought to "conquer the world," it would be attempting to replace the divine might with human assurance and the will to power. The gathering of the nations into the Reign will ever remain the deed of the eschatological power of God. This does not mean that there is nothing to be done. After all, God sends laborers to the harvest. But these laborers must know their place. They must do all that in them lies, and when they have acted, with or without success, know that they are unprofitable servants (Luke 17:10). All is grace.

4. All is grace in the development of mission, as well. Mission has been entrusted to human beings in Jesus Christ. It is *the continuous presence of Jesus Christ*—or, to invoke a theology of the Spirit, with Luke and John, it

is *the power of the Spirit—that sustains and bolsters mission*. And this Spirit is the Spirit of God, as Jesus is God-with-us. The gospel is the "good news of God" (Mark 1:14). It is not the evangelizer who carries the gospel; it is the gospel, the power of God, that carries the evangelizer.

5. Before all else, then, what is essential—just as it was for Jesus—is *transparency to the gospel*, the authenticity of witness. If the flame is burning, the light must shine. Jesus was such a Light (John 8:12, 9:5, 12:46), and he passed the torch to his own (Matt. 5:14-16). It would serve no purpose to carry torches to the ends of the earth if they had been extinguished. This is the deviation with which Jesus reproached the scribes (Matt. 23:15), and this was the object of his warning to those he was sending forth (Matt. 6:23, Rev. 2:5).

6. Nevertheless, while remaining the deed of the Spirit and the gift of the Spirit, mission does not become "purely spiritual" in the Platonic sense of the word. We need only recall our reflections on the Old Testament. In the Bible, the Spirit is not "spiritual" in the sense of disincarnate and atemporal. Just as the New Testament did not "spiritualize" the Old, so neither does the coming of the Spirit do away with the Incarnation. The Resurrection is precisely the divine seal of approval on all that Jesus of Nazareth said, did, and was. Thus, mission retains *all of the concrete human character of the work of Jesus*. As Jesus' own ministry cannot be reduced to a purely verbal message, cannot be restricted to the communication of a teaching, so neither can the mission entrusted to the church by the Risen One be reduced to such a message. To proclaim the gospel as in Mark 16:20 is to do what Jesus is described as doing throughout the pages of the gospel, beginning with Mark 1:14. To "make disciples," as in Matthew 28:19, is to perform the diversified activity by which Jesus molded his own disciples. To be "witnesses" as in Luke 24:48 suggests a total process of shared living, involving a good deal more than mere doctrine.

"As the Father has sent me . . ." Jesus says in John 20:21. But the Father has sent Jesus to give life not only in words but in deeds. The Father has sent Jesus to show forth the works of God, to be God's living parable, to be God's "sign," with his whole being and all his deeds, with his prayer and his intercession, with all his love and with his death.

". . . So I send you," he continues. I send you forth to bear witness not only in words, but in deed and in truth: to intercede and glorify, to proclaim love, to live by love, and if need be, to give your lives for your sisters and brothers.

We must read all of the pages of the gospels if we hope to discover the various faces of mission. These faces are as diverse as the diverse ways in which Jesus shared the hope and anguish of his fellow human beings and identified with the salvific will of God, as varied as such total freedom and such constantly astonishing creativity could inspire. "So I send you": creatures of little faith that we are, full of mingled worship and doubt like the apostles, yet we are sent forth as witnesses of the gospel; and the power of the gospel continues to be exercised through those who are sent.

7. The concrete human condition of the person and the work of Jesus included *membership in Israel*, and Jesus' attitude with regard to his mission continues to pose the problem of the role of Israel. Jesus' viewpoint on Israel is identical with that of the prophets of old: election of the people of Abraham and universalistic scope of this election. Like the Old Testament, Jesus envisages a universalism of judgment and salvation with the people of Israel as the point of departure. On the other hand, the mark of membership in this people is no longer physical descendancy from Abraham, but faith and conversion. Does this mean that the history of Israel is henceforward without meaning? And does the Resurrection, in leveling frontiers, suppress the role of the chosen people? Let us note that, when Jesus wishes to indicate a point of breach with the old order, he does so from a point of departure in the law itself: "You have heard the commandment . . . . What I say to you is . . . ." It is from within Israel's experience that Jesus opens new horizons. It is in Jewish flesh that the Word became flesh and in Jewish flesh that we have seen his glory.[1] It is what Franz Mussner calls Jesus' "being Jewish" that we must never forget, under pain of docetism.[2] On this point as well, the Resurrection has not abolished the Incarnation. Christ the Lord of the world is still Jesus of Nazareth. This will be one of the data on which we shall base the next step in our reflection, with the aid of Luke and Paul, who took a particular interest in this problem.

### PART THREE

# THE PRIMITIVE CHURCH AS A MISSIONARY CHURCH

Our study has taken us from the Old Testament to Jesus and to the Risen Jesus. We have remarked certain constants between Jesus and the Old Testament. But the Resurrection opened new perspectives, of which we had had a glimpse in the actual life and ministry of Jesus.

Let us now turn our attention to the primitive church. How did that church take up Jesus' work? How did it understand the mission that had been entrusted to it by the Risen Christ? We shall interrogate Paul and Luke, in particular—the former a practitioner, the latter a historian, of the mission to the nations. With them, do we not at last encounter an active, itinerant, triumphal conception of mission?

Until not long ago, when a missionary departed for foreign climes from the French-speaking world, it was to the accompaniment of "Partez, Hérauts de la Bonne Nouvelle!" ("Depart, heralds of the Good News")—the "mission march" whose music (Gounod) and words had perhaps more of a romantic ring than an authentically apostolic one. Inspired by the image in Isaiah 52:7, the assembly would sing, "Ah, how lovely are your feet, missionaries!" and come up and kiss the feet of those departing. After all, St. Paul himself had cited the Isaian text and celebrated the "beautiful feet of those who announce good news" (cf. Rom. 10:15). The Book of Acts in its entirety is a development of the metaphor of the feet that march from Jerusalem to Samaria to the ends of the earth (Acts 1:8).

Between the gospels and the Acts of the Apostles, then—from Jesus to the primitive church—do we not have a shift of metaphors in which the image of the gathering of the nations is replaced by that of an apostolic march? Do we not have a new model of mission here, one that will become normative for modern mission? But then must we say that mission in Paul and Acts has betrayed the image of Jesus that we have discovered? Conversely, shall we maintain that mission, actual mission, the mission that has built the church and that continues to function today, was invented by Paul and not by Jesus? But what would Paul himself have had to say to such a suggestion—indignant as he was with those who "wish to alter the gospel of Christ" (Gal. 1:7)? What would he have made of it? To answer this question, we must examine the data furnished by the texts, beginning with the pre-Pauline period so that we may situate Paul in his context.

# 8

# "In Jerusalem, throughout Judea . . ."

*The Acts of the Apostles constitutes our principal source of information on the origins of Christian mission. That book is composed in the form of a missionary account, and, from the outset, proposes a progressive outline of apostolic witness, beginning in Jerusalem and extending to the ends of the earth (Acts 1:8). Following an examination of this outline, we shall examine, in this chapter, the first part of Acts, which is devoted to the testimony rendered at Jerusalem, especially by the Twelve grouped around Peter. The first part of Acts is important. The history of a Paul who, in the second part, sets out for the ends of the earth, cannot be understood independently of this point of departure.*

## THE MISSIONARY PROJECT OF THE BOOK OF ACTS

### GEOGRAPHICAL PLAN OF ACTS

You are to be my witnesses in Jerusalem, throughout Judea and Samaria, yes, even to the ends of the earth (Acts 1:8).

In accordance with the missionary program outlined by the Risen One, the book of Acts will describe the step-by-step advance of the word toward new horizons. In chapters 1-7 the action takes place at Jerusalem. Then, in chapter 7, Stephen's discourse takes its distance from the Temple at Jerusalem, perhaps even incorporating Samaritan motifs.[1] Thus the way is paved for the mission to Samaria, to be described in chapter 8. With the calling of Paul in chapter 9 and the conversion of Cornelius in chapters 10-11, the groundwork has been laid for the mission to the nations, to be formally launched in Acts 13:1-3: there the Spirit, through the church of Antioch, dispatches Paul and Barnabas to the new task to which they have been called. Suddenly the pair are in Cyprus and Asia Minor, thence to be led, by further interventions of the Spirit (Acts 16:6-10), to Macedonia and Europe. The discourses of the "Council of Jerusalem" in Acts 15 show us the deeper reason for this passage to the nations, and the discourse on the Areopagus in chapter 17 is the echo of that encounter of the word with Greece. Then, through the perils of a captivity, Paul will leave for Crete and Malta—"the islands," that biblical symbol of far-off worlds (cf. Isa. 11:11, 41:1, 49:1)—and finally Rome, capital of the far West. The program has been accomplished. The arc of the word has touched the ends of the earth. Paul's final discourse to the Jews of Rome will now show the word to have been delivered from theological fetters, too, as it has been delivered from all physical ones (Acts 28:31).

It is a majestic, marvelously skillful sketch. All interconnections are clearly indicated and carefully explained in discourses placed at key intervals, the whole being artistically centered on the two great figures of Peter, for the Jewish world, and Paul, for the nations—who join hands, from the tableaus of their diptych, in the encounter at Jerusalem in chapter 15, the pivotal point of the entire construction.

### OUTLINE OF ACTS AND THEOLOGY OF LUKE

The outline reflects Luke's theology. The theme of the Word is a dominant one in Luke. In the gospel itself, Luke has proposed a christology of the word, underscoring the prophetical aspects of the ministry and person of Jesus (cf. Luke 7:16). His ecclesiology, too, will be an ecclesiology of the Word. While the church is the central theme of his second book, that church is not defined by its structures, which Luke is prepared to accept in as broad a diversity as possible. Thus, at Jerusalem, we find, first, a directorate of apostles (Acts 2:42, 4:33-35), soon to be complemented by a council of seven representing the Hellenists (Acts 6:1-7), then enlarged by a senate of elders (15:4,6,22ff.). The church of Antioch is grouped around "prophets and teachers" (13:1), while Ephesus has a presidium of "presbyters" (*presbuteroi*, 20:17), also called guardians (*episkopoi*, 20:28).[2] Luke's ecclesiology is not reducible to a canon law. Nor does Luke enter into a reflection on the mystery of the church as body or spouse or temple of Christ, after the manner of Paul. For Luke, what makes the church is mission, and the reality at the heart of the church is the impulse of the Spirit for the increase of the Word.

The church is animated by this Word living within it. The latter impels it to the fore. It finds its cohesion and identity in this Word, and this continual new beginning, to the point that Luke unconsciously interchanges the terms: he says that the church multiplied (Luke 6:1,7, 9:31) and grew stronger (Luke 16:5), or that the Word increased (Acts 6:7, 12:24, 19:20), multiplied (Acts 12:24), and gained strength (Acts 19:20).

## OUTLINE OF ACTS AND HISTORY IN ACTS

Luke's simple, vigorous construction has fired the imagination of Christian generations. Acts has become the book of the origins of the church as the gospel is the book of the history of Jesus. But that Christian imagination has outstripped the intentions of Luke himself and oversimplified his already simplified sketch. It has retained little more than the notion of newborn Christianity's rapid expansion as represented, especially, by Paul's "missionary voyages." The first part of the book is thereby relatively neglected, regarded as the history of a period of indecision and groping. We must not succumb to the same temptation. This image is too schematized. Luke himself would not recognize it. Still less would history.

Like any historian, Luke has sought to bring out certain constant elements and to align the points of his report. Like any theologian, he has endeavored to demonstrate the lines of force operative in the events. But to attempt to cast doubt on his historical honesty would be to attack him unfairly.

The data of general history, and of archaeology, on the one hand, and on the other, the data furnished by the rest of the New Testament, especially Paul, permit us to make a comparative evaluation of this framework and some of its details. The results of our examination are more often favorable than unfavorable to the historicity of Acts.[3]

But the facts are complex indeed. Behind Luke's unified and unifying account, we sense a tension of considerable proportions. Nor does Luke conceal this tension, although he does have a tendency to soften it. The problem of the seven representatives of the Hellenists in Acts 6:1-6 doubtless went well beyond the demand for a welfare department; and the fact that these seven and their charges come in for a special persecution of their own (Acts 8:1) suggests that the solution proposed in 6:3–5 involved a certain compartmentalization of groups. Stephen's theology must have surprised the Judaeo-Christian community of Jerusalem as much as it shocked the Sanhedrin. The "Council of Jerusalem" of Acts 15 may have been composed of two distinct assemblies that failed to reach the same conclusions.[4] The vow of Cenchreae (18:18), the circumcision of Timothy (16:3), the purification of Paul and four disciples at Jerusalem (21:23-24), remain somewhat mysterious details, not easily reconcilable with the theological framework of the whole. Like Heraclitus, Luke has solved the problem of unity by movement. But this flux is composed of well-mixed currents, representing quite diverse church structures and forms of mission.

The exegetes have delivered themselves to ingenious reconstitutions of the various ecclesial milieus that form the substrate of the New Testament.

Thus, for the pre-Pauline period, the following quadripartite schema is proposed:

1. A Jerusalemite Judaeo-Christianity, around James, with a missionary goal in the spirit of Second Isaiah's eschatological gathering of the nations at Jerusalem.

2. A Palestinian Judaeo-Christianity, under the headship of Peter, and more directly engaged in active mission, on the model of the itinerant radicalism described in Mark 6: little teams of two, without equipment or finances, moving at the inspiration of the word and subsisting on what they received from those they encountered in the course of their ministry.

3. Another form of Palestinian Judaeo-Christianity would be that of the apocalyptics, radiant in their postpaschal enthusiasm and eschatological expectancy. Their spokespersons would have been the Christian prophets, and they would be the redactors of the synoptic source $Q$.

4. Thus far, Palestinian Judaeo-Christianity. But there was a Hellenistic Judaeo-Christianity, as well, whose missionary tendencies were more accentuated, in the spirit of the proselytism of the rest of the Diaspora. This would be the Christianity of Philip and Stephen, Barnabas and Paul.[5]

Such reconstitutions necessarily indicate a certain coefficient of uncertainty.[6] One must also consider the possibility of very old Galilean, or even Samaritan, communities. Within Palestinian Christianity itself, the "family of Jesus" constituted a unique church milieu. It has likewise been suggested that elements of Palestinian Judaism could have been influenced by converts from the Qumran community.[7] And where had the church of Damascus come from, which Paul was on his way to persecute (Acts 9:1)? The preceding chapters of Acts have made no mention of its existence. Finally, we hear, the Johannine material enriches this portrait of the primitive church and renders it even more complex.

These questions and hypotheses are not game-playing. They only illustrate what Acts itself proposes for our consideration. The Christian faith sprang from a matrix of superabundant vitality. The forms of community life and the missionary thrusts provided by these forms were varied. We must not imagine the missionary mandate of the Risen One to have been like the order of the day issued by a general staff dispatching its troops in orderly columns to execute a concrete, carefully calculated strategy. The dynamism flowing from the Resurrection and from the gift of the Spirit was felt and acted upon in many ways. At the same time—and this is one of the elements of the profound truth of the Lucan account—this overflowing vitality was permeated by a basic concern for unity. This multiple mission was not content to express itself in anarchical abundance. The various tendencies sometimes collided in tumultuous confrontation, but the encounter was always accompanied by a quest for communion. This is more than an assertion we find in chapters 6 and 15 of Acts. It is also the significance of the composition of gospels representing traditions from various milieus, followed by the formation of a collection of four distinct but convergent gospels, and then the gradual appearance of a canon including the writings of Paul as well as of James or Matthew.

Given these various data, which contemporary research is elucidating more and more satisfactorily, it is not our intent of the moment to attempt a reconstitution of the history of the primitive Christian missions. This would be a vast project. In addition, a background would have to be supplied, in the form of a study of the movements of Jewish proselytism, Palestinian as well as Judaeo-Hellenistic, and then those of Hellenistic philosophical propaganda, especially in terms of Stoicism.[8] Our perspective is theological, and we cannot build a theology of mission on these historical reconstitutions. Interesting as they are, they remain hypothetical. Let us return to the data of Acts, then, giving special attention to some of the main points in the account in an attempt to penetrate their meaning. Perhaps, such as they are, these data from Acts do more justice to the original pluralism of the Christian mission than is generally thought. Perhaps, too, our reflection will produce a more nuanced conception of mission than the schema of the triumphant explosion of the Word in the fantasies of so many reductionisms of the Lucan project.

## "IN JERUSALEM . . ."

### THE WORD AT JERUSALEM

Notwithstanding his framework of the account of a Word that goes forth to the very ends of the earth, Luke tarries long in an account of the initial period at Jerusalem. In Acts, the apostles do not seem impatient to rush down the highways of the world. The first seven chapters observe unity of place: the apostles do not forsake Jerusalem, or even, more precisely, the vicinity of the Temple. Chapter 8 moves into Samaria and toward Gaza; and in chapter 9 we follow Saul to Damascus, where there are some "disciples" (Acts 9:1)—who, however, still belong to the "Jewish community" (9:22).

Lydda, Joppa, and Caesarea will be the next steps, in chapters 10-11. But we are still in Palestine, and there is as yet no question of a planned missionary campaign. If Peter's ministry reached a few pagans, it was because, like Jesus in the presence of the centurion or the Syro-Phoenician, he felt obliged by signs from on high to broaden the habitual circles of his activity. This is especially the case with the battery of visions that will lead to the first baptism of an uncircumcised convert. Again, Peter has not planned to go to Samaria. He seems overtaken by events and in breathless pursuit of them. The moment his task is accomplished, he returns to Jerusalem (Acts 11:2). In sum, until Acts 13:1—thus, for 12 of the 28 chapters that make up the book—the Christian community and its apostolic activity remain solidly ensconced in Jerusalem. Three-sevenths of the Book of Acts transpires in the land of Israel.

If we accept the chronology of Acts, a number of years intervene between Pentecost and the martyrdom of Stephen, before the apostles leave Jerusalem or Paul embarks on his deliberate mission to the nations.[9] With Paul's ministry, Luke moves on to the account of another style of mission; but the attitude he has described in chapters 1-12 must have continued to exist in Palestinian Judaism, and thus to coexist with the Pauline missionary campaigns. It must be recognized that Luke has done justice to this attitude on the part of the Palestinian churches and that he has broadly incorporated it into his construction by giving it sufficient amplitude in the first part of his recital.

### SIGNIFICANCE

What meaning did Luke ascribe to the first part of his work, which continues for so many chapters? Why has he underscored this seeming dilatation on the part of the apostles when it came to responding to the commandment of the Risen One to bear witness to all the nations? An operatic style, in which the chorus sings, "March! March!" throughout the scene without advancing a single step? Or timidity on the part of the apostles, who hesitate to set out on their journey? A "psychological" explanation of this kind would be an unlikely one in the Lucan context. And even from a psychological point of view, it does not suit the portrait Luke gives us of Peter. It was certainly not timidity that led him to go out into the street the day of Pentecost and preach Christ, then to have to face the Sanhedrin. On the contrary, Luke insists on Peter's quality of *parrhēsia*, or apostolic boldness (Acts 2:29, 4:13,29). Another "psychological explanation" is to allege a lack of breadth of spirit on the part of Peter and the Twelve: to see a true missionary launch an authentic mission, we must await Paul—and we are back with the exceedingly tenuous notion that Paul is the true founder of mission. And since Luke insists throughout his account that the actual apostolic initiative belongs to the Spirit, must we then speak of a narrow Spirit in Peter, unlike the Spirit in Paul? And was Jesus himself "narrow," then?

The explanation is rather to be sought in the missionary mandate itself, in Luke 24:47, which specifies: ". . . to all the nations, *beginning at Jerusalem*." Jerusalem is clearly designated as the scene of stage one, preceding any outreach to the nations. This is also the plan indicated in Acts 1:8: ". . . in Jerusalem, throughout Judea . . . yes, even to the ends of the earth." According to this schema, Jerusalem is more than a simple starting point, to be abandoned as soon as possible in order to go elsewhere. Just as in Luke 24:47, Acts 1:8 and the structure of Acts that follows indicate that Jerusalem is of intrinsic importance and that the ministry that is to develop there is literally fundamental, in the sense that it is this ministry that founds the entire subsequent movement of the Word.

The viewpoint of the Acts of the Apostles remains that of the Old Testament and the ministry of Jesus. The call to the nations is a call to join a chosen people. Luke's interest in Israel has been very correctly pointed out.[10] The theme of the fulfillment of the scriptures is no less important in Luke than in Matthew.[11] The people of Israel retain their priority in the apostolate of Jesus and the church, and even Paul, preaching among the nations, will have the custom of visiting the synagogues first and presenting himself as an authentic Jew, a Pharisee and the son of a Pharisee (Acts 23:6), "a Jew . . . brought up in this city [Jerusalem]. Here I sat at the feet of Gamaliel. . . . I was a staunch defender of God" (Acts 22:3).

But more than anything else, it is the theme of Jerusalem that reveals the special value ascribed by Luke to Israel and its center, the Holy City. Jerusalem is the vanishing point of the entire Third Gospel. The narrative opens at Jerusalem in the Temple (Luke 1:5) and concludes at Jerusalem, showing the disciples "in the temple constantly, speaking the praises of God" (Luke 24:53). Then, within this perspective of the whole: the infancy account, which opens with Zechariah in the Temple, concludes with Jesus in his "Father's house" (2:49); the pericope of the temptations is recast to make the temptation at the Temple the climax of the encounter with the devil; and the Resurrection accounts, unlike those of Matthew, will avoid any indication that the Eleven ever set foot outside Jerusalem. And especially: beginning with 9:51 in the construction of the gospel, Jesus is en route to Jerusalem, on a journey that dominates the entire book and endows it with the tone of this ascent.

Not that Luke is a zealot of the Temple walls, or, for that matter, a Judaeo-Christian at all. It is only that, for him, as for Isaiah 2:2-3, it is from Zion that the word must emerge. If, at the end of his journey, Jesus enters the Temple to manifest his authority there (Luke 19:45), it is that he may teach there (19:47-48). All of Jesus' activity at Jerusalem is framed by a prologue that presents him as occupied with teaching and proclaiming the Good News (20:1) and an epilogue that describes him spending the day teaching (21:37). The theme of the Temple in Luke is of a piece with the theme of the Word. Again, this is why the procession of the Word in Acts commences with the presence of the Eleven in the Temple (Luke 24:53; Acts 2:46, 5:12) and tarries in Jerusalem over the course of many chapters. The Temple, for Luke, is more than an edifice. It is the center from which the Word radiates forth to the ends of the earth.[12]

Reciprocally, however, the Word, for Luke, is more than an abstract message. It issues from a Temple and from a people. It is the emanation at once of "the glory of your people Israel" and of "a revealing light to the Gentiles" (Luke 2:32). After all, it is Israel that has been established as "a light to the nations, a means of salvation to the ends of the earth" (Acts 13:47 = Isa. 49:6).[13]

For Luke, as for biblical tradition and for Jesus himself, Jerusalem and the Jewish people, on the one hand, and the dynamism of the Word, on the other, stand in a dialectical relationship. The outward movement toward the nations maintains Jerusalem as its center. It is the call, and not a doctrine, that gathers the nations—a call perhaps vaguely originating with the faith of Israel, but destined to be emancipated from its origins. The plan of the salvation of the nations has its deepest roots in the people of the election and in their Temple. This is why, over the course of several chapters and over a number of years, witness is given at Jerusalem. This is where that witness is to take root.

## THE "TWELVE APOSTLES"

It was not a simple question of tactics to begin with a solid foundation of mission at Jerusalem. It was a matter of the very identity of the church. It is in this sense that the role of the "Twelve Apostles" must be understood.

In our current expression, "the twelve apostles," we have a tendency to accentuate the word "Apostle," and to see in the number "Twelve" just that—a simple numeral, the number of the apostles. Actually, these two elements must be clearly distinguished. "Apostle" and "Twelve," far from being synonyms, have different extensions, and the conjunction of the two terms constitutes not a tautology, but a synthesis.

### THE APOSTLES

The word "apostle" had been on a long semantic journey before it became attached to the "Twelve." It is doubtful that the word comes from Jesus' mouth. Luke is the only one to say that Jesus "selected twelve . . . to be his apostles"—literally, ". . . to whom he gave the name of apostles" (Luke 6:13). The appellation rather reflects a later usage.[14]

When the word appears in the letters of Paul, it is first applied in a broad sense—to Paul himself and various of his associates: Silvanus and Timothy (1 Thes. 1:1), Apollos (1 Cor. 4:9), Barnabas (1 Cor. 9:6), Junias and Andronicus (Rom. 16:7), and the "apostles of the churches" (2 Cor. 8:23) generally. The "apostles" are simply the "coworkers of the Christian mission."[15] They are "missionaries" in the etymological sense of the word.

But a more precise denotation makes its appearance in 1 Corinthians 15:3-7, a text that reports the apparitions of the Risen One according to an earlier tradition that Paul has received. This list of apparitions mentions a group of "apostles" (v. 7) distinct from that of the "Twelve" just cited (v. 5), and yet distinct from that of the "brothers" (v. 6). The word "apostles," then, denoted a group which was broader than that of the Twelve and narrower than that of the "brothers," and which had received the "mission of the Resurrected Christ, unlike the 'brothers,' who could testify to him but had not been sent with the same authority and commission to proclaim the Gospel."[16] It is this acceptation of the term that Paul implicitly employs in laying claim to the title and authority of "apostle." The expression connotes the mission received from the Risen One, a mission which, in the case of the Twelve, had been anticipated at the moment of their dispatch to the mission of Galilee.

## THE TWELVE

The expression, "the Twelve," is the preferred one in the gospels (Mark 3:14, 4:10, 6:7; Matt. 10:5, 20:17, 26:14,20; Luke 9:1,12, 18:31; John 6:67,70,71, 20:24). It is found as early as 1 Corinthians 15:5.

This expression has a proper, specific meaning. In the background we glimpse the twelve tribes of Israel and the twelve patriarchs who are the ancestors of these tribes. The choice of the "Twelve" suggests continuity with Israel, then. It links the Messianic people with the Israel of the Fathers. And yet the Twelve chosen by Jesus are obviously no longer the ancestors or even the ethnic representatives of these tribes. They are the prototypes of a Messianic Israel in which the criterion of membership is no longer carnal lineage, but conversion and faith. Thus, the selection of the Twelve suggests that the umbrella of the apostolic mission will continue to be Israel, if an Israel now called to more depth and breadth.

The mission of the Twelve, then, is not to be understood solely in function of the commission to go forth to the whole world to proclaim the Good News. We find another pole of their ministry expressed in another logion of Jesus, one directly relating to the number twelve: "I give you my solemn word, in the new age when the Son of Man takes his seat upon a throne befitting his glory, you who have followed me shall likewise take your places on twelve thrones to judge the twelve tribes of Israel" (Matt. 19:28).

The parallel of Luke 22:28-30 is inserted in an altogether different context, thus seeming to indicate a floating logion originally distinct from either the Matthean or Lucan context. Luke attaches it to the account of the institution of the Eucharist, and Matthew makes the promise to the Twelve an aspect of the reward promised to generous disciples. In the original, floating logion, there was no question of a reward in heaven. The text had a more basic meaning and defined the function of the Twelve as "judges" of the twelve tribes of Israel. J. Dupont has shown that the terms are to be understood in their literal, eschatological sense.[17] "To judge" does not mean "to rule," and "Israel" is not the church. The Twelve are to discharge the function of assessors in the eschatological judgment, and this with regard to the people of Israel.

This was the original sense of the Lord's words. We may wonder, then, how the Twelve applied them to themselves while they awaited the "restoration of Israel" (cf. Acts 1:6) in the period following the Resurrection. They must have recalled these words, since they had persisted in the gospel tradition. They must also have transposed them in light of the new situation in which they found themselves. In this new context, the logion meant that the role of the Twelve consisted in being the rallying point of the gathering of Israel and the nations before the judgment seat of God (cf. Matt. 25:31-32), and this in the perspective of a centripetal universalism. Meanwhile, "this eschatological prerogative conferred on the Twelve" was not without its earthly, missionary counterpart, linked as it was to a "terrestrial mission vis-à-vis the people of Israel in their entirety."[18] At the moment of the Galilean missionary mandate, Jesus had dispatched the Twelve to lay the groundwork for the eschatological judgment: their proclamation of the gospel would function as a judgment in terms of whether that gospel was accepted or rejected (Matt. 10:5-16 and par.; Luke 10:4-12). It is this same proclamation of the gospel with which the Twelve continued to regard themselves charged when they found themselves alone after Jesus' leave-taking. They adopted a missionary attitude, but it was with regard to Israel that they did so. Although they were not yet seated on the thrones of their glory, the image of the thrones and the definition of their function vis-à-vis the twelve tribes of Israel scarcely recommended a course to the ends of the earth. They remained in Jerusalem not out of timidity, then, or narrow-mindedness, but because this was essentially their mission as the Twelve. They visited the Temple daily (Acts 2:46, 3:1), and it was in the Temple that they preached (Acts 5:12). There was more than piety here. The Temple was the focus of the expectations and mission of the Twelve.

B. Gerhardssohn has suggested that the activity of the Twelve in Jerusalem must have been of the rabbinical type.[19] The "ministry of the word" cited in Acts 6:4 did not necessarily mean a preaching of the gospel, Gerhardssohn holds. Rather, it consisted in a didactic teaching, a "doctrinal labor based on the scriptures and on the tradition received from Christ."[20] They devoted their lives, in "concentrated and persevering fashion, from morning to evening, to prayer and the service of the word" understood in this magisterial sense.[21]

Gerhardssohn is too rigid in his application of the rabbinical model to the primitive church. One can scarcely imagine the Twelve functioning as a "theological commission" or as an "anti-Sanhedrin." It is not clear why they would be deprived of the glad right to communicate the Good News of the Lord Jesus. There is no reason to attempt to cast doubt on the missionary image Luke gives us of the beginnings of the church. Gerhardssohn's thesis does, however, have the merit of suggesting other types of service of the word than that of itinerant preachers along the highways of the world. Actually, the role of the Twelve consisted principally in gathering the "twelve tribes" into the Messianic fold by inviting them to conversion. Thus, the Twelve intended to form a new, regenerate people, which, on the Day of God, would become the rallying point of all the nations of the earth.

The Galilean mission of the disciples had already begun to transfer to the present the eschatological gathering of the people of Israel for judgment. The postpaschal mission at Jerusalem continued to render eschatological perspectives current. Luke prolonged this transfer of eschatology to the concrete realities of the life of the church. He inserted the logion on the participation of the Twelve in the judgment into the context of the Last Supper and an admonition to the Twelve. Somewhat after the manner of John, Luke has added a testament to Jesus' last supper in the form of a little discourse (Luke 22:21-30). In the framework of this testament, the logion of the twelve thrones comes to bear on the postpaschal period of the church and defines a style of apostolic life and exercise of the ministry. The Twelve are to inherit a "dominion" (Luke 22:29). While they must assume this function with the humility of servants (vv. 24-27), they must also bear its responsibility. It is no longer the eschatological judgment that is envisaged, but the direction of the church, and "judging" now takes on the meaning of "governing."[22] But even in the context of the postpaschal mission which Luke gives it, the logion continues to situate the mission of the Twelve in the framework of Israel. The chapters that Acts devotes to the activity of the Twelve in Jerusalem and Judaea underscore the preferential and central role of Israel in God's plan.

It is a concentric missionary aim, then, that emerges from the logion of the thrones. This illustrates the structure of Acts. In the center we have the Twelve, seated at the messianic table and enthroned; round about, regenerate Israel gathers, by the grace of the Risen One and the action of the Spirit; finally come the nations, called to share in Israel's privileges.

### THE TWELVE APOSTLES, A MISSIOLOGICAL SYNTHESIS

The Lucan expression, the "twelve apostles," then, is a synthesis, summarizing the great lines of a reflection on mission.

It associates the two poles of election and universalism, gathering and emergence, poles already defined by the mission of Israel in the Old Testament and the attitude of Jesus. As *twelve*, Jesus' mandatories represent a return to unity and the assembly of those who, in virtue of their conversion, are prepared for judgment. As *apostles*, they are "sent" and represent the dynamism of the word that emerges from Zion.

The Lucan expression, the "twelve apostles," also establishes the connection between an eschatological expectancy and the concrete engagement of the word in the course of history. As "twelve," they evoke the eschatological perspectives of the "restoration of Israel"; as "apostles," they are "sent" to proclaim the gospel of Jesus Christ, which already calls the nations to come together in conversion and faith.

In thus gathering into a single expression the centripetal, eschatological tendencies of the Palestinian church and the decentralized, concretely engaged mission of the Judaeo-Hellenistic and Hellenistic communities, Luke has sought to bring out the profound convergence of two attitudes. Tensions existed, but Luke sought to show that these apparently opposed tendencies were not contradictory. A gathering of Israel and an openness to the nations were but the two poles of the mission that Jesus had entrusted to his own when he chose twelve of their number to make them apostles.

## PETER

The case of Peter is particularly instructive. It is Peter who occupies center stage in the first part of Acts, and there is no reason to doubt this datum of the Lucan account. It corresponds to the fact that, in all of the gospel traditions, Peter's name always begins the lists of the Twelve, and that it is generally he who, for better or for worse, takes the initiative. Peter is not always proposed as a model to be imitated. He doubts, he completely misunderstands, he sometimes reacts as a "satan" (Mark 8:33), he sleeps at the moment of the Agony, he even denies his Master. Even after the Resurrection, he will have need of a dressing-down from Paul in order to be once again "straightforward about the truth of the gospel" (Paul's report, Gal. 2:11-14; here, v. 14). But all of this helps us identify what he represents. Peter is proposed not as a model but as a fulcrum. To say that the faith of Peter is to be the rock on which the church is built is still too idealistic. He is the representative of the church, even in its human weakness, and then, in counterpart, of the divine might that bursts through this weakness, which makes of him the *kepha*. There is only one Rock, the Lord, and Peter is a stone only to the extent that he allows all human sufficiency to be scoured away so that the divine Rock may appear in all its beauty and preeminence. Peter is a limit case of the dialectic between weakness and strength that Paul analyzes in his own case in 2 Corinthians 12:7-11.

It is this dialectic that Luke engages in his portrait of Peter in Acts. In the miracle of the healing of the cripple at the Beautiful Gate, Peter emphasizes that it is not "by some power or holiness of our own" that this has happened (Acts 3:12); it is "in the name of Jesus Christ the Nazarean . . . [that] this man stands before you perfectly sound" (Acts 4:10). In their prayer, Peter and his companions see themselves as a persecuted community, threatened on all sides. They can only ask God to "stretch forth his hand" that the power of the "name of Jesus" may be manifested (Acts 4:23-30). Indeed, a substantial part of Peter's work is accomplished while he is under arrest or in prison (4:1-22, 5:17-42, 12:1-9). All of Peter's great initiatives are commanded by the Spirit (2:14-41, 4:8, 11:12), the name of Jesus (3:6, 4:7-12), or a "voice" from on high (10:13-15, 11:7-9). As in the gospels, Peter's mission is first and foremost an act of God. It is not so much Peter who works for God as God who leads Peter in his task.

Meanwhile, it is by Peter, of course, with or without John as his companion, that this activity is performed. "Peter's career was that of a missionary."[23] It is he who pronounces the first missionary discourse (Acts 2:14-41), intervenes before the Sanhedrin (4:9-12, 5:29-32), pronounces judgment (5:3-9), confirms the passage of the word into Samaria (8:14-17), and especially, for the first time, receives pagans into the community on the basis of faith instead of circumcision (Acts chaps. 10-11). Luke is also at pains to show that all of the great missionary options that will define the ministry of Paul are already present in the apostolate of Peter.

In Luke's outlook, it is the first part of Acts that founds mission. In our haste to "get to Paul," we sometimes tend to see this first part only as fumbling and groping for mission, while the Pauline apostolate will be true, full-fledged mission. From this viewpoint, Peter and his limited field of activity seem paltry. But we must not lose sight of the fact that, in the division of the territories cited in Galatians 2:7-10 and underlying the plan of Acts—Peter being sent to the Jews and Paul to the nations—it is the first mission field that is more important in the eyes of Paul and Luke as well as in those of Peter and the whole New Testament. Ministries are not to be measured by distances covered. Paul may have crossed the seas and reached the extremities of the earth; but the apostolate to Israel retains priority and preeminence.

In the Lucan perspective, the first chapters of Acts are fundamental. They represent the apostolic witness, the age of the privileged witnesses who alone represent the qualities of the apostle listed by Peter in Acts 1:21-22: to have accompanied Jesus from the time of his baptism by John, and to be a witness of the Resurrection. Paul did not fulfill the former condition. Glorious as it was, his work was subordinate to the apostolate of the Twelve. This subordination was not that of a delegated jurisdiction. The matter goes deeper than that. Paul's ministry belonged to the subapostolic order of those who had not been witnesses of the life of Jesus, and who, furthermore, addressed the nations. On both criteria, Paul's order was subordinate to the fundamental order of beginnings represented by the Twelve grouped around Peter, the eyewitnesses who had been sent to Israel. It is these, and first of all Peter, who are apostles par excellence. As with Jesus, the validity and solidity of the missionary witness take precedence over considerations of its extent.

We must turn the Acts of the Apostles right-side-out, so to speak. This may require that we reverse the reading we sometimes make when we begin with Paul. Acts places Peter and Paul in parallel, as the tandem of Peter and Paul is in turn set in parallel with Jesus. This yields a hierarchical construction in which the supreme moment is the era of Jesus, with the apostolic age of Jesus' witnesses subordinated to that era and in turn prolonged into the subapostolic age of the other servants of the Word, of whom Paul is the prototype. To be sure, there is a progression toward the "ends of the earth" in Acts and an openness to the nations; but this does not mean that, from Jesus to Paul, everything is to be ranged along a rectilinear evolutionary course of which the postapostolic age of Paul would represent the pinnacle. For Luke, the postapostolic age in which we live is not the golden age. If there were to be a golden age, it would be the apostolic era. We need only compare the enthusiastic capsules of Acts 2:42-47 and 4:32-35 with the dismal forecasts of 20:29-32: on the one hand, "they devoted themselves to the apostles' instruction and the communal life, to the breaking of bread and the prayers" (Acts 2:42), with "one heart and one mind" (4:32); and on the other, "savage wolves ... distorting the truth," and "tears" in the eyes of Paul himself at the sight of the dangers threatening the community.

This is not to detract from the merit of Paul. Nor was this merit slight in Luke's eyes, in virtue of the new dimension that Paul had bestowed on mission, as we shall see in our next chapter. But we must not forget that these new horizons had already been traced in outline by the ministry of Peter. It is Peter who consecrates the overtures to Samaria (Acts 8:14-17) and to the uncircumcised (Acts chaps. 10-11). It is this attitude of Peter's that founds universal mission, justifies the extension of the word to new worlds and endows this extension with legitimacy and validity. As an apostolic ministry, Peter's ministry is necessarily "missionary."[24] The primacy of Peter is of the order of mission. After all, Peter is defined by a church that identifies with its mission, and he exercises this primacy precisely by situating his mission at Jerusalem, at the heart of Israel.

## CONCLUSION

### PLURALITY AND UNITY

Luke has constructed Acts as a journey (*hodos*), the course (*dromos*) of the Word from Jerusalem to the ends of the earth. To this purpose he has arranged the historical data he has at his disposal in an orderly series that leads the eye toward ever-expanding horizons. Actually, some of the narrative elements he has arranged sequentially occurred concomitantly. The forms of church and of mission cited at the beginning of this chapter, and perhaps others as well, actually developed in parallel. The church of Jerusalem must have continued to prepare the eschatological gathering at Zion even after Paul and the Judaeo-Hellenistic church had launched the mission to the Gentiles.

Must we then regard these two kinds of mission as mutually exclusive, or make a choice between them? Must we prioritize the universal mission of the Pauline type and condemn the Judaeo-Christian attitude, and thank heaven for having taken it off the menu under the impulse of a Pauline dynamism and the shock of the events of A.D. 70? Or on the contrary, shall we renounce Paul, accuse him of unfaithfulness to Jesus and a practical Pelagianism, and censure his endeavor as infected with the activism of the Hellenistic philosophical sects?

Luke says: *Datur tertium*. Not that his is a syncretistic solution of any sort; he scarcely needs to resort to a compromise, since he does not see the two approaches as standing in mutual opposition. He does not belittle the Jerusalemite attitude or regard it as a point of departure to be transcended and abandoned. On the contrary, he devotes chapter after chapter to it, insisting on the foundational role of Peter and the Twelve. He also demonstrates the seminal character of this period: the Jerusalemite mission itself is open to the nations. By way of the Ethiopian minister and the centurion Cornelius, it prefigures the incorporation of the nations. Still, that mission remains faithful to its objective of convoking the renewed people of God, who will constitute the pole of universal attraction. Without this firmly established pole, the Book of Acts would not be comprehensible. The time will come when frontiers will fall, and Paul will bear his project of evangelization to Asia Minor, Greece, and even Rome. But the time of Jerusalem must be well marked, and the chosen people must be called, so that mission may be the gathering, the formation of a people joined by the apostolic teaching in a communion of siblingship and in prayer (cf. Acts 2:42), and not the dissemination of ideas.

Thus, Luke's historical view is a vision of faith. Furthermore, it has basic historical value. Luke has doubtless softened the images and glossed over the differences. But he has a point: the divergent tendencies of primitive Christianity need not be hardened into sectarian oppositions. When Luke describes the church of origins as being of one heart and one soul (Acts 4:32), he is painting an icon, of course. But it would be cynical, and unjustifiably so, to wish to smudge the gilt and cloud the tableau with a concept of hostile churches in a mutual standoff, experiencing their differences in harshness and hostility. Nothing—certainly not the letters of Paul—suggests the lack of a basic will to unity. The ambassadors to the nations intended to gather a people and splice it onto a regenerate Israel. The icon of the primitive church sketched by Luke is beautiful precisely because it has the profound truth of icons—which is not that of material exactitude, but that of an interior light that, precisely, transforms the material traits of the subject.

## DEED DIVINE AND HUMAN

The beauty of the Lucan work is not finicky or mincing. It has the vigor of Jesus' mission. It also shows the creativity of original thought.

1. Like that of Jesus and the people of Israel, the mission of the church is first and foremost the work and *deed of God*. More specifically, in Lucan terms, it is the deed of the Spirit. Before being the Acts of the Apostles, Luke's second book is the record of the Acts of the Spirit. This is no crypto-Pelagianism. The apocalypse of the Spirit on the Day of Pentecost corresponds to the apocalypse of the Messiah in Luke 1:26-38, and the function of this second apocalypse, like that of the first, is to demonstrate the divine origin of the deed about to be narrated. The church *en mission* will find cohesion and identity in this divine strength, which dwells within it and thrusts it onward.

2. But Luke is very interested in human mediation.[25] He has too keen a sense of history for it to be otherwise. Luke wants to reconcile the gospel

message with the fact of time. He wants to display an eschatology in history. This has an effect on his conception of mission. On the one hand, mission will be solidly rooted in the history of Israel. On the other, it will penetrate the geographical and historical fabric of all humanity.

a. With regard to the past: Luke is interested in Israel's past, and he ascribes a positive value to that past. For Luke, Israel is not the Law and the slavery the Law entailed, but the prophets, the Temple, the righteous. Luke is also interested in the gentile past; he finds religion there and the fear of God (Acts 10:2). He finds authentic piety even among the Athenians and endorses the dicta of their poets (Acts 17:22-29). Luke underscores a historical continuity with the past more than an eschatological breach. Luke is open to dialogue. He is the pioneer of the theologies of inculturation.

b. With regard to the human life of the present: Luke is acutely aware of time. Thus, he has a special interest in the human dimensions of salvation. Received by a people in its history, the salvation of God will be experienced and communicated throughout the fabric of human life, including the socioeconomic. The Christian community of Acts will bear the witness of its word, yes, but also of its joy, its prayer, its communion, and its sharing. In presenting this image of a community of an integral sharing of heart and goods alike (Acts 2:44-45, 4:32-35), Luke continues to found the "Christian sociology" that he has already sketched in his gospel (cf. Luke 16, 19:8, 3:10-14). Thus, the Word has descended into socioeconomic realities and taken possession of them. Of these realities Luke would have said, with Paul VI in the "Apostolic Exhortation on Evangelization in the Modern World," that they were "not foreign to evangelization."[26]

### THE PROBLEM OF ISRAEL

And so a problem arises. Acts insists on the priority of Israel. This priority is not only chronological; otherwise it would scarcely have been necessary to devote so many chapters to it in a "first moment." It is theological, as well; otherwise, Israel would not have been the object of the fundamental, foundational ministry of the Twelve and Peter. Nevertheless, in a "second moment," Acts will open up to the nations. Faith will be detached from circumcision, and, with Paul as the representative of the subapostolic generation, the Word will depart for new generations and new frontiers. Will this mean that the umbilical cord has finally been severed? We must return to this question in the light of the second part of Acts, to which we now address our attention.

# 9

# Paul

*We have already met Paul in Acts, by way of a comparison with Peter. In the Christian imagination, Paul is the missionary par excellence, "the Apostle." Our study of the period in Acts that precedes Paul has enabled us to snatch him from this deceptive isolation. Paul remains the great figurehead of Christian mission. However, we must go beyond the grand portrait of Christian hagiography and move as nearly as possible to the testimony of the New Testament. Here we actually find a double image — that of Acts, and that of the self-portrait presented in the letters. First we shall examine these images in separation; then we shall examine the convergences residing in their difference.*

*In the foregoing chapter, we began our examination of Acts. We shall remain with that book for the moment and open our study of Paul with Luke's account of him. Then we shall go back to the writings of Paul himself, to look for the profound motivations of his apostolic dynamism.*

## PAUL IN THE ACTS OF THE APOSTLES

Luke's portrayal of Christian origins was extremely effective. The Christian fancy has been completely caught by the image he has sketched. It is from Acts that we have the figure of Paul as the giant of the apostolate — the figure reproduced, for example, in classic sculpture such as we may behold in the Basilica of Saint Paul in Rome. It requires an effort on our part to comprehend that the sword the apostle carries is the martyr's sword. The stature and posture of the hero of the gospel are too imposing to show the conquistador of faith. Lives of Paul delight in portraying their hero as the tireless voyager, bearing the new faith to the farthest corners of the known world, the inspired strategist progressively broadening the frontiers of the Christian religion. The vision is a militant one, nor does it escape the pitfalls of triumphalism or the ambiguities of a colonial mentality.

But was this actually Luke's view? Have we not more or less unconsciously reread Acts in the light of a particular type of modern, militant,
activist mission? It will be well worth our while to look more closely at the
Lucan portrait of Paul, which may be less "modern," and more nuanced,
than we suppose.

### NEW HORIZONS

Through Paul, the second part of Acts presents a new face of mission.
Paul takes up the human mediation of the word and launches a carefully
planned evangelizing campaign. He goes out to the nations, goes from
Antioch in Syria to Cyprus and Asia Minor, then to Europe, in three campaigns reminiscent of Alexander the Great. He sows the faith in all of the
great centers of the Roman world: Antioch, Ephesus, Thessalonica, Athens,
and Corinth.

In doing so, he inaugurates a new era, and, for the author of Acts,
becomes the symbol of the postapostolic generations that will succeed the
direct, strictly apostolic witnesses. Deprived of the apostolic dignity of eyewitnesses, these generations will yet be the ones to deploy the Word in
space and time, and lead it to new horizons. Thus Paul will encounter, in
his ministry, the great political realities of the Roman world, from his first
sojourn on Cyprus with the conversion of Proconsul Sergius Paulus, to the
judicial proceedings which he will deliberately have had transferred to
Roman jurisdiction. Thus, he will have met the great Greco-Levantine
world of commerce (Acts 16:14-15), Athenian culture (17:18-32), and pagan
religion for better (17:23, 27-28) and for worse (19:23-40).

According to Luke, apart from the case of the pagan devotion to Artemis
at Ephesus, Paul's encounter with the various aspects of the Roman world
is irenic. Paul addresses this world with benevolence and in return receives
a sympathetic hearing. Gospel and earthly realities meet in peace, and in
the encounter, the Word acquires rich new dimensions.

### THE DISCOURSE AT ATHENS

This is especially the sense that Luke attributes to the discourse in the
Areopagus (Acts 17:22-31). The episode has often been treated as an inter-
lude of scant importance. Arriving at Athens and taken by the cultural
ambience of the city, Paul is thought to have committed a tactical error.
He resorts to Greek rhetoric. The unhappy attempt is met with defeat. The
preacher is mocked, and the meeting is adjourned *sine die* (Acts 17:32).
Paul leaves in disgust, swearing never to return. He comes to Corinth and
draws his conclusions: in vain has he sought to resort to "wordy wisdom"
—the only value is the folly of the cross of Christ (1 Cor. 1:17-18). Henceforth he will know nothing but Jesus Christ and Jesus Christ crucified
(1 Cor. 2:1-2). For Paul, this chapter of the dialogue is closed. Only the

scandal of the cross can express the faith and save the world.

This superficially edifying reconstruction of events is actually a very dubious one. It is very disputable methodology to resort indifferently to Acts and the letters for the purpose of reconstituting Paul's states of soul. Furthermore, the episode at Athens does not actually end in failure: "A few did join him, however, to become believers. Among these were Dionysius, a member of the court of the Areopagus, a woman named Damaris, and a few others" (Acts 17:34). Here are a half-dozen converts at the very least, including members of the upper classes. What missionary in these circumstances would have regarded it a defeat to have achieved so much in a single sermon?

Furthermore, there is nothing in the structure of Acts to suggest that Luke is presenting the discourse at Athens as an example of an apostolic blunder. The conference of Jerusalem in chapter 15 had been a key event. Universal mission had been accorded full privileges, and Paul, its representative, would now take center stage. As chapter 16 opens, the reader senses great things to come. Paul's first travel plans fail. The Spirit has other notions (Acts 16:6-7) and conducts Paul and Silas to the Asian frontier, to Troas, a city rich in the memories of ancient Troy. A Macedonian appears in a dream like an angel of the Lord, calling Paul to cross the strait to the land of Alexander, in Europe (16:9). Philippi, the next stop, says Luke, was "a leading city in the district of Macedonia" (16:12). Administratively, Amphipolis was more important. Symbolically, however, Philippi was greater, with its memories of Philip of Macedon and Alexander the Great.

The Lucan construction is obviously calculated to underscore the symbolic value of this shift to the West. And so we have the messenger of the gospel at Athens, which city, while in political subjection to the Roman conqueror, remains the high and holy house of Greek culture. The account will now proceed to exalt that city. A good many important cities of the Mediterranean world have been cited by now. But they have been mere ports of call on the apostolic itinerary and have merited no special portrayal. Athens is a case apart. Luke borrows the style of a travel guide and describes the cultural landscape composed of various Stoic and Epicurean schools, the intellectual climate of affected dilettantism and bantering curiosity (Acts 17:18,21). He even leads us, in the company of Paul, on a tour of the religious landmarks of the city (17:16). This lengthy prologue is an attempt to dramatize the significance of the discourse at Athens: the encounter of the Word with Western culture.

This is the usual purpose of the discourses in the narrative structure of Acts. They are intended to indicate an important turning point in the account and explain its meaning. In the architecture of Acts, the discourse at Athens marks a new stage in the growth of the Word. It presents new content, with its appeal to natural theology and the sages of Greece. It does not stand in isolation, however. It resumes the themes of the preaching to the pagans that have been sketched in the discourse at Lystra (Acts 14:15-17) and that are found in the résumé of the catechesis to the Thessalonians (1 Thes. 1:9-10). For that matter, this discourse to non-Jews merely extends and thrusts to its Christian conclusions the themes of the Judaeo-Hellenistic themes of the diaspora. Thus, this discourse is not presented as an example of failed evangelization. As E. Haenchen says, "Luke would not have described this particular event if he had not seen in it an altogether special meaning: actually, a sort of program for mission." And Haenchen concludes, with Martin Dibelius: "This is how preaching is done; this is how preaching ought to be done."[1]

But this "program for mission" appeals to the poets and philosophers Aratos and Epimenides. Following the example of Hellenistic Judaism, it echoes the great enterprise of Greek philosophy—the quest for Ultimate Reality, from the metaphysical principle underlying the world to thought and the divine, to *kosmos*, *logos* and the *theos*. Luke does not canonize Epimenides and Aratos. On the contrary, he gives their texts a sense that far outstrips the perspectives of, for example, Aratos' *Phenomena*, whose scope was actually only rather pragmatic.[2] In the encounter between the gospel and Greece, Greek thought grows in breadth and depth; but Christian thought takes on new dimensions, as well. The gospel no longer responds only to the expectation of the prophets and their Israel. Now it is thrust into the heart of a cosmological and metaphysical search and dons new mystical aspects. " 'In him we live and move and have our being' . . . 'for we too are his offspring' " (Acts 17:28). Continuity with Israel is now fitted into the larger continuity of the history of the nations. The Word finds new echoes in this larger context: it encounters the fundamental questions of Being and the One, and takes on a universal value, for the West immediately, and for other metaphysical civilizations, such as India, indirectly.[3] "Thus," by the power of the Spirit, "did the word of the Lord continue to spread" (Acts 19:20), touching new worlds. Luke gives Paul a great role in making him the servant of this Word and this growth in the Spirit.

### SOME OBSERVATIONS

In refusing Paul the title of apostle, Luke did not intend to belittle him. He only wished to give him his specific place, which was great enough. Paul is not an apostle in the sense of the office of the Twelve. He is something else—something both more and less than the ministry of the Twelve. On the one hand, Paul is less than the Twelve, since he is neither an eyewitness nor a member of the *numerus clausus* of the Twelve. On the other, he represents more than they, by reason of the new dimensions he confers upon the Word. From this viewpoint, Paul comes on the scene as the model of active, deliberate mission, the first of the long line of great missionaries like Patrick, Augustine of Canterbury, Boniface or Xavier, or the Nestorian monks who carried the gospel clear to China. The Lucan portrait of Paul also makes him a pioneer of inculturation, a forerunner of the attitude of the Fathers of the church toward ancient culture, and a foreshadowing of today's efforts on the part of mission to see the gospel incarnate in the civilizations of the world.

It would be a misunderstanding of Paul and his mission, however, to neglect all but his activist, voluntaristic traits. Paul then would be the entrepreneur of mission instead of the servant of the Word that Luke saw in him. Acts paints a more balanced portrait. An examination of some of the lines of this portrait will help us appreciate its nuances.

1. According to Acts, *Paul is entirely at the disposal of the Spirit*. None of the great steps of his ministry are taken as the result of a deliberate decision. They are all taken at the instigation of the Spirit. It is the Spirit who, in Acts 13:2, demands that Paul and Barnabas be set apart for the work to which they have been called, who sets a seal of approval on the admittance of the uncircumcised (Acts 15:28), and who manipulates the conditions of the second journey, blocking the two envoys' routes so that they come to find themselves on the threshold of Europe (16:6-10). And when Paul undertakes the great journey of the Captivity, which will take him to Rome, he does so as a prisoner of the Spirit (20:22; cf. 21:4,11). The new horizons opened up by Paul's mission are first of all opened up by the Spirit, and if Paul, who is generally inferior to the Twelve, is superior to them in some respects, it is the Spirit who bestows this greatness upon him.

2. For Luke, *the Spirit acts amidst a people*. The Spirit is given to the church, and Paul presents himself as a person of the church. The mandate of the Spirit to begin the work of the nations is given in a context of worship and with a community laying on of hands (Acts 13:2-3). Official acceptance of the uncircumcised is sanctioned by a decision of the Holy Spirit and the church of Jerusalem (15:28). It is through the prophets of the communities that the Spirit guides Paul's steps (21:4-10). Indeed, it is by the mediation of Ananias and the church of Damascus that Christ had informed Paul of his vocation (9:11-16). Luke does not isolate Paul on a hagiographical pedestal. He shows him surrounded and borne up by a community which will be the locus in which the Spirit will act to launch and guide his mission.

3. According to the plan of the composition of Acts, *this community is intimately bound to Israel*. In the foregoing chapter, we established the overall viewpoint of Acts: evangelization begins "in Jerusalem." Apostle to the nations that he is, Paul yet remains faithful to this perspective. The Paul of Acts remains a true child of Israel: "I am a Jew," he tells the crowd at Jerusalem (Acts 22:3) — not, "I was a Jew" — and he goes into detail (22:1-4). He accepts the authority of the high priest (23:5) and is eager to place the problem posed by Jesus' Resurrection in a context of the Jewish problematic (23:6-9, 24:21), to the point where the party of the Pharisees actually takes his side and cause (23:9); at most, any differences are "over issues in their own religion" (25:19).

Luke cites these words of Paul, not to make him a sly litigant playing his cards from under the table, but, on the contrary, to show us that his "game" is altogether open and aboveboard. Throughout his missionary campaign among the nations, Paul is only serving the God of the Fathers. True, he proclaims a "new way," which his opponents may call a "sect" (Acts 24:14). But neither side imagines faith in Christ to be a new religion. Throughout his ministry, Paul will continue to assign precedence to the Jews, and, everywhere he goes, he will first visit the synagogue or Jewish place of prayer (Acts 13:5,14,44, 14:1, 16:13, 17:1-2,10, 18:4,19, 19:8).

But does not the end of the book finally make a break with Israel? The encounter with the Jewish community of Rome is presented in curious fashion. Paul's Jewish compatriots have received him with an open mind (Acts 28:21-22); but because his first sermon does not succeed in establishing a unanimous conviction (28:23-25), he seems to lose confidence in his people and cites Isaiah's dismal threat: "You are to make the heart of this people sluggish, to dull their ears and close their eyes; Else . . . they will turn and be healed" (Isa. 6:10).

Thus, "this salvation of God has been transmitted to the Gentiles—who will heed it!" (Acts 28:28). Neither the logic nor the psychology of the narrative seems to justify this solemn conclusion. Paul could scarcely have hoped to establish unanimity among his auditors in a single sermon. And why should the little group of Jews at Rome be regarded as representing all Israel? Everywhere else, whether with the Jews at Antioch in Pisidia (Acts 13:42-45,48-51), at Corinth (18:4-8), at Ephesus (19:8-10), or with non-Jews at Athens (17:32-34), Paul had obtained the same mixed result that every missionary must expect. At the level of the account, nothing justifies the dramatic conclusion drawn by Paul from this semidefeat. This being the case, are we not dealing with a literary artifice, by which the author of the account would signify that, while faith in Christ was born in Israel and must acknowledge this origin, the moment has come to cut the cord? Was this not precisely the situation that Luke could observe when he was writing his book, after the caesura occasioned by the Jewish revolt of A.D. 70 and the destruction of the Temple? Israel had fallen; was the church not "on its own" now, and must it not regard the call to salvation as now addressed to the nations, independently of Israel?

This could be the meaning of the conclusion of Acts. It is to be observed, however, that the book does not quite conclude with the verses 25-28. There are two more verses, and these tell us that Paul received all who came to him at Rome, proclaiming the Reign to them (Acts 28:30-31). A variant reading specifies that "all" means "Jews and Greeks" alike. Despite its critical tenuousness, this reading does have the merit of expressing Luke's meaning more clearly. Like Isaiah, Luke envisages a remnant of Israel that will accept the Word and continue to discharge the role of catalyst of the chosen people until the end of time. Has he not emphatically and repeatedly underscored the fact that thousands, indeed, *muriades*, tens of thousands (Acts 21:20), of Jews had embraced the faith (2:41, 4:4)? Has he not, throughout the pages of his gospel and of Acts advanced the theory of the righteous who accompanied Christ, from Zechariah and Elizabeth (Luke 1:5-6), Mary and Joseph (1:27), and Simeon and Anna (2:25,36), to the members of the synagogues of Beroea (Acts 17:11-12), Corinth (18:8), Ephesus (19:33), and Rome (28:24) who accepted the faith and, with the Twelve, composed regenerate Israel? For Luke, Israel the faithful exists, and the conclusion of Acts has no intent of being on the wrong side of the question after so many pages of evidence so assiduously amassed.

It would be a mistake, then, to see in the conclusion of Acts the theme of the "rejection of Israel." Luke's problem is not abstract.

It is that of a Christian church composed for the most part of Gentiles, but likewise attached to a self-image as the legitimate heir of the promises made by God to Israel. It is a matter of this church's identity.[4]

But how could this church still lay claim to a legitimacy of succession? The answer is, on the one hand, that the remnant of Israel subsists, and, on the other, that the hardening of the heart of the chosen people (Acts 28:25-27 = Isa. 6:9-10), like the gathering of the nations (Acts 13:47 = 26:23 = Isa. 49:6), is part and parcel of the prophetic message. In the last analysis, scripture views events, including defeats, as substantiating the continuity of God's plan for Israel. The conclusion of Acts resumes the theme of Jesus' inaugural discourse at Nazareth: the scriptures show that Jesus is indeed the Messiah who has been promised to Israel (Luke 4:18-27). At the same time and by the same token, he is "a revealing light to the Gentiles, the glory of . . . Israel" (Luke 2:32). Through all the hazards of defeat and rejection, God's plan unfolds in all continuity, just as the prophets had foretold it.[5]

4. Nevertheless, we must balance this continuity with a consideration of the *novelty introduced by the nations.* We have seen an example in the discourse at Athens. But it is the second part of Acts, in its entirety, that shines with the joy of the overture to the nations. This joy must have been strikingly expressed in the report Paul submitted to the assembly of Jerusalem: "They made their way . . . telling everyone about the conversion of the Gentiles as they went. Their story caused great joy among the brothers" (Acts 15:3; cf. 11:18).

Here we have a capsule of the entire atmosphere of the Pauline mission in Acts. The times inaugurated by Paul's ministry are indeed the "times of the Gentiles" (Luke 21:24), the period when the nations, hearing the gospel, echo it in their lives, their thought, and their culture. Joyfully, Luke foresees a new age of mission.

The religious community can now apprehend the world differently. Now comes the time, as Troeltsch says, of adaptation and compromises, but also the time when, through the rediscovery of the world as creation (cf. Acts 14, 17), new, positive relations between the Christian community and nature or culture can spring up.[6]

5. One final remark apropos of the portrait of Paul in the work of Luke: The second part of Acts is often summed up with a reference to the three missionary journeys. But let us observe, first of all, that the schema of the three journeys is questionable: the division between the second and third is far from crisp and clear. In Acts 18:22, the church that Paul greets is, likely enough, that of Caesarea. Even if it is more probably the church of Jerusalem, Luke passes over this visit too hurriedly for us to regard it as an important juncture in the text. Besides, the very disposition of the great blocks of the account suggests a different division of the Pauline ministry. In Acts chapters 13-20 Paul acts, or rather, the Spirit thrusts Paul to act and to develop his initiatives. But in chapters 21-28, Paul is a prisoner of the Spirit (20:22). Between the part in which Paul has the initiative and the part in which he is in the Spirit's thralldom, the division is neat and clear: eight chapters of activity and eight chapters of passivity. From a chronological viewpoint, this would be disproportionate: the eight chapters, 13-20, cover some twelve years of active ministry, while an equal number of chapters are devoted to the three years of captivity. Thus, Luke regards these three years as an important period, indeed, the most important period of Paul's entire ministry. It is during these three years that Paul will implement the program that has been outlined for him in his calling: "to bring my name to the Gentiles and their kings and to the people of Israel," while at the same time discovering "how much he will have to suffer for my name" (Acts 9:15). It is through these sufferings that he will be able to address these "kings" (24:10, 25:2-8), these "Israelites" in the Temple (22:3-21), and the Sanhedrin (23:6-9). It is especially in this "passion" that he will reach Rome, the "ends of the earth."

Above all, it is in the course of this captivity that Paul will identify most closely with Jesus. In the parallel construction of the Lucan compositions, Paul's captivity in Acts chapters 21-28 is the counterpart of that of Jesus in Luke chapters 22-23, as also of Peter's in the first part of Acts. The "Acts of Paul," the second part of Acts, takes up the theme of Jesus' journey, and, just as the latter is a journey through suffering toward an ascension (*analēmpseōs*, Luke 9:51), so also Paul's journey, in fetters and tribulation (Acts 20:23), gradually progresses toward the moment when the Word will take wing "with full assurance, and without any hindrance whatever" (Acts 28:31), as we have it in the triumphal note of the conclusion of Luke's work.

There is less passivity, then, than passion in Acts chapters 21-28. The final viewpoint of Acts on Paul's mission is in agreement with that of the Gospel of Luke. When all is said and done concerning Paul's activity, zeal, initiatives, and success, yet the essential remains unexpressed. By his suffering, Paul, like Jesus, has entered into the mystery of the pure divine power. Joachim Jeremias has said of Jesus that he did not convert the world, he died on the cross. The Book of Acts does not swerve one iota from this basic Christian intuition. To be sure, Paul went forth to convert the nations. But above all, he reproduced his Master's passion, and it is at the heart of this passion that he attained the goal of his course.

## PAUL AS SEEN THROUGH HIS OWN EYES

The letters of Paul constitute a unique documentation on the missionary awareness of the primitive church. In the context of a gigantic apostolic effort and in the face of incessant opposition and incomprehension, a missionary, who is also a thinker and a writer, opens his heart and shares his introspection and theological reflection. No other book of the Bible, with the possible exception of Jeremiah, offers such access to the subjectivity of a servant of the Word.

The wealth of this documentation renders the commentator's task all the more difficult. Entire volumes have been composed on the problem of Paul's missionary goal. In the effervescence of projects, ideas, outlines, positions, and reactions, how are we to identify the elements we require for a systematic presentation? How may we avoid forcing Paul's living thought onto the Procrustean bed of our paltry schemata?

We must set limits, of course; at the same time, we must avoid unnecessary subjectivity in our choice of what we regard as important. With a view to avoiding subjectivity, we shall listen to Paul himself define his apostolic identity. Lest we extend ourselves unduly, we shall limit our study to the Letter to the Romans. The choice of this letter as a missionary document may not seem obvious. However, as we shall see, it is framed by a pair of texts that describes the way in which Paul saw his role. These texts are Romans 1:1-17 and 15:15-25. The position of these texts at the beginning and end of the letter makes them particularly significant. From a point of departure in the "inclusion" they form, we shall attempt to retrace the missionary thinking of Paul as we have it in the Letter to the Romans. A comparison with Luke, presented later in this chapter, will enable us to generalize the observations that we shall have made in this precise context.

### TWO PARALLEL TEXTS AND AN "INCLUSION"

The few phrases with which Paul, addressing the community of Rome, describes his apostolic identity, frame the entire letter. We are not dealing with *obiter dicta*, then. These two passages—Romans 1:1-17 and 15:15-25— express views that govern the construction of the Letter to the Romans and assign all of the theological developments of the letter their proper place in Paul's personal conception of mission.

| *Romans 1:1-17* | *Romans 15:15-25* |
|---|---|
| ... Paul, a servant of Christ Jesus, called to be an apostle and set apart to proclaim the gospel of God.... | ... A minister of Christ Jesus ... with the priestly duty of preaching the gospel. ... |
| Through him we have been favored with apostleship, | God has given me the grace ... |
| that we may ... bring to obedient faith | ... to win ... to obedience |
| all the Gentiles, | ... the Gentiles ... |
| among whom are you who have been called.... | consecrated by the Holy Spirit ... to be a minister of Jesus Christ ... |
| The God I worship in the spirit by preaching the gospel of his Son.... | so that the Gentiles may be offered up as a pleasing sacrifice. ... |
| For I long to see you.... | I ... cherish the desire to visit you. ... |
| I have often planned to visit you.... | I hope to see you.... |
| I am eager to preach the gospel to you.... | ... to bring assistance to the saints. As soon as I can set out for Spain ... |
| I am not ashamed of the gospel. | It has been a point of honor with me ... |
| It is the power of God leading everyone who believes in it to salvation, the Jew first, then the Greek. | ... by the power of God's Spirit ... from Jerusalem all the way around to Illyria. |

The two texts express the same ideas, often in identical terms, if in a slightly different order: 1. The apostolic identity is defined by the proclamation of the Gospel ... 2. ... And more specifically, its proclamation to pagan peoples. 3. Priority, however, belongs to Israel. 4. The apostolic task is described as an act of worship or sacrifice. 5. Faith is a matter of obedience. 6. Paul is proud and confident of the apostolate ... 7. ... Since he can rely on the power of the Spirit. 8. Paul intends to visit Rome.

The parallelism of the two texts is so clear that we need not hesitate to explain one in terms of the other. Thus, 15:16 sets forth the service of the gospel as an act of "worship in the spirit": like a priest or Levite, the apostle prepares the sacrificial offering constituted by the faith of the Gentiles. The power of God that is the gospel in 1:16 is described in greater detail in 15:19: it is that of "mighty signs and marvels, by the power of God's Spirit." As for his goal of visiting Rome, Paul saves his heavy artillery for the conclusion of his letter. He has given the reasons for his journey in 1:13-15 — but only in general, as a desire to "do some fruitful work," and to "preach the gospel." He makes these reasons altogether clear in 15:24: he seeks the material and spiritual patronage of the church of Rome for his Spanish project.

Thus, the conclusion of the Letter to the Romans returns us to the introduction and makes some final specifications. It takes up the same themes and concretizes them. It is doubtless owing to the greater precision of chapter 15 that our text from that chapter has always been acknowledged as a description of the "ministry of Paul."[7] Chapter 1, on the other hand, has been treated as a mere "theological introduction." Actually, both texts have the same scope: never having visited Rome, Paul introduces himself to the Christians of that city, presenting himself as an "apostle" in the context of a concrete missionary project, that of carrying the gospel to Spain.

### SELF-PORTRAIT OF A MISSIONARY

We need only examine this pair of texts in order to discover Paul's conception of his missionary identity. A brief exegesis will bring out the highlights of this self-portrait.

### Romans 1:1-16

*"Paul"*: Paul introduces himself at the beginning of this letter without any mention of coworkers. This is quite exceptional on his part. He usually mentions the other members of his apostolic team (1 Cor. 1:1; 2 Cor. 1:1; Phil. 1:1; Col. 1:1; 1 Thes. 1:1; 2 Thes. 1:1). The reason for this exception is doubtless that he is embarking on a new stage in his apostolate. By now Paul has installed his teams from Jerusalem and Antioch in the various churches that he has already founded. Now a new apostolic team must be made up, and this addition constitutes an important aspect of the "assistance" Paul expects to receive from Rome.

*"Servant of Christ Jesus"*: Paul is a "servant," like the Servant in the Old Testament, and like Jesus himself. We observe that Paul not only steps into the place of the old prophets, but in the same breath replaces the name of Yahweh with that of his Master in the consecrated formula he employs.[8] At the same time, he undertakes to follow Jesus, the Servant of God.[9]

*"Called"*: The apostolate is not primarily a task taken up on one's own initiative. Primarily it is a mandate received. The ambassador must be commissioned (cf. 2 Cor. 5:20; Eph. 6:20).

*"Apostle"*: Here, as frequently, Paul insists on his title of apostle. It is his principal title, the one he cites in the exordia of all his letters, beginning with First Corinthians (thus, not in First or Second Thessalonians or in Philippians). In the Letter to the Galatians (chaps. 1-2, 6:11-18) and in Second Corinthians, he defends his right to this title passionately and at length. But the word "apostle" does not yet have, in Paul, the sense it will have in Luke. In his first letters, "apostle" seems only to be used in the

sense of missionary (1 Thes. 2:7, Phil. 2:25, and perhaps 1 Cor. 12:28). But from the way in which Paul has now come to defend this title, it appears that, for him, the word has taken on connotations of an official mandate from Christ (Gal. 1:1,11-16, 2:7-10), guaranteeing the integrity of the gospel (Gal. 1:8-9, 2:14-16, 6:14-16; 2 Cor. 10:4-8) and thereby, confidence (2 Cor. 3:12, 7:4; Eph. 3:12, 6:19; Phil. 1:20) and a parental authority (1 Thes. 2:11-12; 1 Cor. 4:15, Philem. 10; Gal. 4:19). With Luke, Paul would be willing to acknowledge that he is not of the Twelve, and that he has not had contact with the earthly Jesus: he is a miscarriage in the apostolate. But unlike Luke, he makes little of the importance of this physical contact with Jesus (2 Cor. 5:16); and, more than Luke, insists on the essential value of his own encounter with the Risen One (Gal. 1:15; 1 Cor. 9:1, 15:8-10; 2 Cor. 4:6) and on the legitimacy and continuity with Christ that this encounter guarantees him: he is Christ's authentic ambassador (2 Cor. 5:20).

*"Set apart to proclaim the gospel of God"*: The instrument of this ambassadorial office is the gospel. The apostolate is defined as the proclamation of the gospel, and its authority is none other than that of the gospel. The message makes the ambassador. Thus, it is the Good News that makes the apostle; without it the latter is nothing. Also, this gospel is the "Gospel of God." It is from God himself that the Good News comes, and it is God who is at work through it. God, in effect, makes his appeal through the ambassador (2 Cor. 5:20). Thus the Gospel is the "power of God" (Rom. 1:16).

*"Through him [Christ Jesus] we have been favored with apostleship"*: The apostolic vocation is a grace (cf. 1 Cor. 12:28; Rom. 12:3) before being a responsibility. It is a gift before being an activity. In Paul's mind, it is even a reserved charism: like every charism—except that of love—it represents a particular function in the body. Paul would doubtless admit that every Christian has an apostolic responsibility, although he does not speak much about it. He would surely not, however, tolerate such a watering-down of the sense of the word "apostle" that the word would denote no more than a conscious, committed faith. He appeals to his "apostolate," his apostleship, by virtue of which he has a singular mission vis-à-vis the nations, a mission distinct even from that of Peter (Gal. 2:7-10). This vocation confers upon him a specific responsibility and the authority of an extraordinary ambassador. God does not have as many ambassadors as recipients of the message. From this standpoint, Paul is not simply a model for successive generations of apostles to come. He is the Apostle of the Nations.

*"The God I worship in the spirit by preaching the gospel of his Son"*: The parallel text in Romans 15:16 will explain in what this act of worship consists: the faith of the nations that are "consecrated by the Holy Spirit" is a sacrifice agreeable to God (cf. 1 Cor. 6:20, Rom. 12:1, Phil. 4:18). In regarding himself as a minister who arouses faith, Paul sees himself as discharging the quasi-liturgical function of a minister who prepares the offerings.[10] Paul is a synthesis of prophetic and liturgical ministries: he is

the minister of a cultus whose fundamental act is the proclamation of the Word.

## Romans 15:16-21

Since Romans 15:16-21 converges so extensively with the exordium of the letter, we have already had occasion to consider the greater number of its key elements. We need only examine the specifications that Paul makes with regard to his missionary project in the last verses.

*"From Jerusalem . . . to Illyria"*: Illyria is today's Yugoslavia and northern Greece. The Acts of the Apostles does not speak of a ministry in Illyria. But as Illyria includes northern Greece, Paul may be referring here to his activity in Macedonia, calling it Illyria in order to stress its proximity to Rome. Seen from the capital of the Empire, Greece started in Illyria. Durazzo (Dyrrachium), in today's Albania, was one of the ports of the Ignatian Way, which linked the Adriatic with the Bosphorus by way of Thessalonica and Neapolis.

*"All the way around"*: Literally, "in a circle" (*en kuklōi*) having Jerusalem as its center. Doubtless we must understand this in a theological rather than a topographical sense.[11] It is not evident that Paul worked in a closed circle beginning from Jerusalem. But Jerusalem was certainly the point of reference for all his activity (Gal. 1:18, 2:1).

*"I have completed preaching the gospel of Christ"* (literally, "I have accomplished the gospel"): In this context, Paul clearly regards his task as having been completed wherever he has already been, and the only thing that remains for him to do is to go to Spain (v. 24), at the ends of the earth, where nothing lies beyond but the great ocean. Thus, the gospel will have been proclaimed everywhere: a blitzkrieg strategy, described here in sweeping strokes.

But how could Paul gauge that the places where he had now preached represented the whole of his task except Spain? He surely knew very well that he had not covered Africa, of which the North, at any rate, constituted a considerable part of the Roman Empire. The East, as well, all the way to India, had been known since the campaigns of Alexander. Perhaps he judged that, in the great division of the lands to be evangelized in the Jerusalem accord (Gal. 2:7-10), Africa and the East belonged to the Judaeo-Christian jurisdiction of the "circumcised." Alexandria in Egypt and Babylon were the great Jewish centers for Africa and Asia, respectively. The arc of the Jewish Diaspora described in Acts 2:9-10 effectively begins in Persia and extends through Asia Minor to Egypt and Libya. West of that, only Rome is mentioned. But this arc, with its advance point of Rome, corresponds exactly to the part of the Greco-Roman world where Paul has not brought the gospel. Surely this is not to be explained by chance or by negligence.

In any hypothesis, we may observe the way in which Paul conceives his task. He does not think it is his responsibility to convert all the pagans or to bring the whole world to the Christian faith. He would have fallen far short of such an assignment, with his scattered little communities of believers here and there in the immense Mediterranean world. "Conversion" is God's affair, and, for Paul as for the entire Bible, the gathering of the peoples is an affair of the last days. Nor is it up to Paul to form Christians in depth. Even the administration of baptism is not his task (1 Cor. 1:14-15), except by way of exception (1:16). To be sure, baptism was administered and the Eucharist was celebrated, and Paul approved these sacramental practices (Rom. 6:3-11; Gal. 3:27; Eph. 5:26; 1 Cor. 11:23-24, 10:16-21). But they were not his own assignments. His task was to "preach the gospel" in all eschatological haste, leaving conversion to God and formation in depth and the celebration of the sacraments to other human beings. Paul was an ambassador, in the strict sense.

It would be a mistake, however, to extrapolate to hasty practical conclusions. Today we hear it questioned whether baptism is really necessary, since Paul seems to exclude this external rite in 1 Corinthians 1:14-15. Or again, in view of Paul's tactics, we hear the proposition of spending a long time in the formation of Christian communities, in seeing to their adequate material and spiritual equipment, labeled Pelagianism: the only valid ministry is peripatetic, a rapid movement from place to place that would leave the neophytes, each time, with their faith and their Bible. These conclusions are based on a misunderstanding. We wish to see Paul as the model of the missionary, the leader of the long column of envoys of the gospel down the generations. And this may be the Lucan image. But it is not how Paul sees things. Paul does not pose as the model of anything at all. He sees himself as having been assigned a unique ministry, that of eschatological ambassador to the nations. Such is the very special charge that he has received, and all of his activities and priorities are subordinated to this responsibility, which is his and his alone.

We may not legitimately generalize from the Pauline methods, then, under pain of getting things precisely backwards. In Paul's mind, what is significant and of universal validity is precisely the eschatological significance of the salvation proclamation and the confidence we may have in the victorious power of the grace of God at work in that proclamation. Paradoxically, Paul is the prototype not of generosity, a sense of initiative, and the spirit of apostolic enterprise; Paul is the prototype of faith and of the certitude that all is in the hands of the divine grace and might—the conviction that one is no more than an ambassador, and that the efficacy of one's activity resides entirely in the power of the message, a power that is the triumphal sign of the eschatological victory of God. He expresses this same concept elsewhere and in other images, when he says: "Neither he who plants nor he who waters is of any special account, only God, who gives the growth" (1 Cor. 3:7). It is this faith in the eschatological power of God, at work in the proclamation of the Good News, that is at the heart of the Pauline ministry—and not the human qualities, extraordinary as they are, demonstrated by the apostle in making this proclamation.

It is this eschatological consciousness that is at the basis of Paul's impatience to go to Spain. He feels that he is on the point of "completing preaching the gospel": he has only one more step to take. Again, in Romans 10:14-21, when he lists the links in the chain of evangelization, ascending from "calling" to faith, from faith to hearing, from hearing to preaching, and from preaching to being sent, Paul is not visualizing an infinite cycle. He does not say that those who have "heard" and "believed" must now regard themselves as being sent forth in turn, to relaunch the movement of the gospel. The question does not arise; after all, already "their voice has sounded over the whole earth, and their words to the limits of the world" (Rom. 10:18 = Ps. 19:5).

To return to Romans 15: it is this same eschatological consciousness that dictates Paul's concern "never to preach in places where Christ's name was already known" (Rom. 15:20). This is more than simple apostolic courtesy or respect for jurisdictional boundaries. It was urgent that the message be heard by all (verse 21). It was no longer the hour for repeated labors on the same terrain, for slow preparation of the soil. Now it was time to sow the seed, and God had already "given the growth" with a view to the harvest (1 Cor. 3:6).

## THE LETTER TO THE ROMANS AS A MISSIONARY DOCUMENT

Accordingly, the two texts of Romans 1:1-16 and 15:16-21 are mutually corresponding and complementary, the first placing more emphasis on the interior aspects of the apostolate, the second showing the position of this apostolate in the framework of the divine economy.

Framing it like a pair of braces, the two texts place the Letter to the Romans in a missionary perspective. From Saint John Chrysostom to Thomas Aquinas to Martin Luther to Karl Barth, the density of the Letter to the Romans has been an object of great admiration. It is the "heart and marrow of all the books," Luther assured us — a "summary of Christian doctrine," according to Melanchthon. But the dogmatic wealth of the composition and systematic rigor of its presentation must not sidetrack our interpretation, and distract us from the missionary scope of the whole. Paul was on his way to Rome not to seek a chair of theology but to win support for what he considered would be the last step of his apostolic career.[12] He propounds his gospel in detail in order to persuade the church of Rome to patronize the last step in his apostolic enterprise. His theological exposé is couched in the context of a missionary project, and this is the comprehensive viewpoint of his letter. The Letter to the Romans is a missionary charter, then, justifying the overture to the nations (chaps. 1-8), while respecting Israel's election (chaps. 9-11). The overture to the pagans is justified by the universality of grace: "All men have sinned and are deprived of the glory of God. All men are now undeservedly justified by the gift of

God . . ." (Rom. 3:23-24). For, "despite the increase of sin, grace has far surpassed it, so that, as sin reigned through death, grace may reign by way of justice leading to eternal life, through Jesus Christ our Lord" (5:20-21). Thus, salvation is no longer reserved to those who have been circumcised in the name of the Law (chap. 7). Now it belongs to all who have faith, Jews and Greeks alike: the token of salvation, of the liberation and the glory of the children of God, is the gift of the Spirit, the gift given to all who are in Jesus Christ (chap. 8), to all who "love God" and are called in accordance with God's design (cf. 8:28).

The grace of God as the ultimate occasion of mission, faith as the sole fundamental demand, liberation from sin and salvation as final goal, the gift of the Spirit as pledge of this salvation, and with this gift, what Paul calls justification, that is, the experience of a rediscovered faith and a filial relationship with God—such is the missiological synthesis set forth by Paul in the first part of his letter, in chapters 1–8. To grasp the import of this majestic synthesis, we must actually see what Paul understood by sin, law, flesh, and death, all of these kinds of slavery from which human beings are liberated by salvation. They are hostile powers and their sway is universal. The Pauline viewpoint is not individualistic. "Sin" is more than individual fault. "Transgressions" (paraptōmata) are multiple, but "sin" (hamartia) is more frequently used in the singular.[13] It is a proper name. It is the name of a tyrannical Power that is crushing the world (Rom. 5:12-14). Law is not merely the expired Jewish law: it is the law to which Adam, and consequently all humanity, had already been subjected (cf. 7:7-11). Here we must see all constraint, all moral, social, and political alienation of human freedom, as coming from without.[14] The flesh is more than individual sensuality: it is the divided, dissipated "I" (Rom. 6:19), incapable of self-control (7:18, 8:3), hostile and vindictive (Gal. 5:20), and manipulated by the death instinct (7:5, 8:6). As for death, it is more than the end of earthly existence: it is the profound corruption affecting human existence at every level (8:20-22).

Paul is proposing a vast analysis of existence, then, reminiscent of certain prises de conscience of modern thought. Paul's reflection on the Law recalls the modern critique of institution and power. His thinking on "flesh" reminds us of certain intuitions of Freudianism on the profound traumatisms affecting the human psyche. Contemporary ecological insights into the cosmic dangers threatening a depraved, polluted world can help us understand what Paul meant by "death" and by the "corruption" that overpowers creation (Rom. 8:21). And lurking behind all these sinister Powers? Dame Hamartia, Sin as mistress of the gallows, who "pulls the strings" in this heartbreaking game of life and death.[15]

Paul's deeply pessimistic analysis is presented in a context of the final judgment and the eschatological days of wrath (Rom. 1:18). But while the content of his thinking is so akin to so many successive pessimisms that have prevailed among humanity over the centuries—from the Upanishads

and the Buddha to the various forms of our modern philosophy of nausea—
in Paul this somber tableau is only the springboard to a consideration of
the splendor of God's grace. In the face of the "revelation" of wrath springs
the parallel "revelation" of the saving justice of God (cf. Rom. 1:17-18),
and the gospel is the propagation of this "revelation."

Thus, the gospel of Paul far transcends any individualistic viewpoint. It
takes on social, political, and cosmic dimensions. The "salvation" it proclaims penetrates the entire depth and breadth of human existence.

But what of the people of Abraham in this universalistic vision? Did
Israel's election still have a meaning? The question was of personal concern
to Paul, since the Israelites were his "kinsmen," *kata sarka*, according to
the flesh (Rom. 9:3). It was also of theological concern to him, as he was
convinced that "God's word has [not] failed" (9:6), and that "God's gifts
. . . are irrevocable" (11:29). Thus, the second part of his letter, in chapters
9-11, takes up the problem of sin and salvation once again, this time from
the specific standpoint of Israel's recent history and the hardening of its
heart.

The very fact that the letter goes on to treat of the problem of Israel is
one more indication that its aim is not to become a treatise in spiritual
theology, but to reveal the deeper motivations of a particular apostolic
strategy. As Feuillet has shown, chapters 9-11 prolong the reflection underlying the whole letter.[16] The first eight chapters have justified the apostolate
to the pagans. What, then, of Israel? If there is no more Jew or Greek
(Gal. 3:28), then has Israel vanished? Paul catches himself up short and
devotes three chapters to a reformulation of the central place of Israel in
the divine plan. He recalls the privileges of the chosen people (Rom. 9:1-
5). But "God's gifts . . . are irrevocable" (11:29). True, "in respect to the
gospel, the Jews are enemies of God." Still, "in respect to the election,
they are beloved by him because of the patriarchs" (11:28). Israel remains
the sacred root (11:16). The hardness of its heart is but a passing phase: it
will last only "until the full number of Gentiles enter in, and then all Israel
will be saved" (11:25-26).

This last text is far from clear. Does Paul mean that the Jews will be
converted after all? Or only a remnant? Or again, are we to understand
that, along the pathways of some providential route of its own and without
explicit faith in the gospel, Israel will find salvation? The question is dis-
puted.[17] Equally mysterious is Paul's assurance that, while Israel's "rejection has meant reconciliation for the world," its reintegration is to be a
passage from death to life (11:15). Does Paul mean that "acceptance" on
the part of the Jews will signal the end of the world and the resurrection
of the just, or does he only mean that Israel's return will be a new departure
in God's salvific plan? It is all very enigmatic, and Paul finally confesses
this (11:33-36). Did he have a clear understanding of it himself? However
this may be, his ultimate conviction is that Israel cannot constitute a road-
block to the onward march of the gospel. Temporarily thrust aside, Israel

nonetheless retains its status as holy root: even in the perspective of a ministry to the nations, Israel is the trunk of the tree (11:16). Israel is a plenitude (11:12), the beginning point and end point of the plan of salvation.[18]

Missionary identity, foundation of the mission to the nations, content of the gospel as proposed by this mission, grand coordinates of the missionary strategy—such, then, in a few strokes, is the content of the Letter to the Romans. If we were to seek a biblical treatise on the theology of mission, this letter would come the closest to satisfying our desires. But original as Paul's thinking and behavior may have been, both are still quite "biblical." Paul does not swerve one whit from the orbit traced by the Old Testament and determined by the double focus of Israel's election and God's universal call. The two great parts of his Letter to the Romans—chapters 1-8 on the universality of salvation and chapters 9-11 on the irreversibility of the privileges of Israel—might well constitute a classic compendium of what the prophets had proclaimed and Jesus had fulfilled. The only difference is that, for Paul, the times had been accomplished and the hour had arrived (Rom. 13:11-12): the moment had come for the predictions of the prophets to be translated into act and the salvation brought by Jesus Christ proclaimed to the world.

## FROM PAUL TO LUKE: CONSTANTS AND VARIABLES

### A TRAJECTORY

Although the Book of Acts and the letters of Paul deal with the same subject and emerge from the same Judaeo-Hellenistic Christian milieus, they are very different, and it is interesting to compare them. Between Paul and Luke, between Paul's self-portrait and the picture of him that Luke paints, it has been a long journey, with its years of experience and missionary reflections.

The basic difference between the two is to be found in their view of the times. Paul is convinced he is living in eschatological times. Now is the favorable time; now is the day of salvation (2 Cor. 6:2). The hour has come to rise from sleep, for the night is far spent, and day draws near (Rom. 13:11-12). By contrast, Luke speaks from the midst of a church that, over the years, has had the experience of a time grown long. He knows that, in our ignorance of the times and moments of the final restoration, ours, in the strength of the Spirit, throughout all times and places, is the responsibility of witness (Acts 1:7-8).

Where Paul sees the revelation of wrath and the last judgment upon sin, Luke perceives a continuing history, one that reaches back into Israel's past and the history of the nations, and ahead to their gradual response to the gospel. While, for Paul, the Spirit gives life, in contrast to the flesh of death (Rom. 8:6,13; cf. 2 Cor. 3:6), for Luke the Spirit inspires an "increase of the word." Paul has already beheld the prolongation of faith in love (1 Cor. 13) and seeks to perceive the meaning of this love in the context of racial and social antagonism and sexist discrimination (Gal. 3:28). Luke will go beyond these declarations of principle and strive to define a concrete attitude of shared ownership (Acts 2:42-47, 4:32-35; cf. Luke 3:10-14, 19:8-9), ethnic compromise (Acts 15), and recognition of women's role among the people of God (cf. Luke 1-2, 8:2-3; Acts 1:14, 16:14-15, 18:1, 21:9) – the blueprint for a Christian social project.

Paul's eschatology leads him to a prophetic attitude of condemnation of sin. He sees the world as the eschatological battleground, where wrath is unchained in one last apocalypse of evil while the Good News echoes the revelation of God's saving justice. His style of evangelization, then, will be as rapid and as dumbfounding as the day of the Lord that he announces. Luke has recovered the meaning of history and is more interested in rates of growth, the ins and outs of the current situation, and the concrete repercussions of the activity of evangelization on the human vital and social fabric. Paul is more sensitive to the definitive, decisive character of the irruption of the divine grace, and this in the context of an apocalyptic pessimism. Luke has developed a theology of time and will be more attentive to human mediations.[19]

While very different, these two types of mission are not contradictory. They form a continuum in the history of Christian mission. The more Pauline missiological attitude will be marked by an eschatological haste and by a denunciation of the injustice of the world, from Paul to Augustine to liberation theology. The more Lucan type of missionary undertaking will insist on the continuity of inculturations, will place the accent on dialogue, and will accept the slow progress of human becoming and acting. This will be Thomas Aquinas's position with regard to the renewal of medieval theology, Aristotelianism, and the Arabic and Jewish philosophers of his time. This, again, will be the orientation of Vatican Council II vis-à-vis the modern world in its Pastoral Constitution *Gaudium et Spes*. It would be futile to attempt to choose between the two tendencies, and to condemn one in the name of the other. Both belong to the New Testament, and each has its validity and its pitfalls. The thrusts of the Spirit in either direction should be perceived as expressions of the variety of gifts issuing from the same Spirit (1 Cor. 12:4). St. Francis Xavier raced from continent to continent with the same eschatological impatience as Paul. Father Charles de Foucauld buried himself amidst the Touaregs of the desert. "It is one and the same Spirit who produces all these gifts, distributing them to each as he wills" (1 Cor. 12:11).

## NOVELTY OF PAUL

We have now examined the trajectory pursued by the theology and practice of mission in its evolution from Paul to Luke. But Paul himself represented a factor of novelty vis-à-vis the Old Testament and the church of Christian origins.

1. With lucid rigor, Paul has perceived the practical consequences of the universality of sin and grace. In the face of these realities, circumcision and uncircumcision no longer have any significance. Henceforth, only *faith in Christ Jesus* counts for anything.

2. Thus, he *moved into action*, and in systematic fashion. Few in antiquity, and probably no one in the ancient church, had as broad a sense of the *oikumenē* as did Paul. Nor did many feel the strength of divine grace in human weakness as intensely as he or throb with the will to devote so much intelligence and heart to the work of God.

3. Paul's apostolic intensity was honed to a keen edge by his *sense of the eschaton*. He intended to complete preaching the gospel (cf. Rom. 15:19), to bring it to full realization in the sphere that had fallen to his lot. When he analyzes the elements of mission in Romans 10, Paul does not envisage their resumption, in cyclical fashion, in successive generations. While Luke sees Paul as the pioneer and prototype of the new postapostolic mission, Paul regards his role as unique. He is the prophet, the Servant of the last times (Rom. 15:16; Gal. 1:15).

4. Likewise unique is Paul's *mission to the Gentiles*. In the allotment of territory between Peter, who is dispatched to the Jews, and himself, who goes to the nations (Gal. 2:8-9), Paul was convinced that the evangelization of Israel came first—that his role was secondary vis-à-vis the mission to Israel. However, he was equally convinced that he had been charged with a specific mission directly by Christ (Gal. 1:1,11, 16-17). He had asked of the apostles not delegation, but only recognition, to be expressed by extending the right hand in token of communion (Gal. 2:9-10). Thus, there is neither subjugation nor independence here, but, on one side, the conviction that a new field had opened up, and had been entrusted to him by Christ, and on the other, an awareness that this new field was not detached from the rest of the plantation that was Israel (Rom. 11:16-24).

5. Was not this notion of the unique position of his ministry rather presumptuous? Paul fears the reproach of braggadocio (*kauchēsis*). But especially, he fears to base his work on any human assurance. In order to exorcise all temptation to self-sufficiency, he conscientiously *lists his weaknesses* and accepts his apostolic failures with serenity. These only demonstrate that the power at work in his ministry is that of the Risen One and his Spirit.

6. It is the *creativity of the Spirit*, then, that manifests itself in the Apostle of the Nations. The extraordinary, unpredictable nature of the Pauline enterprise is, for Paul himself, the mark of the Spirit. In a context of the life and perspectives of the primitive church, the explosion of the missionary, theological, and even literary genius of Paul was absolutely unforeseeable. Peter and the Twelve must have been astonished when this missionary phenomenon tumbled down on their heads out of the Damascus sky (Gal.

1:18-23). Paul himself never ceased to be amazed at what was happening during his ministry and went into endless ecstasies over this "mystery" (Rom. 11:33-36, 16:25-27; 1 Cor. 2:6-10; Eph. 3:1-12,20-21; Col. 1:25-29). It could only be the work of the Spirit, who ever creates what is new and never ceases to surprise us.

## CONSTANTS

Despite all this novelty, certain constants appear between Paul and the rest of the primitive church and even the Old Testament. These constants are the key elements of mission.

1. Mission is first of all an *act of God*. The gospel is the gospel of God. It is God who calls the apostle: it is God and the divine grace that accompany and sustain that apostle's activity. One does not make oneself an apostle. "Apostle" means someone with a mandate. The mandatory bears the message, authority, and power of another—of the Other, in the case of an apostle.

2. Thus, *the power of mission is the Word* that it bears, or rather, that bears it. The gospel is the power of God for salvation (Rom. 1:16), and the power of the gospel is more basic than the activity of evangelization. The latter suffers from the admixture of human activity, while the gospel is divine strength directly. From "belief" to "preaching," and from "preaching" to the one "sent," the concatenation is uninterrupted in Romans 10:14-17: there is no appeal by mail, no techniques of mass persuasion, no efforts mounted to change someone's mind. Actually it would be easy to find techniques of communication and rhetoric in Paul. But the summary he presents in Romans 10 certainly shows what he regards as his strong points, and his strongest point is the strength of the gospel.

3. "What Christ has done through" Paul has been not only in words, but also in acts—in "signs and marvels, by the power of God's Spirit" (Rom. 15:18-19). The gospel is more than discourse—it is might and the action of the Holy Spirit (1 Thes. 1:5). Paul has "performed . . . with great patience the signs that show the apostles, signs and wonders and deeds of power" (2 Cor. 12:12). But the clearest sign he has shown is that of bearing the "brand marks of Jesus in my body" (cf. Gal. 6:17). The supreme sign given to human beings has been the sign of the Crucified, and the ultimate discourse "the message of the cross" (1 Cor. 1:18-25; here, v. 18). This is the very sign that Paul exhibits, and this the very "message," the same language, that he speaks by his apostolic life. Here is where the source of his pride in his ministry resides. He returns to it time and again: 1 Corinthians 4:9-13; 2 Corinthians 1:4-7, 4:7-15, 6:4-10, 11:23-30, 12:6-10. This is likewise Luke's intent in devoting half of his account concerning Paul to the journey of the captivity, in order to have a parallel with the passion of Jesus. Thus, a line of force is prolonged in Paul that has already underlain the gospels. Paul has traveled the world over carrying the Word. But this Word, which

he carries on his lips and in his flesh, is that of the cross: "Continually we carry about in our bodies the dying [nekrōsis] of Jesus, so that in our bodies the life of Jesus may also be revealed" (2 Cor. 4:10).

4. Thus, Paul is utterly convinced of the principle that we have seen to underlie the activity of Jesus: that *transparency to the message* is incomparably more important than the activity performed in regard to that message. He identifies himself with the mystery of the cross. He founds his ministry on his experience of the power of Christ's resurrection and his share in Christ's sufferings (Phil. 3:10). He expresses this concept of transparency explicitly when he speaks of his calling and his ministry in terms of a light shining first within himself and then radiating all around him (2 Cor. 4:4-6, Gal. 1:16, Eph. 3:9). His ministry does not emanate ultimately from him, however. He only radiates "the splendor of the gospel showing forth the glory of Christ, the image of God" (2 Cor. 4:4; cf. 2 Tim. 1:10).

5. For Paul, as for the rest of the Bible, mission is the *function of a people*. Paul is jealous of his communion with the church of Jerusalem, lest he have run his course in vain (Gal. 2:2), and he makes certain that James, Cephas, and John extend to him the hand of communion (Gal. 2:9). Luke underscores the mandatory role of the church of Antioch (Acts 13:1-3), and the Letter to the Romans implies that Paul expected from them not only logistical, but also theological support. Acts and the letters show Paul performing his mission in the spirit of teamwork. Paul does not operate in isolation. He works as a member of a group. He is unwilling to encroach on foundations laid by others (Rom. 15:20-21). He knows the limits of his jurisdiction (2 Cor. 10:13-16). He is as persuaded of the solidarity of the body as he is of the complementary of its functions (Rom. 12:4-8).

6. This community is gathered about Israel — "God's Israel" (Gal. 6:16), broadened to the dimensions of all the nations. "Theirs [the Israelites'] were the adoption, the glory, the covenants, the law-giving, the worship, and the promises ... and from them came the Messiah (I speak of his human origins)" (Rom. 9:4-5).[20] Paul cannot accept Israel's definitive rejection any more than can the rest of the New Testament: "God's gifts and his call are irrevocable" (Rom. 11:29). The movement toward the nations started out from Israel, and it will end with Israel: "All Israel will be saved" (Rom. 11:26). From this viewpoint, Paul is more reserved than Luke with regard to the nations. In Luke's account, the arrival of the nations is welcomed and joyously described. In Paul, it is always tinged with nostalgia. His heart is pained when he sees the Gentiles rush in, with his people shunted off to one side (Rom. 9:1-3). In Acts, the overture to the Gentiles is a conclusion, the goal toward which all history has been traveling (Acts 1:8, 28:28). To hear Paul, his march to the pagans is only a tactical detour, subordinate to the great strategic goal of Israel's salvation. In going forth to the nations, Paul hopes to arouse Israel's jealousy, and thus bring his people home (Rom. 11:11-14). On a stage of world dimensions, Paul plays the role of the resentful lover. Despite the failures of Abraham's descen-

dancy, it is the chosen remnant that remains the apple of Paul's eye and God's.

7. With all of the *concretion of the life of a community*, mission in Paul takes on the socioeconomic dimensions of the life of that community. Paul may not have sketched as systematically as Luke a program of Christian sociology, but he has sung the praises of charity (1 Cor. 13) and, more concretely, taken up a collection for the poor of Jerusalem, which he has called by the beautiful name of *koinōnia* (2 Cor. 8:4, 9:13). He has proclaimed that there is no longer either Jew or Greek, slave or free, man or woman (Gal. 3:28). He has risked his freedom and his life for the overthrow of ethnic antipathies, taken up the defense of the slave Onesimus, and admitted women to his apostolic teams.[21] His teaching on freedom and law, life and death, sin and grace is less abstract than it might appear. Actually he is proclaiming the overthrow of oppressive, unjust, annihilating structures. In Paul as in the Old Testament, sin and death are not individual factors, but powers that enthrall and throttle the image of God in us.

8. The people of God gathered in faith are a *praying people*. In his analysis of the missionary action in Romans 10, invocation is the last stage before salvation: prayer is the pledge of salvation, and the mark of those who are to be saved: "Everyone who calls on the name of the Lord will be saved" (Rom. 10:13). The Spirit, given as pledge and foretaste of heavenly glory (cf. Rom. 8:23, 2 Cor. 1:22) prays in us with inexpressible groans (Rom. 8:26), and enables us to cry out—in tongues or in plain talk?—" 'Abba!' (that is, 'Father')" (Rom. 8:15). The Spirit intercedes for us and is at the heart of our intercession for the saints (Rom. 8:26-27). The Spirit knows the depths of God and gives us access to the mysteries of the wisdom of God (1 Cor. 1:7-10).

As L. Cerfaux has said, Paul was an "Apostle in the presence of God."[22] He was moved by an "apostolic mysticism."[23] His letters abound in prayer in all its forms: not only thanksgiving, blessing, doxology, and hymn,[24] but also in intercession, impetration, and even ecstasy (1 Cor. 14:15-16, Rom. 8:15-16, Gal. 4:6). As it abounds in his letters, so must it abound in his ministry. The picture Luke sometimes paints of a Paul surrounded by the prayer of the community (Acts 16:25, 20:36, 21:5,20, 27:35, 28:8,15) sins rather by discretion than by exaggeration. Prayer does not figure in the summary of the missionary career that Paul leaves as a testament to the elders of Ephesus (Acts 20:18-35); but the assembly ends in prayer (Acts 20:36). Luke, the evangelist of prayer, will sum up the apostolic task in two words: prayer, and the service of the Word (Acts 6:4). Such was surely Paul's view as well, as it had been of Jesus and the prophets. Prayer was a central aspect of his apostolic combat (Rom. 15:30). It was the mark of the faith community that he sought to establish:

Present your needs to God in every form of prayer and in petitions full of gratitude. Then God's own peace, which is beyond all understanding, will stand guard over your hearts and minds, in Christ Jesus (Phil. 4:6-7; cf. Eph. 5:18-20, 6:18; Col. 3:16-17).

But he had formulated this goal from his first letter onward and had proposed it to his new Christian community: "Never cease praying, render constant thanks; such is God's will for you in Christ Jesus" (1 Thes. 5:17-18).

The objective of God's plan could not have been described more clearly: to create a people whose life was prayer.

# 10

# The Gospel of John
# as a Missionary Synthesis

*Have we not reached the mountaintop with Paul? Could we possibly have
anything to learn of mission from John? Need we speak of the Fourth
Gospel at all in a study of missionary theology? John is called the mystic,
the theologian, the seer, the friend of Jesus; he does not stand out in our
minds as a representative of mission. Here is a perhaps too neglected
aspect of the Johannine work. After all, John's name is attached to a
"gospel." But "gospel" means Good News. John must be writing of mission, then.*[1] *E. Cothenet has admirably formulated the missionary scope
of the Fourth Gospel:*

*Even apart from the Prologue, with its emphasis on the universality
of the activity of the Logos, a number of episodes manifest John's
interest in mission. Only Luke and John ascribe any importance to
Samaria. In this first part, centered on the proclamation of Life, the
woman of Sychar represents not only the people of her village, but
all those whom the Father seeks (4:23) in order to make them
adorers in spirit and truth. The conversation with the disciples (4:34-
38) forms the Johannine counterpart of the mission discourse in the
Synoptics (Matt. 10 and par.). Significantly, the episode concludes
with the proclamation of the choir of Samaritans: "We know that
this really is the Savior of the world" (4:42; cf. 3:16). The next scene
brings in a royal official (4:46-54), whose faith will be communicated to his whole house (4:53; cf. Acts 10:44-48, 16:15,31-32, etc.).
Jesus' absence from the Festival of Tabernacles gives the people to
suppose that he is out teaching the Greeks (7:35). These same
Greeks reappear as Passover draws near, and their request to "see
Jesus" manifests the arrival of the Hour (12:20,23). Attentive to
data that might clarify the meaning of the Passion, John is careful
to point out that the inscription on the cross was in three languages:*

*Hebrew, Latin, and Greek (19:20). The Jews who read it were offended; but for John it represented the universality of redemption. Thus, in discreet but repeated strokes, John founds the missionary vocation of the church on the history of Jesus.*[2]

*Let us analyze the Fourth Gospel, then, in broad strokes, giving special attention to this missionary perspective.*

## THE PROLOGUE

"In the beginning was the Word . . . ." So opens the Gospel of John in our current translations. No translation is innocent, even with a phrase as simple as this six-word proposition. In translating the Greek word *logos* as "Word" with a capital *w*, our translations recall all the theological controversies, all the heresies and councils, on the Trinity and the Incarnation from ancient times onward.

It is altogether legitimate to introduce the theology of the Word in this way. It is justified by the conclusion of the Prologue: "No one has ever seen God. It is God the only Son, ever at the Father's side, who has revealed him" (John 1:18). The Greek text says, literally, ". . . has done his exegesis." Jesus is the Father's exegete. The Word is the exegete of God. The Fathers of the church, along with a good many theologians and mystics, have tiptoed to the edge of the abyss of the mystery upon which John's Prologue opens and peered into its depths.

In modern times, a historico-critical exegesis has sought the origins of this theme of the Johannine *logos* in Mandaeism, Hermetic and gnostic literature, Stoicism, and Neoplatonism. Closer to the biblical milieus, we hear John compared with Philo, the rabbinic Memra, the Wisdom of the sapiential books, and especially, the Old Testament theme of the creative Word. The value of this research is that, by way of comparison or contrast, it brings out various aspects of the Prologue, illustrating the deep roots of Johannine thought in the complex milieu in which that thought developed.

But we must not neglect an important aspect of the semantic value of the Johannine logos—the sense of created word, the most frequent meaning of logos in the New Testament: the word of Good News, the Word proclaimed and preached in the Christian kerygma. This meaning is rather obscured by the capital *w* in "Word," which without further ado orientates our thought in theological, ontological directions.[3] And yet, the meaning of "word," with a lower-case *w*, is one of the most obvious senses of the word logos. In the New Testament, the logos is the "message of the gospel" (Acts 15:7), the word of the Reign (Matt. 13:19), the word of salvation (Acts 13:26), of grace (Acts 14:3, 20:32; Luke 4:22), of truth (John 17:17, Acts 26:25, 2 Cor. 6:7, Eph. 1:13, Col. 1:5). Most often it is simply *the* "word," summing up all that Christ brings us (Mark 2:2, 4:14,15,16,17,20,33 and par.; 8:32,38). This word has a dynamism of its own: it becomes a synonym for the church; or better, it expresses the profound, dynamic reality at the heart of the church (Acts 4:29, 6:7, 12:24, 19:20). It is even the reality deep within Jesus: *qua* sent, Jesus is the Word sent, says Acts 10:36 (cf. Luke 4:32). It is the Word that the apostles serve (Acts 6:4), and it is to it that the Christian community is entrusted as if to a living being, to a shepherd or protector (Acts 20:28-32). The Book of Revelation describes the Christ Word as riding through the universe like a conquering knight (Rev. 19:13).

With this last text we are in the Johannine milieu. It provides us with a transition from general New Testament usage to Johannine usage. Indeed, the meaning of "word" in the sense of "proclaimed gospel" is anything but foreign to John's usage. The Word in John is what Jesus says (12:48, 14:24, 15:3). It is believed in (2:22, 4:50). It is heard (5:24, 8:43). It is kept (8:51,52,55, 14:23, 15:20, 17:6). One abides in it (8:31,37). It is the word of truth (17:17), the very word of the Father (14:24, 17:14, 10:35), to be transmitted in turn by those who receive it (4:41, 17:20; cf. 1 John 1:1-3).

The Johannine theme of the word is the equivalent of the Markan theme of gospel and akin to the Lucan theme of testimony. It can be summed up in the declaration with which John concludes his account of Jesus' ministry, before beginning his narrative of the last days:

> I have come to the world as its light,
> to keep anyone who believes in me
> from remaining in the dark.
> If anyone hears my words and does not keep them,
> I am not the one to condemn him,
> for I did not come to condemn the world but to save
>     it.
> Whoever rejects me and does not accept my words
> already has his judge, namely, the word I have
>     spoken—
> it is that which will condemn him on the last day.
> For I have not spoken on my own;
> no, the Father who sent me
> has commanded me
> what to say and how to speak.
> Since I know that his commandment means eternal
>     life,
> whatever I say
> is spoken just as he instructed me (John 12:46-50).

Let us observe the position of this text at the end of the first part of the Gospel of John. It performs the function of a conclusion. It is a résumé of all that Jesus has said and done. This epilogue forms an "inclusion" with the prologue of chapter 1. The same themes recur: word, light, coming into the world, life, origin in the bosom of the Father. Thus, we cannot divest the prologue of John of the meaning of the Word as light and salvation, which is so clear in the epilogue. As we have seen, Luke has personalized the evangelizing Word. The Johannine reflection on the logos is not unconnected with that of Luke; but while Luke has pursued the extension of this theme into history, into its development in the church, John, quite the contrary, returns to the most profound theological, divine sources of the logos. Mark has spoken of the "good news of God" (Mark 1:14), and Paul has seen in the gospel the power of God: the logos of the cross is "the power of God and the wisdom of God" (1 Cor. 1:24). In the same sense, but even more profoundly, John scrutinizes the depths of God. The Word of the gospel, light as it is for every human being (John 1:10), is also the Word of the Creator, light in the primordial darkness (John 1:4). Paul expresses the same movement of thought in Second Corinthians: "God, who said, 'Let light shine out of darkness,' has shone in our hearts, that we in turn might make known the glory of God shining on the face of Christ" (2 Cor. 4:6). Light of creation, light of Incarnation and of glory, inner light of hearts: this is the very movement of the prologue of John. But John goes back still further when, beyond creation, he sees this Word in the very eternity of God, "in the beginning." The Book of Revelation, too, will speak of the "everlasting good news" (Rev. 14:6).[4]

## THE BOOK OF SIGNS

The first part of the Gospel of John, mounted between the prologue and the epilogue of 12:46-50, has been called the "book of signs." The word "sign" occurs there again and again, a *leitmotiv* expressing all that Jesus does (2:11,18,23, 3:2, 4:48,54, 6:2,14,26,30, 7:31, 9:16, 10:41, 11:47, 12:18,37). After chapter 12, the word "sign" will not recur before the gospel concludes, in 20:30.

The scope of these "signs" is indicated from the very outset, on the occasion of the first miracle: "Jesus performed this first of his signs at Cana in Galilee. Thus did he reveal his glory, and his disciples believed in him" (John 2:11). The "signs" worked by Jesus are an anticipatory manifestation of his glory. Those who see his acts already perceive the glory of the Word (cf. John 1:14). By faith, believers, transcending visible things, open their eyes to "much greater things" (John 1:50; cf. 9:35-39). Thus, signs accompany faith. In John 4:46-54, on the occasion of the second "sign" (verse 54), the royal official "and his whole household thereupon became believers" (v. 53). Again, contrasting Jesus with the Baptist, who had never "performed a sign," John declares that "many came to believe in him" (John 10:41-42).

It is true that signs were not enough to cause faith. They could correspond to a simple hankering after the wondrous, as in 2:18. In this case the faith that they aroused was imperfect and ambiguous. Thus, while "many believed in his name, for they could see the signs he was performing,"

Jesus, for his part, did not believe in them—"would not trust himself to them" (2:23-24). Or, once more, in 6:14, the faith aroused by the sign of the multiplication of the loaves is only inchoative, and it will take the whole discourse on the Bread of Life to guide this faith to the point of decision (6:60-68). Meanwhile, even if their value is incomplete, the signs never fail to pose a question. It is they that give pause to Nicodemus (3:2), the crowd at Jerusalem (7:31, 9:16, 12:18), and even the chief priests and the Pharisees (11:47).

The conclusion of the book of signs sums up this Johannine theme:

Despite his many signs performed in their presence, they refused to believe in him. This was to fulfill the word of the prophet Isaiah:

Lord, who has believed what has reached our ears?
To whom has the might of the Lord been revealed?

. . . Isaiah uttered these words because he had seen Jesus' glory, and it was of him he spoke.
There were many, even among the Sanhedrin, who believed in him; but they refused to admit it. . . . They preferred the praise of men to the glory of God (John 12:37-43).

Here we find the same link between signs and glory as in 2:11. The signs manifested the glory of God. They should have led to faith. A failure occurred: such was God's plan, foretold by the prophets and realized in the pusillanimity of the "crowd" and their leaders. But the shadow cast by this failure only serves to set in bolder relief the great theological perspective of the book of signs:

I have come to the world as its light,
to keep anyone who believes in me
from remaining in the dark. . . .
For I [came] to save [the world]. . . .
I know that [the Father's] commandment means
    eternal life (12:46-50).

This theological outlook is a missionary one, as well. These accounts have been committed to writing not so much to provide a historical explanation of how the disciples and the crowds came to believe or to refuse to believe. These accounts have come into existence rather to present to the "world" the dilemma of faith or its rejection, life or death, sentence or salvation. This book is written for the reader or hearer, and that reader or hearer is challenged by these signs and the Word that accompanies them. The story of Jesus, his disciples, and the "crowd" reaches readers in the gospel. These are placed on their guard against the risk to be run by those

who think they see and only make themselves blind. It is to these readers
that Jesus says: "I have come to the world as its light." For the coming
generations of those who will not have beheld Jesus and will not have been
able to touch him (cf. 20:29), the Fourth Gospel, through signs that appeal
to faith, transmits the coming of the Word. During Jesus' lifetime, these
signs were given to raise questions that would lead to faith those who had
been their eyewitnesses; in the Gospel of John, these same signs are committed to writing to place in the same position those who have not seen
and yet will receive the invitation to believe.

The book states this explicitly in its original conclusion, which, as the
*Traduction Oecumenique de la Bible* title says, expresses the "intent of the
evangelist":

> Jesus performed many other signs as well — signs not recorded here —
> in the presence of his disciples. But these have been recorded to help
> you believe that Jesus is the Messiah, the Son of God, so that through
> this faith you may have life in his name (John 20:30-31).

The commentators dispute the precise import of this text. Are we to
understand that the Gospel of John was written to bring readers to faith
in Jesus? In this case, it has been written with a missionary intent: it has
been written for non-Christians, nonbelievers, in order to lead them to the
faith. Other exegetes, however, hold that the meaning of the text is: "These
[signs] have been recorded that you may continue to believe, that you may
be strengthened in authentic faith." Here, the Gospel of John would have
been written for Christians who wavered — who had been excommunicated
by the synagogue, who were undergoing persecution, or who had been led
astray by heresy.[5]

It would actually be difficult and hazardous to seek to specify John's
audience too precisely. Raymond E. Brown is doubtless correct in suppos-
ing a complex audience for John, made up of an outer world of "Jews,"
"Greeks," and partisans of John the Baptist, and within the pale, among
believers, of crypto-Christians who hid their faith, Judaeo-Christians of
wavering faith and Christians of apostolic churches that might have been
a cut or two above the "Johannite" churches on the social ladder.[6] In this
context, the readers of the Fourth Gospel could have been being called to
faith if they did not as yet believe, to strengthen or correct their faith if
the latter was still too timid or somehow lacking, and to reenter the unity
of faith in the case of different groups who might have stumbled in the
various manners of their attachment to Christ. In this complex situation,
any attempt to distinguish in the Fourth Gospel between simple pastoral
reinforcement and actual missionary extension of the faith can only be
theory-spinning.

Distinctions between "pastoral theology" and "missiology" are made in
terms of later classifications of doubtful value. When Paul wrote his letters

to the Christian communities, he was performing his apostolic ministry in literary genres or "languages," of which some elements would today be called missionary language (kerygma, catechesis), while others would be said to belong rather to "pastoral theology" (exhortation, admonition, instruction, directive, liturgical indication, ethical reflection, and so on). Meanwhile, Paul would have been very surprised to hear that there was going to have to be a distinction between the apostolic or missionary elements of his writings and the pastoral. His response would have been that, in his letters as in the rest of his activity, he was totally committed as an apostle.[7]

It is the same with John. In writing his gospel, he had in mind the different groups that his book was to reach. These groups were mixed — composed of believers, unbelievers, and poor believers. It was into this complex humanity that the Word must come. And indeed John addressed the logos to them all, that they might believe and have life. His gospel is an appeal for faith, and the word that he transmits is addressed to all, be their faith nonexistent, inchoative, defective, vacillating, or imperfect.[8]

Indeed, we observe that in John 2:11, when the evangelist says that "his disciples believed in him" after the first sign, this implies that they were already his disciples, and yet that the glory of the first sign leads them to faith. Again, Jesus says, after Lazarus' death: "For your sakes I am glad I was not there, that you may come to believe" (John 11:15), as if their act of faith would be brand-new. Yet again, 13:19 and 14:29, the words "so that . . . you may believe" refer to the postpaschal period (cf. 2:22), as if the disciples' faith were to be born only after the Resurrection. The explanation is that, for John, faith is always nascent. It is never completely acquired. It must ever spring up anew, from a ceaselessly revived sense of wonder, from an ever-renewed contemplation of the divine glory. In the light of the manifestation of this glory, continually reported by the gospel, all must discover their lack of faith. Faith, in John, is not a simple mental view. In a context of the tensions and divisions affecting the churches of the close of the first century, who could claim to be totally "believing"?

Finally, in any attempt to specify "the intent of the evangelist" as expressed in the conclusion of his work, we must not lose sight of the contextual bond between this conclusion and the sentence climaxing the apparition to Thomas in the pericope immediately preceding: "Blest are they who have not seen and have believed" (20:29). The emphasis on the verb "believe" in verses 29 and 31 reveals a precise thematic bond. Jesus' last words to Thomas open windows on the generations to come.

> From this moment forward, the group addressed is no longer only the eleven disciples gathered at this particular point in space and time. Every reader of the gospel who has faith is included in Christ's final beatitude, till the end of time.[9]

Now John can end his book. In the light of Jesus' last words in that book, we see the Fourth Gospel as constituting a missionary call to a vast people, scattered in space and time, of persons who "have not seen." As 1 John 1:1-4 will say, what the witnesses have seen, heard, contemplated, and touched, the gospel will communicate to all. The chain of "seeing" and "saying," initiated with the Baptist (John 1:32) and the first disciples (1:39,46-50) and continuing to Calvary (19:35) and the tomb (20:8,18)—this chain that goes back to the Only Son, who resides in the bosom of the Father (1:18)—is about to be extended from generation to generation by the gospel. Acts was the book of the geographical extension of the Word; the Fourth Gospel pursues this extension in time. Having traced the Word back to the eternity of God, it also follows its prolongation throughout the generations. Thus John's conclusion echoes down all the ages of those who have not seen, the Word that has come from deep within God and has been revealed to the world, that it may have eternal life, the glory and grace of the only Son (1:14).

Thus, John 1 and John 20, the Prologue and the Epilogue, converge in one great missionary concern, to embrace, in a single regard, the Word emerging from God from the "beginning," made flesh in Jesus Christ, revealed in the divine glory of the signs and the Exaltation, and addressed to the world—to the limited group of witnesses who have seen, as well as to the immense people of those who have not seen, in order that, believing, all may have life in its (his) name.

## THE BOOK OF GLORY

Our investigation of the theme of "signs" has already brought us to the conclusion of the Fourth Gospel.

Now we must return to the second part of that gospel (John 13-20), the part that no longer speaks of "signs," but reveals "plainly, without talking in veiled language" (John 16:29), "the glory of an only Son coming from the Father" (1:14).

### THE GLORY OF LOVING

Paradoxically, the account of the Passion will be the Book of Glory.[10] For John, the glory of God is the manifestation of the very depths of the divine being, and thus of the divine love, for God is love (1 John 4:8,16). It is this love that is revealed in Jesus (John 3:16), and most of all in the gift of his sacrifice, which manifests both his love for his Father (14:31, 15:10) and us (13:1,34, 15:9,13), and his Father's love for the world (3:16).

C. H. Dodd has shown that the Gospel of John is constructed as a progressive revelation that reaches its climax in *agapē*, love. While the key words of the first twelve chapters of John are "life" and "light," the vocabulary of love, which has appeared only 6 times in the first part of this gospel, comes to predominate in chapters 13-17 (31 times), replacing the themes of "light" (completely absent) and "life" (occurring only 6 times).[11] "His [the evangelist's] intention, then, is to accentuate this essential truth: that the definitive reality of life and light is given in *agapē*."[12]

## LOVE AND JUDGMENT

This important observation on the part of the great English exegete calls for a complementary remark: the love theme is accompanied in the Fourth Gospel by the theme of judgment, and the latter occupies an equally important place. The gospel of life, light, and love is also the gospel of judgment. Indeed, the curve followed by the use of the vocabulary of judgment in John follows that of the light and life themes. While in the first twelve chapters the verb "judge" occurs 17 times and the noun "judgment" 9 times, in chapters 13-20 judgment is mentioned only 4 times (the verb twice and the noun twice). We must say, then, what Dodd has said of light and life: for John, love is the "definitive reality" of judgment.

This conclusion may seem paradoxical, but it must be drawn if we are to understand the Fourth Gospel correctly.

John's gospel is a gospel of judgment, too. This is a major theme there, on the same order as the themes of light and life. Nor does it disappear in the second part of the book. On the contrary, the Passion is presented as a judgment—indeed, as a double judgment: that passed upon Jesus and that passed upon the world.

John builds his account of the Passion on two levels. Seemingly—to human eyes—Jesus is condemned as an imposter. In reality—in God's eyes—the world has pronounced its own sentence. When Pilate exhibits Jesus to the crowd, saying, "Look at the man!" (John 19:5), unbeknownst to himself he is presenting the eschatological judge who receives sovereignty, glory, and power (cf. Dan. 7:14). When the chief priest decides to destroy Jesus, he makes himself the prophet of the Shepherd who will gather all dispersed Israel together into one (John 11:49-54). The guiding thread of the Johannine account of the Passion is the reversed verdict: "Now has judgment come upon this world . . ." (12:31). The moment has come when the Spirit "will prove the world wrong . . . about condemnation." To human eyes, it is Jesus who is judged and condemned; but in reality it is "the prince of this world" who "has been condemned" (John 16:8,11).

Johannine love must thus be understood in function of the other side of the coin. Johannine love goes hand in hand with judgment. It is not a spineless "love," some analgesic jelly smeared over the world's injustice. It is a courageous, lucid love, a love that denounces evil, injustice, and the powers of this world (John 16:8-11). It is the love of the One who, while our Father, and measurelessly close to us, is also the Holy One (John 17:11; cf. 1 John 2:21) and the One who "consecrates" and sanctifies those who will be called to association with that Holy One (John 10:36, 17:17); the

One who is truth that cannot lie (1 John 2:20-21), who is light in which there is no darkness whatever (1 John 1:5), and the One who will be rejected by those who prefer darkness because their deeds are nefarious: for this is judgment (John 3:19-20). The viewpoint is the same as in Mark 16:16: while believers receive salvation, those who close themselves off to faith risk condemnation. The theology of liberation has called attention to this conflictive aspect of salvation: Christian charity is also exercised in the prophetic denunciation of evil.[13] But conversely, John recalls that judgment itself is to be situated in a perspective of love.

## LOVE, JUDGMENT, AND THE MISSION OF THE SPIRIT

The glory of the cross, then, is the glory of loving. This is its victory over the world (John 16:33). The cross is glorious because it is the supreme manifestation of the One who is at once and indissolubly the God who is Love and God the Holy.

It is from this cross that the Spirit will spring forth (John 19:30,34-35; cf. 7:38-39, 20:22), who gives peace to the world (20:21) in deliverance from sin (20:23). It is not out of a simple apologetical concern, then, that Jesus shows his disciples his hands and his side at the moment of his sending them forth (20:20): the Spirit, and hence the mission animated by the Spirit, actually flow from this heart and these open hands. The Spirit sent by the Father teaches all things and recalls all that Jesus has said (14:26), enabling the disciples to bear witness in their turn (15:26-27)—a witness of peace (14:26-27), yes, but also of judgment on the "world" that does not accept this Spirit (14:17). It will be a witness of blood and water (1 John 5:6-10)—of the water that gives life and of the blood that represents the violence of the world.

It is in function of these themes that we must understand the passage in which the disciples are sent forth to mission, the passage with which the Book of Glory concludes (John 20:20-23). "He showed them his hands and his side," from which the Spirit had issued. Also, he tells them: "Receive the Holy Spirit." In virtue of this gift of the Spirit, the mission to which Jesus had been sent passes to his disciples: "As the Father has sent me, so I send you." Like Jesus' mission, that of the disciples' mission will have two faces. It will be a mission of peace: "If you forgive men's sins, they are forgiven them." But it will necessarily involve the other side of the coin, as well: "If you hold them bound, they are held bound."

Spirit, sending, peace and forgiveness of sins, judgment and binding of sins—here we have a synthesis of missionary theology woven about the gift of the Spirit. From the outstretched hands and open heart of Jesus exalted, the Spirit spills out on the world, to be received in peace or rejected in judgment. Here, in its entirety, is the profound reality of mission.

## THE GREAT MISSIONARY PRAYER OF JOHN 17

In John 17, the meaning of the book of exaltation is summarized in the form of prayer. This chapter is the keystone of chapters 13-20, and the prayer it expresses is at the heart of the mystery of the glorious cross.

### JOHN 17: MISSIONARY PRAYER

John 17 is commonly entitled the "Priestly Prayer of Jesus." The designation is a correct one. This prayer indeed expresses the oblation, consecration, and intercession of Christ the priest. However, the word "priest" does not appear in the text, while the verb "send" (*apostellein*) occurs seven times. It is an "apostolic" prayer, then, a missionary one: Jesus presents himself here as the one sent by the Father, and prays for the disciples whom he will send forth in their turn. Jesus is the Father's missionary to an unrivaled degree—to the very consecration he effects in his sacrifice. The disciples share in this consecration and mission of the Son. Thus, John's entire missionary concern is summed up in this prayer.

Along the same lines, we observe the parallelism between John 17:18 and 20:21:

| *John 17:18* | *John 20:21* |
|---|---|
| "As you have sent me . . . so I have sent them. . . ." | "As the Father has sent me, so I send you." |

Another parallel occurs between John 17 and the missionary mandate of Matthew 28, in the use of the verb "give": "Full authority has been given to me both in heaven and on earth," says Matthew 28:18; this is the foundation of mission. The same theme recurs, nearly identically, in John 17:2: ". . . Inasmuch as you have given him authority over all mankind." The rest of the prayer will explain in what this "gift" consists: it is the gift of the disciples (v. 2,6,9,24), the gift of a deed to be accomplished (v. 4), the gift of the Word (vv. 8,14), of the Name (vv. 11,12,26), of glory (v. 2), of power (v. 2), and, in sum, of "all" (v. 7). Thus, John 17 presents, as in a paraphrase, in the form of prayer, the great texts of the sending forth to mission by the Risen Christ.

This great missionary vision will be laid out in three installments: Jesus sent (vv. 1-5), the disciples sent (vv. 6-19), and those who will believe over the course of time (vv. 20-26).

### JESUS SENT (VV. 1–5)

In the prayer's first verses, Jesus prays for himself and asks for his glorification. This prayer is not a selfish one. As in the other texts of the sending forth to mission, resurrection means mission: Jesus' glory is the power to give everlasting life (v. 2). This glorification is the founding act of mission. In it, Jesus the One sent makes himself and the Father known (cf. Matt. 11:27). Receiving "authority over all mankind," Jesus can grant eternal life (cf. Matt. 28:18). The glory received has been communicated to those who know him and who know the Father. Such was the mission, "the work," that he had received.

### THE DISCIPLES SENT (VV. 6–19)

The great missionary prayer then passes on to various aspects of the disciples' mission:

1. The disciples have been "given" by God, and thereby taken from the world (vv. 11,15-16)—set apart and consecrated (vv. 17,19). These are themes of calling: Paul, too, has emphasized that the apostle must be called, "set apart" (Rom 1:1, Gal. 1:15).

2. The disciples have received the Word of Jesus, which is the Word of the Father (vv. 7-8,13-14). It is this Word that has consecrated them. Their faith has identified them with the Word they have received (vv. 17,19).

3. The Word with which the disciples' faith is thus identified is a Word proceeding from the divine unity. Hence, in their life, the disciples are to carry to the world the image of the divine unity (v. 11).

4. The Father's sending of the Son is succeeded by the Son's sending of the disciples to the world (v. 18). We observe that, while v. 18 speaks of a sending, the following verse does not seize upon the *communication* of truth, but returns to the theme of *consecration* to truth. Up to a certain point, the analysis of the evangelizing action in John 17 is reminiscent of Paul's in Romans 10:14-15: calling, sending, hearing, faith. It differs from it, however, in its focus on the spiritual event taking place in the soul of the one sent: consecration, identification with the truth. The envoy remains before all else a "disciple." Associated with Jesus' mission, those sent remain fundamentally "his." To be sure, they are to proclaim the gospel; but more specifically, and more profoundly, they are called to be one with the truth of the Word: it is the Word that will have the initiative in the deepest heart of their mission.

### THOSE WHO WILL BELIEVE (VV. 20-26)

The same insights are afforded in the third part of the prayer, which extends to all who, over space and time, will ever believe in the word of the disciples (v. 20). They, too, will know the glory (vv. 22,24) and name of the Father as Jesus has known it and made it known (vv. 25-26). But this glory and this knowledge are ever the glory and the knowledge of love:

> . . . that they may be one, as we are one —
> I living in them, you living in me —

that their unity may be complete.
So shall the world know that you sent me,
and that you loved them as you loved me. . . .
so that your love for me may live in them,
and I may live in them (vv. 22-23,26).

This is a very poignant text. But we must not forget to situate it in the concrete context of the tensions prevailing in the primitive church. The pluralism in which the Christian communities at the close of the first century lived was not without its confrontations. We only catch an occasional glimpse of these conflicts over the course of the Fourth Gospel.[14] They will come to violent expression in the Johannine letters (2 John 7-11, 3 John 9-11). Thus, the prayer for unity is an expression of anguish and at the same time an act of faith in the face of the discouragement occasioned by these rents. The source of Christian unity is to be sought not in the poverty of human goodwill, but in the very oneness of Father and Son. Thus it becomes the manifestation of this unity to the eyes of human beings: "so shall the world know."

And so the prayer also engages believers' own responsibility. Addressing the world, believers are the vehicles not only of a verbal message, but also, and especially, of their identification with Jesus and the Father, of their consecration in unity. Thus, the Prayer for Unity is at once a mystical text and a missionary text. The disciple is not isolated in an individual spiritual experience. He or she has a responsibility to the world: "that the world may believe" (v. 21). But in order to perform this duty to the world, it is not enough to proclaim the Word. One must live the Word, enfleshing the profound oneness of Father and Son, and present to the world, in the love of the community, the image of the glory and presence of God.

Thus, according to John 17, to be sent is first of all to *receive* knowledge, the manifestation of glory, the intimacy of Father and Son.

This acceptance of the Word of truth makes the envoy someone *consecrated*, someone belonging to God, protected by God, set apart from the world without being taken from it.

As someone consecrated, the one sent bears the earthly reflection of God's glory, the *glory of love and unity*. It is through this love and this unity, then, that the one sent exercises his or her responsibility toward the world, "that the world may believe."

Thus, the purpose of mission is to share with the world, in the concrete context of its anguish and its antagonisms, the very joy of the Son, the glory that he has received, the love that he shares with the Father. Mission shares with the world the communion of Father and Son.

## CONCLUSION

In its very original way, the missionary vision of John brings us once again quite close to Old Testament perspectives.

In John as in the Old Testament, the basic impulse of mission is the glory of God, whose splendor attracts the nations. But in John this glory is the radiance of an infinite love: it is a glory "filled with enduring love" (John 1:14).

In John as in the Old Testament, the glory of God bursts upon the world through the Messiah (cf. Isa. 9:1-4, 49:9). It is in Jesus, the Word made flesh, that we have seen God's glory (John 1:14, 17:1-5). But we have seen this glory on a cross, in a love thrust to the point of the total sacrificial consecration of death (John 17:19). It is in this "exaltation" that the glory that will attract all women and men will be made manifest (John 12:32).

As in the Old Testament, in John the glory of God is manifested through a people (cf. Isa. 60). But the glory that radiates from this "consecrated" people is that of a total transparency to the Word of love: "Consecrate them by means of truth—'Your Word is truth'" (John 17:17). The sign of this transparency will be a love capable of assuming human tensions and divisions, and thus of ensuring unity. If this people of believers manages to show forth the glory of loving in unity, then the world will have seen the glory of God and will know love (John 17:23).

Seen through John, then, mission is God coming to the world in the divine Word, light, and life, coming in the Spirit of God to cause the glory of the divine love to flash forth in that world.

Mission is the *gift of the Son* to the world, the Son that is the incarnation of the Word of God, the living image of the Glory of God, and the supreme act of God's Love.

Mission is the invitation to the world to gather, by faith in the Word, in the *oneness of a people*—a people called to bear witness, amidst lies and hatred, to truth and love, a people called to reproduce in their oneness the image of the mystery of communion that lies in the depths of the Godhead.

The missionary scope of John, then, is fully as genuine as that of the rest of the New Testament—just as conscious of the world's expectancy. But it distinguishes itself by its spiritual depth. It peers into the inner experience of those sent, to discover there, at the heart of mission, and amidst the hostility of the world, the "knowledge," intimacy, glory, love, and joy of God. John 17 extends to the disciples and to all who are to believe, the mystical depths of which the Prologue has afforded a glimpse in the Verbum. John will sum it up in the words of the Risen One: "As the Father has sent me, so I send you" (John 20:21). Behold the mystery of the intimacy of Father and Son that mission is to extend to the world.

If the Fourth Gospel has not always been recognized as a missionary text, it is because Johannine perspectives depart too far from those of our habitual image of mission. But precisely, this "mystical" image of mission is an invitation to broaden and deepen our way of seeing and to transcend our unhappy dichotomies between action and contemplation, grace and human responsibility, interiority and other-directedness, spiritual experience and social commitment, theocentrism and anthropocentrism, monastic and missionary calling. Ascetics and apostles alike will always have need of this gospel. Ascetics must remind themselves of their responsibility to the "world," in the footsteps of the Word made flesh. Apostles of the mystical depths of the Word that they bear to women and men, with this reflection in mind, both will better understand that their missions merge in that of Christ, who is indissolubly Word and Flesh.

# PART FOUR

# CONCLUSIONS AND QUESTIONS

We have come a long distance from the call of Abraham to the Gospel of John. We have seen various attitudes toward God's salvific plan for the world. Out of this swarm of tendencies, can we identify certain constants and draw some conclusions? Or must we perhaps simply allow this disconcerting variety of views to serve as a basis for our own self-examination? The questions posed by a movement are as important as the convictions that inspire that movement. Indeed, our only too human certitudes are ever in need of examination and continual conversion to God, who ceaselessly repeats to us:

> My thoughts are not your thoughts, nor are your ways
>     my ways, says the LORD.
> As high as the heavens are above the earth,
>     so high are my ways above your ways
>     and my thoughts above your thoughts
>                             (Isa. 55:8-9).

# 11

# The Ways of Mission

*The Old Testament did not ignore the nations. Its thinking with regard to other peoples was determined by the two poles of election and universalism. We altogether distort Israel's attitude when we attend only to the first pole, and even more when we reduce it to a narrow "exclusivism."*

*The novelty of Jesus Christ manifests itself in two movements.*

*The first movement is the coming of Jesus, the first "missionary," the eschatological ambassador of God sent forth to gather the messianic people. This people is composed, first, of the scattered sheep of Israel; but it is also open to the nations, whose eschatological assembly is prefigured by the Samaritans and pagans who believe in Jesus and receive salvation even now. Jesus proclaims the Word that gathers this people together, while overturning their expectations. He translates this Word into acts—into concrete deeds and attitudes. He identifies with this Word. He is this Word.*

*When his Resurrection liberates this Word and gives it universal scope. It hastens the eschatological movement. At the impulse of the Spirit, the laborers will begin to gather in the harvest, inviting Jews and Gentiles alike to enter into the communion of the new people of Abraham, the people whose mark is faith in Jesus Christ.*

## DIVERSITY

This long, rich history is characterized by diversity. Even in the Old Testament, of the two poles of election and universality, certain passages place more emphasis on the former, others on the latter. Old Testament universalism itself, corollary of a faith in one almighty God, takes various forms, from a universalism of domination, in which the nations are subjected to the Lord of Hosts and his representative, Israel, to a universalism of salvation; from a universalism of sin to a universalism of the love of God, from a centripetal universalism calling all nations to Zion, to a decentralized universalism, which, to be sure, is rare in the Old Testament.

The New Testament will go to the nations. But here once more, we must not attempt to reduce a complex reality to just one of its terms. The missionary movement that ensued upon the Resurrection was expressed in a great variety of attitudes. Its two great axes are constituted by Peter's mission to the Jews and Paul's to the nations, in terms of the accord ratified at Jerusalem (Gal. 2:9). But within these two comprehensive movements, many were the different paths of New Testament mission.

The "Palestinian mission" itself was necessarily quite a complex affair, including as it did a number of different orientations, beginning with a certain sedentarism on the part of Judaeo-Christians and the Twelve, then branching out to styles as varied as the rabbinical training of disciples in the Matthean style, the itinerant movement of charismatic "missionaries," and a certain better organized movement with Peter at its center, not to mention a Galilean mission of which we know little and about which we can only conjecture.

In an outward movement, there was the mission of the Judaeo-Hellenistic Christians, heir to the open attitude, methods of propagation, and themes of the Jewish diaspora. It was this Judaeo-Hellenistic Christianity that embarked on the Samaritan mission, one of the most successful of the New Testament age, although the New Testament speaks so little of it. Along the trajectories of the Jewish diaspora, Judaeo-Hellenistic Christianity laid the foundations of the communities of Damascus, Antioch, and perhaps even Rome. Luke, somewhat the prisoner of his plan in diptych, does insufficient justice to this movement, whose importance we surmise only when we see Saul welcomed by the community of Damascus, receiving the mandate of that of Antioch, or counting on that of Rome to endorse the last stage of his ministry, which will take him to Spain at the ends of the earth.

At all events, it is from the heart of this thrust of Judaeo-Christianity that the Pauline mission was born. But the Pauline type itself is not a simple one. The fashion in which Luke reports it in Acts does not perfectly coincide with the image that Paul gives of it in his letters. A rather consistent difference resides in the fact that Paul saw himself as the missionary charged, along with his collaborators, with proclaiming the gospel to the ends of the earth in eschatological haste and the hope of completing the preaching of the gospel of Christ (cf. Rom. 15:19). Luke sees Paul as the model of the postapostolic mission, and hence of the successive generations that will take up the relays of the evangelizing task. Another difference is that Paul insists more on the power of the gospel, of which he is but the feeble servant, useless steward, and lowly ambassador, while Luke brings out the importance of the active mediation of the human agents of evangelization.

We should also have to add the "Johannine mission," or rather, the various types of mission carried on by the vast movement of the Johannine churches. As a later composition, the product of a number of redactional stages, the Fourth Gospel presents a pluralism of forms of church and mission. In Jewish fashion, it envisages the gathering of the consecrated people (John 10:16, 11:49-52, 17:21), and it knows that "salvation is from the Jews" (4:22). But it also speaks disparagingly of the Jews, at times almost as if they were foreigners. Certain *obiter dicta* betray an interest in the diaspora, along the lines of Judaeo-Hellenistic Christianity (7:35, 11:52). An entire chapter is devoted to the Samaritans (4:1-42) and may reflect traditions of the Samaritan mission that we find mentioned in Acts 8. But John also cites the coming of the pagans and sees in it a sign of the glorification (12:20-33). In the Gospel of John itself, then, we have a glimpse of a number of different forms of first-century mission.

This variety of types of mission in the Bible will constitute our first conclusion. It is impossible to reduce this rich diversity to simple formulas like an opposition between a particularism and concentric movement characteristic of the Old Testament and a universalism and outward movement proper to the New. Still less may we range all of these forms along a linear evolutive trajectory that would begin with the Old Testament and finally come to the New. What would the point of arrival be? Jesus, who hardly ever left the territory of Israel? Matthew 28:19 or 19:28? Paul or John? The only way to make a selection, to set a *terminus ad quem* to this hypothetical evolutionary line, would be arbitrarily to prioritize one or other of these forms.

No biblical datum supports any assigning of privileged value to any of these forms. Any choice we might make would have to proceed from an a priori judgment of our own of what mission ought to be—a dangerous method indeed, as it would curtail the impact of the Word of God by dictating to it its conclusions in advance. We must be willing to be challenged by the rich variety of biblical data, including above all its unexpected elements. If there are biblical forms of mission that fail to correspond to our own idea of mission, then this is precisely where we should pause. Such is the case, for example, with the Old Testament, with Jesus' attitude, or with the Johannine conceptualization—all of which have forced us to transcend our ready-made schemata and review our way of understanding even the attitude of Paul.

This biblical pluralism corresponds to the diversity of what we actually see in mission today. The situation differs enormously between the mission addressed to the neopaganism of the lands of ancient Christendom and that directed to those whom the call of the gospel has not yet reached; between a mission intended for the peoples of solid, old religious culture, as in Asia, and one addressed to those who have been despoiled of their culture by a devastating colonialism, as in Latin America; between receptive milieus, as in tribal societies, and the context of the lands of Islam; between the capitalist world and the Marxist world. Then, within these various overall categories of society, once more the forms of a missionary presence vary a great deal, depending on whether that presence is clerical, lay, or monastic, whether it is that of persons engaged in a direct apostolate or of persons whose apostolate is that of witness, sharing, the media, dialogue, the struggle for liberation, or the ministry teams of local churches. These analyses could be multiplied ad infinitum. Curiously, while the model proposed to the Christian imagination has so long been fairly uniform, the reality of mission continues to be exercised in rich variety. In the face of impoverishing ideological reductions, the Spirit continues to distribute a multiplicity of gifts and calls, entirely as that Spirit wills (cf. 1 Cor. 12:11).

## CONVERGENCES

However, this variety does not mean that there are no convergences.

1. The Bible is shot through with a dynamism that expands the activity of God to world dimensions. Even faith in one, all-powerful God entails the corollary of a divine domain, the Reign of God. God's love must extend to the entire world, to every creature. The ultimate theological foundation of mission is this movement of God toward creation. *Mission is first and foremost the God who comes*.

2. God comes to create a people of God: for the Old Testament, Israel; for the New Testament, the church.[1] Thus, election is the complementary pole of mission. It signifies that mission is more than propaganda, the recruitment of adepts, or even simply the spreading of the truth. It is an ingathering. From the call of Abraham in Genesis 12:1-2 to Jesus' missionary testament in John 17, this theme will grow in depth, and John will give it its most theological form, presenting the unity of the disciples as emanating from the oneness of the divine Trinity itself. But John is only the climax of an element that we find throughout the Bible, in the prophets, as in Isaiah 2:2-5 and 60:1-17, in the Psalms (Pss. 87, 122), or, again, in Jesus' choice of the Twelve or the Pauline doctrine of the church. Mission is not the act of a prospector staking out a claim. *Mission is exercised in function of a people, creating this people and in turn developing through it.*

3. At the heart of this people is the *word* that calls it, gathers it in, judges it, and guides it. This Word is the efficacious word of almighty God, and has all the dynamism of the explosive joy of the Good News—of the gospel that is the power of God leading to salvation (Rom. 1:16). But it is also a Word as sharp as any two-edged sword (Heb. 4:12), and it will slice its way through equivocations, hypocrisy, and subterfuges to leave a person naked before God—sinful and liable to judgment, but loved and saved, as well. The activity of evangelization must ever remain humble and know that it is an unprofitable servant of the gospel. The whole force of evangelization depends on the authenticity with which the evangelizer pronounces the Word.

4. This Word became flesh in the person of Jesus of Nazareth, and in the messianic people which he has gathered to himself and which relays his activity. The evangelical discourse is not uttered in words alone. It is also pronounced in signs and power, actions and attitudes, life and death.

As the Old Testament, the ministry of Jesus and the witness of the primitive church have explicitly shown, *mission is as concrete as the life of a people*, not only in the "religious" aspects of this life, but in the entire social, cultural, economic, political, and ecological concretion of human existence. It is not merely individual "souls" but a *people* who are judged and called to conversion, loved and saved, set apart and gathered to unity. It is this entire people, throughout the various aspects of its life, that is to bear witness before the world of the Word that dwells within it. In the solidarity and communion of this people, manifested even at the level of socioeconomic exchange, Luke will show forth one of the principal forms of evangelical expression. John will elevate this oneness to the status of ultimate parable of the divine glory.

5. Thus, this people is characterized by the authenticity of the witness it bears the word, its consecration in truth, its intransigence vis-à-vis the Evil one, and its love of unity. *This people is also characterized by prayer.* The chosen, saved people of the Old Testament renders honor and thanksgiving to the Lord, and the deliverance from Egypt climaxes in the canticles of Moses and Miriam (Exod. 15:1-21). Again, it is the glory of liturgical worship that draws the nations to Zion. Jesus expresses his vision of the Reign in the Lord's Prayer and in his consciousness of his mission as expressed in the form of thanksgiving (Matt. 11:25-27). In John 17, the program Jesus bequeaths his disciples becomes intercessory prayer. Paul gives thanks and prays "continually" (1 Cor. 1:4) and thrusts the analysis of the missionary activity beyond faith to invocation (Rom. 10:13-14). Like Jesus, who is the Apostle and High Priest of our profession of faith (Heb. 3:1), Paul the Apostle is conscious of having been charged with the "liturgical ministry" of the oblation of the nations (Rom. 15:16). In the vignettes that Luke has sketched by way of a description of the apostolic church, he has painted the icon of this community gathered in both a communion of goods and in prayer (Acts 2:42-47; cf. Luke 1:46-55,64-79, 2:14,20,29-32,38).

6. *The gathering of all the peoples into one is the eschatological deed of God.* The Old Testament says so, and Jesus remains loyal to this viewpoint. But Jesus introduces a new element, as well: that of a Reign of God at hand, and thus an eschatological realization that has burst in upon the present. Furthermore, the divine action, which, according to the apocalyptic tradition, was exercised from on high either by direct divine intervention or through the ministry of angels, is now found to have been entrusted to human beings—first of all to the human being Jesus, and then to those who, in his footsteps, will be sent forth to the harvest. Thus, *eschatology descends into human history.* But it is an eschatology in course of realization and not an eschatology fulfilled. What the human mediation of Jesus and his "own" does is to posit signs, tokens, of the final ingathering. Jesus does not convert all of the pagans, nor does Peter, or even Paul. Mission is the deed of human mediation. As such, it will never see total success in this present, transitory age. It will ever bear the mark of human weakness and

incompleteness. Jesus himself bore this mark. His ministry was requited with defeat and death. But precisely therefore, throughout all of its defeats, mission will ever be the *vessel of the hope* bestowed upon it by its faith in God and its awareness that what it does, however poorly and uselessly, is the deed of the Almighty, the Sovereign of the Future.

## QUESTIONS

These biblical constants raise many problems.

Which has priority, God's eschatological activity or human mediation? The Old Testament and the beginnings of the Christian mission place more accent on the former. Paul, and especially Luke, have a clearer vision of the need for the latter. Are we, therefore, to allow ourselves to be borne along by the power of the gospel, or are we to rely on a zeal for evangelization and an activity springing from this zeal? Carried to extremes, the first attitude would lead to passivity, the second to a missionary Pelagianism.

Are we to proclaim the Word boldly, "whether convenient or inconvenient" (2 Tim. 4:2)? Or rather should we proclaim it through the testimony, perhaps indeed the silent testimony, of our lives? While Paul knows naught but the word of the cross (1 Cor. 2:2), Luke, in Acts, will feel the impact of a particular quality of faith, prayer, and sharing (Acts 2:42-47). But here again, carried to an extreme, Paul's inspired prophetic vigor could degenerate into aggressivity and arrogance, while Lucan patience could eventually become disguised resignation.

Spiritual liberation? Or concrete liberation, incarnate in all of the aspects of the history of a people? The Old Testament, with its long history, is a better expression of the concrete dimensions of the divine action. This viewpoint is certainly not contradicted in the New Testament; but it is less explicit there. Furthermore, the New Covenant goes beyond stone tablets and institutions and is written on hearts, plumbs the depths of a person's inmost being (Jer. 31:33). To strike a balance between interiority and realism is easier said than done. The reduction of salvation to a concrete program would be tantamount to reducing the Reign of divine grace to a purely human utopia and purely human action, bereft of any of the dynamism or perspective of Christian hope. Conversely, a purely eschatological or "spiritual" conception of salvation would simply be Manichaeism-in-practice, and the concrete realities of existence would be thrust aside as "merely material"—the attitude of the practical rejection of the Old Testament that we so frequently encounter in Christians who are shocked at the carnal language of these books. And we recall the debate over liberation theology, a theology having the merit of revalidating both the Old Testament and the concrete aspects of the salvation message.

Word of condemnation or word of reconciliation? Does God judge the world or save it? In the prophets and even in John, the two attitudes are

combined. God condemns the world; God loves the world and saves it. To
distinguish two senses of the word "world" would be a facile, and tempting,
solution. But it is scarcely clear that a like semantic ploy would resolve the
tension between prophetic condemnation and messianic reconciliation. Liberation theology and third-world theology have helped us rediscover the
meaning of the word "judgment" for our own times: there are sinful, del-
eterious attitudes, situations, and structures to which we may not close our
eyes and which we must denounce. Recently, however, Chinese theologians
have been saying that it is a theology of reconciliation of which countries
stand in need once they have had their liberating revolution. Paul, who,
with a violence worthy of an Amos, had stigmatized the universal sway of
sin (Rom. chaps. 1-3), saw his apostolic role as a "ministry of reconciliation"
(2 Cor. 5:18) and peace (Eph. 2:14-17), and John weaves the affirmation
(John 9:39) and negation (3:17) of a judgment of the world around the
theme of the love that God has for that world (3:16).

To put the problem another way: we might wonder whether, in the way
we call on the world to have faith, we ought to place more emphasis on
breach or on continuity. That is to say, on one side we have Paul, who
proclaimed a world, Jewish and pagan, altogether delivered over to sin, the
better to be able to emphasize the gratuity of the divine grace (Gal. 3:22;
Rom. 5:20). On the other hand, we have Luke, who loves to find tokens of
faith both in the piety of Israel (Luke 1:6, 2:25,37) and in the good works
of the nations (Luke 7:4; Acts 10:2, 13:7), including even pagan religious
thought (Acts 17:28).

We could go on with these seeming antinomies—which ultimately lead
to the paradox of the Most Holy God, the Utterly Other, who infinitely
transcends human weakness, but who is also Love, and who becomes the
Utterly Near one by creation, covenant, and incarnation.

Seen from this perspective, the antinomies of mission are not problems
to be solved with an option for one term over the other. In our faith in
God, we cannot divorce the Most Holy from Emmanuel, the ever-present,
hidden God.

But it would be too much to demand of our poor human finitude always
to attempt to implement a harmonious synthesis and maintain perfect equilibrium in our words, actions, and behavior. Attaining such equilibrium is
easier said than done. Rather we must live, as a people, the antinomies of
mission, conscious of the complementarity of the various sensitivities and
options, refusing to allow ourselves to be imprisoned by one tendency exclusively, willing to examine ourselves in the light of a contrary, or rather,
complementary, intent.

An isolated tendency becomes sectarian. Faith in the Most Holy God,
in isolation, can produce a legalistic or Jansenistic rigidity. But if we will
only know the Utterly Near, we may forget that that One is God, and faith
will founder in finickiness. If we insist on continuities and inculturation
unilaterally, we may be overwhelmed by the ambient mentality and lose

our prophetic distance vis-à-vis the ambiguities of society. If we regard only discontinuities, we shall build a rootless religion, detached from the experience of reality—bodiless, and thereby lacking a true soul. An exclusive attention to mission's "not yet," with the ingathering of the peoples left to the purely eschatological action of God, will be in danger of serving as an excuse for the passivity of a tired, disillusioned church, surely too shabby a witness of the God who comes with power. But at the other extreme, an arrogant, triumphalistic church, smug in its structures and its words, would know no longer either hope or the humility of the Servant. A salvation conceived in purely spiritual terms will sweep away the Incarnation; while a liberation reduced to purely human factors will destroy the meaning of God's transcendence, grace, and Reign.

These antinomies could be solved only by reducing them to one of their respective terms. But this reduction would mutilate divine reality. The only "solution" will be to remain open—open to the call of God who invites us, through one another, to emerge from our cramped positions or sectarian rigidity, our too tightly knotted theories, our too narrow syntheses.

## ISRAEL OR THE MONGOLS?

The problem of Israel should be approached in the same way.

It is a problem that we find at each stage of our study, not only in the Old Testament, but in the words and practice of Jesus, of Paul, and of Luke. "Salvation is from the Jews" (John 4:22). It is remarkable that this formula is found in John, who, of the New Testament writers, is perhaps the most hostile to "the Jews."

That salvation is *from* the Jews in the biblical perspective is abundantly evident. But what remains? Has not Israel lost its privileges? Is there any role left for Israel today? Can we construct a theory and practice of mission that would leave Israel out of account? This has practically been done; and worse has been done, in an actual attempt to destroy the Jewish people. But, as we have seen, no biblical author, in either the Old or the New Testament, can envisage universal salvation apart from Israel.

What, then, will be the current place of Israel according to the flesh? Israel is of great value "in every respect," Paul answers. "First of all, the Jews were entrusted with the words of God" (Rom. 3:2). Faith in the one God is the foundation of biblical revelation, and Israel is the people of that faith. Israel is the people of the Bible—not only the people to whom the Bible has been entrusted, and by whom it has been transmitted to the world, but the people formed by the Bible who incarnate it, who draw their existence from the Covenant, the Law, the Land, the Promises, from all of these themes of which the Bible is made. We can read the Bible, but God has not willed to be revealed and to save the world only by a book. God acts through the divine word at the heart of a people. Thus, Israel has unique value as *living witness of the Bible and of the God of the Bible.*[2] Like the revelation of God, the revelation of the human being, too, has been entrusted to the people of Israel.[3] In the long history it recounts, the Old Testament, without complacency, but without complexes, either, reveals the realities of flesh and blood, hope and failure, injustice and disorder, war and peace, life and death that make up the warp and woof of the human condition, and there is no basis for the notion that through the coming of the Word made flesh, these realities have evaporated in a process of dis-incarnating "spiritualization." The New Testament, too, takes human beings in all dimensions of their existence. But it is the Old that gives us the more explicit image of the human being, before God, in the world. Once again, that image is no bookish one. It is the entire life of a people, who continue to bear, in their memory and destiny, the anthropological concretion of the Covenant and the Promises.

And so the dialogue with Israel still has validity today. It is the dialogue with that which constitutes the integral dimensions of Christian faith: a sense of God and a sense of the human being before God. It is surely no coincidence that Christian alienation from Israel over the course of the centuries has been accompanied by a growing insipidity of Christian faith and a loss of contact with the realities that make up human life.

What, therefore, will be the future role of Israel? Can the "fullness of the nations" be realized only with Israel's return? Does that return belong to the eschatological harvest of God, or does some responsibility lie with human laborers? Will the salvation of Israel occur through its recognition of Christ? Or will it be along Israel's own paths, instead, without explicit faith in Jesus? If Israel is called to faith in Jesus Christ, are we speaking of all of the descendants of Abraham or only of a remnant? And will this remnant be the pious remnant of the observers of Judaism or the profane remnant of those whom life experience will have detached from the Law? Exegetes and theologians dispute the meaning to be ascribed, especially, to the reflections of Paul in Romans chaps. 9-11.[4] The very fact of the dispute is evidence of how deeply shrouded in mystery Paul's insights are. For Paul himself, the mystery abides, and his mediation respects the secret of the divine plan. We can only conclude, with him: "How inscrutable his judgments, how unsearchable his ways! For 'who has known the mind of the Lord? Or who has been his counselor?' " (Rom. 11:33-34).

With Paul, then, let us retain at least this: that the Christian worldview cannot ignore Abraham's descendancy—all that it has been in the past and all that it continues to incarnate today. It is important for Christian mission to rediscover its bonds with the Jewish people.

A recovery of the meaning of Israel in a Christian conception of history and of mission must not mean a return to a Judaeo-Christianity that would eschew an overture to the nations. Not that we have done so, by and large. But certain studies "rehabilitating" Israel seem to disparage the mission to the nations. In a colloquium of exegetes assembled to discuss Romans chaps. 9-11, one of the participants declared: "In the order of signification, the return of Israel is scarcely on a par with the conversion of the Mongols."⁵ From an Asian standpoint, this condescending reference to "Mongols" is annoying in the extreme. Here is a people not to be cheapened — whose extraordinary dynamism has been sketched by René Grousset, among others, and who, from China to Hungary, and from the steppes to India, have had a powerful effect on the history of Eurasia.⁶ The mission to the Grand Mongol of Franciscan Jean de Montecorvin, from 1294 to 1328, itself anticipated by a more anonymous missionary movement on the part of the Nestorian churches, represents one of the finest moments in the history of the Christian missions.

Even apart from the specific case of the Mongols and their merits or demerits — to return to a general theological viewpoint — we cannot regard the great peoples of the world, even the less celebrated peoples or tribes, as insignificant. Human life is precious in the sight of the Lord, whether it be that of the Jews or the Egyptians or the Kushites of Africa or the Ninevites or the Elamites and the peoples of Ophir (perhaps India), toward the East, of Yavan and the Islands to the West, or the Scythians and other barbarians of the North.

Thus the nations count, and "in the order of signification." Paul himself, who acknowledged the central place of Israel in his apostolic outlook, would certainly not have tolerated the assertion that his ministry to the nations was a trifling affair. Yes, he felt the need to have his new ministry approved by the church of Jerusalem (Gal. 2:2-9) and to receive the endorsement of the "pillars" of that church in token of communion (Gal. 2:9). But communion did not mean subordination, and Paul did not see his mission to the nations as a simple corollary of Peter's mission. It was its dialectical counterpart (Gal. 2:7-8). He had received his vocation of apostle to the pagans directly from Christ (Gal. 1:1,15-16), and this mission had its own dynamism and horizons, although not independently of Israel's election. In Romans 11:16-24, he uses the image of the graft. Israel is the stock and the nations the graft. The graft becomes integrated with the stock, while bringing to the stock the new vitality and fecundity of its own unique origins.

Luke, as well, in Acts, while insisting even more clearly than Paul on the connections of the pagan mission with the church of the apostles, likewise brings out the radical novelty of the overture to the nations. He devotes long chapters to retracing its origin (Acts chaps. 10-11) and meaning (Acts 15). He shows it as inspired by special interventions of the Spirit (Acts 10:19,44-48, 11:12,15-16, 13:2-4). The entry of the Word into the pagan world is signaled by the announcement of the angel of the Lord to Cornelius (10:3-7,22,30, 11:13), like the angel's annunciation to Mary had signaled the dawn of the Messianic age. With its new horizon — the particular dynamism animating it, the ever unforeseeable creativity it demonstrates, its overthrow of the structures of the people of God, and even its way of conceiving its relationship with the Lord — the mission to the Gentiles represents a profound mutation, qualitative as well as quantitative, in the evolution of the chosen people.

The question of the respective role of Israel and the nations in Christian mission returns us once more to the same binomial of election and universalism, neither of whose terms can be ignored without destroying the equilibrium of God's plan. To look down on the "Mongols," or any other people, is to ignore the mighty breath of that Spirit who, from Peter and Paul down through the centuries, has given life to the Messianic people. At the same time, were it to cut its ties with Israel, the mission to the nations would be in danger of becoming nothing but wind, and no longer the divine breath — an empty canister, devoid of divine and human substance.

## CONVERSION OF MISSION

Seen in the light of the Bible, mission evinces the dynamism of deep-reaching force vectors: the presence of the God who comes, the power of the Word and the creativity of the Spirit, the election of Israel and the march of the nations, liberation from every slavery and the call for a universal gathering to the unity of the divine love.

All of this may appear rather abstract. Concretely, it means that mission is continually called to a multiple conversion:

A basic *conversion to God*: God is the One who comes, and all else beside is the deed of the love with which God deigns to enlist human beings as partners in the divine work. It is God who calls, and to God that one is called. Like pilgrimages, all missionary journeys, for the evangelizer as well as for the evangelized, end with this return to center — as did Jesus' own journey:

> Father,
> all those you gave me
> I would have in my company
> where I am,
> to see this glory of mine
> which is your gift to me,
> because of the love you bore me before the world
>     began (John 17:24).

*Conversion to the Word of the Gospel*: This is the power of mission, far more than any efficacy of the activity of evangelization. To be sure, there is a missionary activity. The Lord of the harvest has called laborers to cooperate in the harvest. The gospel must be proclaimed loud and long, with apostolic boldness — with the *parrhēsia* in which Paul saw a sign of apostolic authenticity (1 Thes. 2:2; 2 Cor. 3:12, 7:4; Eph. 3:12, 6:19). But it is even more essential to proclaim the gospel forthrightly and clearly. As with Jesus, the Word made flesh, the life of the apostle must identify with the Word in a transparency as perfect as human weakness will allow. Did not Paul himself say that he had come, not with superior eloquence or with human ingenuity, but with the science of Christ, and Christ crucified (1 Cor. 2:2)?

*Conversion to the Spirit* who is the soul of every apostolate, who sent Jesus himself (Luke 4:18), and then the disciples (Luke 24:49; Acts 1:8), who will always create the new, who will always open new horizons, whose gifts constantly surpass human expectations, planning, and effectiveness, whose creative power will never cease to astound us, and who will lead us to the wonder of the revelation of the children of God and the marvel of access to no less than the "deep things of God" (1 Cor. 2:10).

*Conversion to the church*, as well as, at the same time, the *conversion of the church*: The church is the fullness of the One who was filled with God (Eph. 1:22-23), the holy Temple of the indwelling of the Spirit (1 Cor. 3:16) and the glory of God (2 Cor. 6:16). In the church Christ lives as the Father lives in him (John 17:23-24). But the church is also everlastingly summoned to return to this trinitarian center, to this focus of the Spirit, to transparency to the Word, to the concrete unity of the divine love. The church is rich, but with gifts from another, strong, but with a strength not its own. If the Letter to the Ephesians sees it filled with the very plenitude of God (Eph. 3:19), the Gospel of John makes the oneness of the church and its share in the divine love a humble, almost anguished prayer. The fullness of love that makes the church remains ever a free, and, from the viewpoint of human weakness, fragile, gift.

*Conversion to hope*: Mission is called to believe that the power of God is greater than human degradation and destitution—that through the deaths constituted by all our failures and shortcomings the life of Jesus is made manifest (2 Cor. 4:11), that the power of the Resurrection comes into play even, and especially, when all is lost (Phil. 3:8-11). Has not the defeat suffered by Jesus and Paul alike in the mission to the Jews been the reconciliation of the world, and has that defeat not issued in the hope that the reintegration of the Jews will be a life emerging from death (Rom. 11:15)? But conversion to hope also means that, in the present age, one is never saved except in hope, and that a hope in hand is a hope no longer (Rom. 8:24)—that God's "power now at work in us can do immeasurably more than we ask or imagine" (Eph. 3:20), and thus that the Reign will always infinitely transcend all human constructions, including those of the church. Indeed, the bankruptcy of ecclesiastical triumphs over the course of the centuries—from the age of Constantine to medieval Christianity to the mission to the Great Khan and the other subjugators—continually reminds the church that it is still *in via*, and that to become comfortable with its success would be to renounce its call precisely to exceed, in God, its own expectations.

We could go on listing the various forms taken by this continuous call to conversion that God has instilled at the heart of mission: conversion to the image of the Servant, in a renunciation of all pridefulness vis-à-vis others and the world; conversion to hearing, not only a hearing of the Word and the Spirit, but a hearing of the world, where God, "in bestowing his benefits, . . . has not hidden himself completely, without a clue" (Acts 14:17; cf. Acts 17:28); conversion to prayer, in mindfulness that the most important missionary words of Jesus took the form of prayers—the prayer of the Our Father for the coming of the Reign, the prayer of missionary awareness of Matthew 11:25-27, the prayer of consecration of those he sent forth in John 17; and finally, a conversion to silence:

Those who have well understood Jesus' words will be able to understand his silence, as well. That silence will bring them to full spiritual maturity; and now their own words will have the force of action, and their silences the meaning of a discourse.[7]

# Epilogue

Many are the paths of mission. Ultimately, they all follow the way of Jesus: emerging, going elsewhere (Mark 1:38), they return to Jerusalem (Mark 10:32; cf. Luke 9:51), and from there, by death and the Resurrection, lead to the glory and oneness of God. Here we should regard the history of mission without being too much the prisoner of an image of the Pauline, itinerant mission—a poorly understood image, at that—and allow the variety of paths of the Spirit to meet our eyes and to show, with Paul as with John, with Francis Xavier as with Charles de Foucauld, with a de Nobili as with a Monchanin, with the great convert-makers as with the martyrs, the route that led all of these "to know Christ and the power flowing from his resurrection" (Phil. 3:10), and in the Resurrection, the glory and love of the Father. As the mystics, in the ways of contemplation, must learn to renounce their own lights, and even mystical experiences, if they would reach the true Light, so is missionary action called to discover, in awe, deep within its own weakness, the true power of God (2 Cor. 12:9-10). The apostles go forth to conquer the world, and are conquered (Phil. 3:12). They go forth to proclaim the Word, and receive the Verbum and learn silence.

They go forth to the ends of the earth and are ever recalled, to the bosom of the divine unity. They go forth with all of their zeal, to discover the power of the Spirit. They go forth all hopeful, and discover hope. They go forth to give, and they receive.

Then they can make their own the "new song" that is, perhaps, for mission, what the Song of Songs has been for mysticism.

*I*

Sing to the LORD a new song,
　　for he has done wondrous deeds.
His right hand has won victory for him,
　　his holy arm.
The LORD has made his salvation known:
　　in the sight of the nations he has revealed his
　　　justice.
He has remembered his kindness and his faithfulness
　　toward the house of Israel.

All the ends of the earth have seen
the salvation by our God.


### II

Sing joyfully to the LORD, all you lands;
break into song; sing praise.
Sing praise to the LORD with the harp,
with the harp and melodious song.
With trumpets and the sound of the horn
sing joyfully before the King, the LORD.


### III

Let the sea and what fills it resound,
the world and those who dwell in it;
Let the rivers clap their hands,
the mountains shout with them for joy
Before the LORD, for he comes,
for he comes to rule the earth;
He will rule the world with justice
and the peoples with equity (Ps. 98).

*"He comes . . .":* Mission is God's. Amidst the human, yes, and the ecclesiastical, bustle, and gently mocking it, it is God who comes.

*"He will rule the world with justice . . .":* In a world fallen prey to all manner of imbalance—what we may call flesh, death, and sin, but also exploitation, injustice, and pollution—the love of God comes in a judgment that refuses to tolerate evil, and brings salvation. This salvation is not the skimpy individual salvation that tallies up merits and deserts. It is a universal salvation, "revealed before the nations" and embracing "the furthest reaches of the earth," the "rivers and the sea," the "mountains" and the very soil.

*"He has remembered his kindness and his faithfulness":* The people are enslaved and debased, but God's love is unfailing. God triumphs over all injustice and oppression, infidelity and sin, and thus a people covered with shame is restored to the dignity of being loved.

The proclamation of the Good News is this declaration of universal peace. It is a song of joy and a cosmic liturgy to the dimensions of the salvation it celebrates. All the music in the world, all the harps and lyres, all the horns and trumpets, all the cymbals and tambourines, will never be able to orchestrate all the joy of this news: "He has done wondrous deeds"! "The Lord has made his salvation known"! "He comes . . ."!

And the end of the Bible will echo this News.

"Yes, I am coming soon!"

And the church responds, in faith and trust:

"Amen! Come, Lord Jesus!" (Rev. 22:20)

In this gladsome counterpoint of promise and trust, mission sings a "new song."

# Notes

## 1. A PRELIMINARY QUESTION

1. This is how Jewish tradition saw it. The *midrashim* recount Abraham's struggles with idols and his missionary attitude toward his hosts in the desert. Cf. J. P. de Menasce, "Traditions Juives sur Abraham," in *Abraham Père des Croyants, Cahiers Sioniens* 5 (1951):191-94. These traditions have been adopted in Islam (Qur'an 2:260, 21:33,68-69, 29:23). Cf. Y. Moubarac, "Abraham en Islam," ibid., pp. 201-202, 206-207.

2. The exact sense of this verse is discussed in *Traduction Oecumenique de la Bible*, p. 62. The conclusion reads: "This v. 3 expresses the intention of the 'Yahwist' tradition: to show that, through Abraham and all his descendancy, the totality of the nations is blessed by the Lord. It is significant that the story of the patriarch and his people begins with a promise of blessing that humanity is called on to accept."

3. E. Castro, *Freedom in Mission,* 1985, p. 65, cited by K. Blaser, "La remise en valeur du Dogme Trinitaire dans la Théologie actuelle," *Études de Théologie et Religion* 61 (1986/3):406. In the third part of his article, Blaser comes to missiological aspects of the trinitarian dogma and cites especially Lesslie Newbigin, *The Relevance of Trinitarian Doctrine for Today's Mission* (1962); and A. Rétif, *La Mission: Éléments de Théologie et de Spiritualité* (1962); as well as Vatican II. Let us also notice the earlier observations of Y. Raguin, *Théologie Missionaire de l'Ancien Testament* (Paris: Seuil, 1946), pp. 15-28.

## 2. TWIN POLES OF ISRAEL'S MISSION: ELECTION

1. *Bible de Jérusalem*, n. on Ezek. 40:16.

2. We find sardonic observations of the same kind in Christian missionary literature that is far from always being in the style of *Lettres Édifiantes*. See, for example, the sometimes bitter reflections of Msgr. de Marion-Brésillac in *Documents de Mission et de Fondation*, ed. J. Bonfils and N. Douau (Mediaspaul, 1985), pp. 15-121.

3. "A foreigner went to find Shammai, saying to him: 'Make me a proselyte, on condition that you teach me the entire Torah while I stand on one foot.' The other thrust him away with the mason's square he held. He went to find Hillel, who made him a proselyte, saying to him: 'What is hateful to you, do not to your neighbor. Behold the entire Torah. The rest is but explanation. Go learn it'" (Talmud, II, Mo'ed Sabbat B, 30b, cited by J. Bonsirven, *Textes Rabbiniques des deux premiers siècles chrétiens* [Rome: PIB, 1954], p. 153, no. 633).

4. Cf. R. Martin-Achard, *Israël et les Nations*, pp. 9-10; Joachim Jeremias, *Jésus*

*et les Païens*, pp. 7-13. I have broached the question in "Aratos est-il aussi parmi les prophètes?" in *La vie de la Parole: Mélanges Grelot* (Paris: Desclée, 1987), pp. 249-53.

5. Cf. P. E. Dion, *Dieu Universel et Peuple élu*, pp. 21-25.

6. J. McKenzie, "The God of Israel," in *The Jerome Biblical Commentary*, ed. Raymond E. Brown, J. A. Fitzmyer, and Roland E. Murphy (Prentice-Hall, 1968), 2:739.

7. C. Westermann, *Dieu dans l'Ancien Testament* (Paris: Cerf, 1982), pp. 41-44, 51-59.

8. "We cannot separate God's salvation from his blessing. They are at one. Each aspect is important: on the one hand, the singularity and uniqueness of the history of God with his people; on the other, harmony with other religions" (ibid., p. 69).

9. Ibid., p. 51.

10. Ibid., pp. 55-56.

11. The *Bible de Jérusalem* speaks of Jeremiah's "oracles against the nations." For the section in Isaiah, both Jerusalem Bible and *Traduction Oecumenique de la Bible* employ the title, "Oracles sur les Nations," oracles "upon" the nations; but the corresponding note in the Jerusalem Bible says: "Chapters 13-23 are oracles against the foreign nations" (p. 1106).

12. *Traduction Oecumenique de la Bible*, p. 778.

13. At least this was the reconstitution of the movement of the text according to the first edition of the *Bible de Jérusalem*. The second edition proposes an arrangement of the text more like that found in *Traduction Oecumenique de la Bible*: verses 1-5 would report the Moabites' request, and v. 6 the negative response to that request. This seems less probable: one would then have to place on the lips of the Moabites a reference to the Davidic theme when this theme is so typical of Isaiah, and make the entire lament of verses 7-12 a long piece of cruel irony. Cf. Lucien Legrand, "The Humanism of Isaiah," *Indian Ecclesiastical Studies* 3 (1971): 204-10.

14. Except perhaps in 21:12. The very beautiful texts of Isaiah 18:7 and 19:16-24 are later. See chapter 3.

15. In this sense, P. E. Dion speaks of a "dynamic universalism" (*Dieu Universel et Peuple élu*), p. 144.

## 3. TWIN POLES OF ISRAEL'S MISSION: THE NATIONS

1. In Ps. 47, it is not clear whether the intention is explicitly universalistic. The peoples (*àmmim*) invited to clap their hands and the "princes of the peoples" that gather (v. 10) are perhaps the tribes of Israel and their chiefs: these would constitute the "people of the God of Abraham." The "nations" (*goyim*) are certainly well named (vv. 4, 9), it is true, but only to be able to say that God subjects them to himself.

2. We have, for example, the prudent observations of *Traduction Oecumenique de la Bible*, pp. 1261-62.

3. Cf. chap. 2, n. 7.

4. P. Volz, cited by Martin-Achard, *Israël et les Nations*, p. 13.

5. H. H. Rowley, *The Faith of Israel: Aspects of Old Testament Thought* (London: SCM, 1956), p. 185.

6. In 42:1, *Bible du Centenaire* and van der Ploeg translate: "He will give the nations to know [the true] religion." But this translation of *mishpat* as "religion" is doubtful and has not been employed in other translations. See the discussion of the text in Martin-Achard, *Israël*, pp. 23-28.

7. See the discussion on the authenticity of the text in Dion, *Dieu Universel et Peuple élu*, pp. 49-53. Like Martin-Achard, Dion leans toward authenticity.

8. André Feuillet, "Un Sommet Religieux de l'Ancien Testament: L'Oracle d'Isaïe XIX, 16-25 sur la conversion de l'Egypte," in *Mélanges Lebreton* (*Revue de Sciences Religieuses* 39 [1951]:65-87).

9. Martin-Achard, *Israël*, p. 41.

10. Cf. Dion, *Dieu Universel*, p. 98; Martin-Achard, *Israël*, p. 41.

11. A. Lods, *Histoire de la Littérature Hébraïque et Juive* (Paris: Payot, 1950), p. 527.

12. Cited in E. Tobac, "Malachie," in *Dictionnaire de la Théologie Catholique*, vol. 9/2, col. 1752. Cf. Clement of Alexandria, *Stromata*, V, xiv, 136 (PG 9:200).

13. As we read in *Traduction Oecumenique de la Bible*, p. 1633.

## 4. SOME CONCLUSIONS AND SOME QUESTIONS

1. See also the use of this concept in the Vatican II Constitution on Revelation, *Dei Verbum*, no. 15.

2. For M. Löhr, in 1896, "on the level of thought as on that of action, mission plays an exceedingly limited role in the Old Testament" (cited by Martin-Achard, *Israël et les Nations*, p. 11). One could even express certain reservations regarding the first pages of Martin-Achard's work, where the problem is presented. Amos's universalism, we are told, is to be discounted because it "does not issue precisely in a missionary attitude" (p. 9). Nor may we speak of mission when we are dealing with a "normal process of integration." The "proselytism" of the post-Exilic era, especially in Hellenistic Judaism, does not count, either, since it is exercised outside "official circles" and is simply national propagation by naturalization (p. 10). But if we discount all this, what is left? The rest of Martin-Achard's book happily transcends the limits set in the preface and examines the Old Testament perspective in depth.

3. G. W. Peters, *A Biblical Theology of Missions* (Chicago: Moody Press, 1972), p. 22.

4. The Decree for the Jacobites of the Council of Florence (1442). Cf. *La Foi Catholique*, p. 147.

5. K. L. and M. A. Schmidt, "*Paroikos*," in *Theologisches Wörterbuch des Neuen Testaments*, 5:845.

6. Lucien Legrand, "L'étranger dans la Bible," *Spiritus*, no. 102 (February 1986), p. 66.

7. Ibid., p. 57.

## 5. "THE GOSPEL OF JESUS CHRIST"

1. R. Pesch, *Das Markusevangelium*, HTKNT, vol. 2/1 (Freiburg i. B.: Herder, 1976), p. 76.

2. I have made a beginning of this task with regard to the texts relating to the

missionary mandate of the Risen One: "The Missionary Command of the Risen Christ: I. Mission and Resurrection," *Indian Theological Studies*, 23 (1986):290-309; "The Missionary Command of the Risen Lord: II. Mt. 28:16-20," *IndTS* 24 (1987):5-28.

3. See chap. 6.

4. Cf. Lucien Legrand: "Barefoot Apostles? The Shoes of St Mark," *IndTS* 16 (1979):201-19; F. Vouga, *À l'aube du Christianisme: Une surprenante diversité* (Aubonne: Éditions du Moulin, 1986), speaks of an "urban, bourgeois Christianity learning to manage mission" (p. 25; cf. pp. 67-70).

5. Cf. C. Perrot, *Jésus et l'Histoire*, JJC, no. 11 (Paris: Desclée, 1979).

6. See the note in *Traduction Oecumenique de la Bible, in hoc loco*, p. 831.

7. *Traduction Oecumenique de la Bible* correctly translates: "Le Seigneur a fait de moi un messie" ("The Lord has made of me a messiah"), *Traduction Oecumenique de la Bible*, p. 872. The theme of the evangelizer is found again in the inter-testamentary literature. Thus, at Qumran: ". . . That he may be according to your truth who proclaims the Good News in the time of your goodness, evangelizing the lowly according to the abundance of your mercy, consoling those who are contrite of spirit and afflicted, to give them everlasting joy" (1 QH 18:14-15), and in Ps. Sal. 11:1: "Proclaim in Jerusalem the messenger's Good News! God visits Israel, to bestow upon it his grace. . . . Jerusalem, don your garments of glory! . . . For God has proclaimed the happiness of Israel henceforth and forever! . . ."

8. Cf. Jacques Dupont, *Les Béatitudes*, vol. 1, EB (Paris: Gabalda, 1969), pp. 123-39.

9. Fernando Belo, *Lecture Matérialiste de l'Évangile de Marc* (Paris: Cerf, 1974); Eng. trans. *A Materialist Reading of the Gospel of Mark* (Maryknoll, NY: Orbis Books, 1981).

10. The old manuscripts themselves are completely at a loss here, at least with respect to their geography. Witnesses as early as the Chester Beatty papyrus (P 45), among others, omit this detour to the north and east.

11. Cf. A. Alt, "Die Stätten des Wirkens Jesus in Galiläa," *ZDPV* 68 (1951):51-72; Joachim Jeremias, *Jésus et les Païens*, pp. 28-30.

12. Cf. Lucien Legrand, "Deux Voyages: Lc 2,41-50; 24,13-33," in *À cause de l'Evangile: Mélanges offerts à Dom Jacques Dupont* (Paris: Cerf; Bruges: St André, 1986), pp. 409-29.

13. Cf. E. M. Meyers and J. E. Strange, *Les Rabbins et les Premiers Chrétiens* (Paris: Cerf, 1984), pp. 39-40. According to these authors, one must not raise Yohannan ben Zakkai's *mot* ("Galilee, Galilee, you hate the Torah") to the status of a key to the interpretation of the religious life of Galilee. Josephus gives us an altogether different picture of the situation in Galilee at the time of Jesus.

14. F. Comte, "Capharnaüm," *Bible et Terre Sainte* 38/1985, p. 21.

15. And perhaps in Matthew 15:39, according to a variant reading of particularly doubtful authenticity.

16. The recent excavations at Sephoris (cf. *BA* 49 [1986]:4-19) have rekindled speculation on possible contacts between Jesus, living at Nazareth, and that neighboring garrison city. See R. A. Batey, "Is Not This the Carpenter?" *NTS* 30 (1984):249-58; "Jesus and the Theatre" *NTS* 30 (1984):563-74.

17. M. du Buit, *Géographie de la Terre Sainte*, vol. 1 (Paris: Cerf, 1958), p. 177.

18. See the authors cited in R. Pesch, *Markusevangelium*, p. 285.

19. Adolf von Harnack, *Die Mission und Ausbreitung des Christentums in den ersten drei Jahrhunderten* (Leipzig: Hinrichs, 1924), pp. 39-41.

20. "The Matthean Christ reproaches the Pharisees with a relentless proselytism that sought to convert persons not to the true God, but to their own ideas, whether by making them fanatics of rabbinical legalism, or by preventing them from entering the Reign by this same legalistic intransigence" (P. Bonnard, *L'Évangile selon Saint Matthieu*, CNT no. 1 [Neuchâtel: Delachaux Niestlé, 1963], p. 338). The same author explains in a note: "In his well-documented study (*Proselytenwerbung und Urchristentum*, Berlin, 1960), Ernst Lerle has devoted four excellent pages to Matthew 23:15. Against Harnack, and now Joachim Jeremias, he shows that the 'woe' of this verse does not bear on the simple fact of Jewish proselytism, which Jesus does not condemn in principle, but on what the Pharisees have made of this missionary activity. (Cf. the same construction in 23:23,25, where the *hoti* does not immediately introduce the object of the curse: it is not external cleanliness that is condemned, but the fact that it substitutes for the interior)" (ibid.).

21. Rudolf Bultmann, *L'histoire de la tradition synoptique* (Paris: Seuil, 1973), p. 198.

22. Joachim Jeremias, *Jésus et les Païens*, p. 22; cf. P. Bonnard, *L'Évangile selon Saint Matthieu*, p. 232. In the context of the final redaction of Matthew, which concluded with the sending forth to the nations, the restrictions formulated in Matthew 10:5-6 and 15:24 must have been understood as having temporary validity, applying only to the prepaschal period. But it is always possible that, in the framework of the Judaeo-Christian tradition used by Matthew, these restrictions were considered as having absolute value. The discrepancy between Matthew 28:18 and the restrictive texts above indicates that, as the synoptic analysis shows, the history of the composition of the First Gospel was doubtless rather complex.

23. Ibid.

24. Joachim Jeremias, *Jésus et les Païens*, p. 25.

25. See chapter 2, above.

26. On this logion, see especially Jacques Dupont, "Beaucoup viendront du Levant et du Couchant . . . (Mt 8,11-12; Lc 13,28-29)," in *Études sur les Évangiles Synoptiques*, BETL, no. 70, vol. 2 (Leuven: University Press, 1985), pp. 568-82 (= *Sciences Ecclésiastiques* 19 [1967], pp. 153-67).

27. Jacques Dupont, "Beaucoup viendront du Levant," p. 570. We have the same interpretation in J. Zumstein, *La Condition du Croyant dans l'Évangile selon Matthieu*, OBO, no. 16 (Fribourg: Presses Universitaires; Göttingen: Vandenhoeck & Ruprecht, 1977), pp. 362-71.

28. Jacques Dupont, "Beaucoup viendront du Levant," p. 570.

29. Ibid., pp. 574-75.

30. Ibid., p. 581.

31. Joachim Jeremias, *Jésus et les Païens*, p. 63.

32. Cf. ibid., pp. 44-47.

33. G. Lohfink, *L'Église que voulait Jésus*, p. 371.

34. The logia of Matthew 9:37-38 and John 4:35-38 fit together so well that C. H. Dodd sees them as a single saying split in two (C. H. Dodd, *Historical Tradition in the Fourth Gospel* [Cambridge: University Press, 1963], pp. 388-405).

35. The theme of the angelic harvest is rare with the rabbis. Their opinion is expressed in a midrash on Psalm 8 reporting a discussion about whom God is speaking to in Joel 4:13: "Apply the sickle, for the harvest is ripe. . . ." Rabbi

Pinehas (v. 360) responded, invoking the authority of Rabbi Hilqia (v. 320): "He says it to the angels." But the majority of the rabbis thought that God was addressing the Israelites. The discussion takes place a good deal later than the New Testament era, but it is indicative of the tension among the rabbis between an apocalyptical tendency insisting on the role of the angels and a more anthropological tendency. We observe the same tendency in the pages of the New Testament, some time before. See texts cited in H. L. Strack and P. Billerbeck, *Kommentar zum Neuen Testament aus Talmud und Midrasch*, vol. 1 (Munich: Beck, 1926), p. 672.

36. Cf. Lucien Legrand, "Was Jesus Mission-Minded?" pp. 87-104.

37. This reflection on Jesus' part is found explicitly only in Matthew. In the parallel text of Mark 7:29, the reference to faith is only implicit. ("For such a reply, be off now! The demon has already left your daughter.") Matthew insists particularly on faith as a condition of salvation: cf. J. J. Zumstein, *La Condition du Croyant*.

38. J. Friedrich, "*Kērussō*," in *TWNT* 3:699.

39. See also Jonah 1:2, 3:2; Joel 2:1, 4:9, Zephaniah 3:14, Zechariah 9:9.

40. See the list of these terms, with the corresponding Greek words, in J. Friedrich, "*Kērussō*," p. 702.

41. J. Delorme, "Aspects Doctrinaux du Second Évangile," ETL 43 (1967), p. 82.

42. J. Friedrich, *L'Évangile*, pp. 43-44.

43. Ibid., pp. 44-51.

44. "If Jesus used the verb and the noun, the verb must have been the one to be more used in discourse, and so Luke has been more faithful to the sources. Mark's merit is that, by his frequent use of the substantive, he extrapolates from Jesus' preaching more faithfully. Mark represents the preaching of the community according to the spirit of Jesus (J. Friedrich, *L'Évangile*, p. 60).

45. Curiously, Luke, who seems to structure the prayer of the Agony on the liturgical form of the Our Father, does not cite this petition in his version of the latter (Luke 11:2-4).

## 6. THE RISEN CHRIST

1. This is developed further below.

2. It is possible that, in its original tradition, Jesus' words to Peter in John 21 likewise constituted a missionary commandment: until now, Peter had acted in his own name; now he will act in the name of another (cf. Willi Marxen, *The Resurrection of Jesus of Nazareth* [London: SCM, 1970], p. 87).

3. Generally speaking, the Synoptics make no effort to present the Resurrection accounts in parallel fashion.

4. This is true even of the official documents of the church. According to the index of *Actes du Concile Vatican II: Textes Intégraux* (Paris: Cerf, 1966), pp. 791-94, Matthew 28: 16-20 is cited in the documents of Vatican Council II 18 times in whole or in part, and Mark 16:15-16 even more frequently (20 times). But Luke 24:45-46 appears only once (but Acts 1:8, 5 times). As for John 17:21, another important "missionary" text, there are only 4 occurrences (2 of them in the "Decree on Ecumenism"), and none of these is in the context of mission.

5. J. Delorme, "La Résurrection de Jésus dans le langage du Nouveau Testament," in the collection, *Le Langage de la Foi dans l'Écriture et le Monde Actuel*,

LD, no. 72 (Paris: Cerf, 1972), p. 165. The text cited by Delorme is from H. Schlier, *La Résurrection de Jésus Christ* (Mulhouse: Salvator, 1969), p. 49, who explains: "Through the apparitions, it is the kerygma itself that effects the Resurrection."

6. W. Trilling, "De toutes les Nations faites des Disciples," in *La Bonne Nouvelle de la Résurrection*, p. 124.

7. This parallelism between Mark's longer ending and his exordium strengthens the oft-expressed opinion that, in the framework of a later addition to Mark's original conclusion, verses 15-18 deserve to be considered apart, as having a more Markan stamp than the rest (Hahn, Michel). According to E. Linnemann, these verses are actually the "lost" conclusion of Mark: "Der (wiedergefundene) Markusschluss," *Zeitschrift für Theologie und Kirche*, 1969, pp. 265-67.

8. D. Mollat, "L'Apparition du Ressuscité et le don de l'Esprit (Jn 20:19-25)," in *La Bonne Nouvelle de la Résurrection*, p. 92.

9. J. Guillet, "La Bible à la naissance de l'Église," in *Le Monde Grec et la Bible*, ed. Claude Mondésert (Paris: Beauchesne, 1984), p. 60.

10. See our n. 7, above.

11. Although it does not always figure in the translations, the word "but" is in the Greek text, at the beginning of verse 42, in the form of the adversative *de*, whose occurrence is all the less negligible for having its antithetical *men* at the beginning of verse 41. Thus, verses 41 and 42 are to be understood in conjunction, as the terms of a mild opposition: on the one hand, there has been a numerical increase due to preaching (v. 41); *but* account must also be taken of the quality of life of the new community (v. 42), which will also have its repercussions (v. 47).

12. For the opposite conclusion, see J. Hug, *La Finale de l'Évangile de Marc*, EB (Paris: Gabalda, 1978); W. Farmer, *The Last Twelve Verses of Mark*, SNTSMS, no. 25 (Cambridge: University Press, 1974).

13. See note 7, above.

14. See, for example. L. Schenke, *Le Tombeau Vide et l'Annonce de la Résurrection*, LD, no. 59 (Paris: Cerf, 1970), p. 55.

15. The formula is that of Eugene J. Maly, "The Gospel according to Mark," in *The Jerome Biblical Commentary*, vol. 2, ed. Raymond E. Brown, J. A. Fitzmyer, and Roland E. Murphy (Prentice-Hall, 1968), p. 59 ("the fundamental *praeconium paschale*").

16. Cf. Lucien Legrand, *L'Annonce à Marie: Une apocalypse aux origines de l'Évangile*, LD, no. 106 (Paris: Cerf, 1981).

17. E. Lohmeyer, *Das Evangelium des Markus*, KEKNT, no. 2 (Göttingen: Vandenhoeck & Ruprecht, 1967), p. 45; J. Radermakers, *La Bonne Nouvelle de Jésus selon Marc* (Brussels: Institut d'Études Théologiques, 1974), p. 418.

18. Cf. L. Marin, "Les femmes au tombeau," cited by Radermakers, *Bonne Nouvelle*, p. 431.

19. R. Fuller, *The Formation of the Resurrection Narratives* (London: SPCK, 1972), p. 67. Cf. T. E. Boomershine, "Mark 16:8 and the Apostolic Commission," *JBL* 100 (1981):236.

20. W. Trilling, "De toutes les Nations," p. 130.

21. P. T. O'Brien, "The Great Commission of Matthew 28:18-20: A Missionary Mandate or Not?" *RefTR* 33 (1976):73.

22. "Promises of a constant, sovereign assistance accorded to the messengers of Christ in the world" (P. Bonnard, *L'Évangile selon Saint Matthieu*, p. 419).

23. The exact translation of the text is a matter of dispute. Are we to understand:

"They worshiped, but some doubted," or, "They worshiped, but doubted"? (The meaning is certainly not: "Those who had doubted, worshiped," as Lagrange had proposed.) In either translation — especially in the second — the overall image is that of a confused, vacillating response. Trilling is doubtless correct to suggest that actually, the doubt is that of the whole community, whose faith, like that of the apostles, will never be more than an *oligopistia*, a "little faith" (W. Trilling, "De toutes les Nations," p. 129).

24. "We must regard Matt. 28:18-20 very simply and forthrightly as a well matured, coherent conclusion of the entire gospel, in which conclusion we may perceive, with all of the consequences for salvation history, the manifestation of the heavenly *Kurios* — the present efficacy of that manifestation and the hope it offers for the future" (Anton Vögtle, "Das christologische und ekklesiologische Anliegen von Mt 28:18-20," in *Das Evangelium und die Evangelien* [Düsseldorf: Patmos, 1971], p. 272).

25. G. Bornkamm, "Der Auferstandene und der Irdische," in *Zeit und Geschichte: Festschrift Bultmann zur 80. Geburtstag*, ed. E. Dinkler (Tübingen: Mohr, 1964), p. 185. See also the discussion in P. T. O'Brien, "The Great Commission."

## 7. SOME REFLECTIONS ON JESUS AND HIS MISSION

1. "The gospel opens with the Logos doctrine because the author is addressing an audience reared in the religion of the Hellenistic elite, and hopes by this notion of the Logos to smooth the way to the central intention of the gospel, and from there to proceed to the historical reality of his account, a reality entirely rooted in Jewish tradition . . . 'for salvation is from the Jews' (4:22)" (C. H. Dodd, *L'Interprétation du Quatrième Évangile*, LD, no. 82 [Paris: Cerf, 1975], pp. 379-80). Thus, a profound correspondence obtains between John 1:14 and 4:22.

2. Franz Mussner, *Traité sur les Juifs*, p. 193. Mussner lists a number of points defining this "being-Jew" of Jesus. We might add the conception of a universalism centered on, and prioritizing, Israel.

## 8. "IN JERUSALEM, THROUGHOUT JUDEA . . ."

1. Cf. M. Scharlemann, *Stephen, a Singular Saint, Analecta Biblica*, no. 34 (Rome: PIB, 1968). See also A. Spiro's note in J. Munck, *The Acts of the Apostles* (New York: Doubleday, 1967), pp. 285-300.

2. Cf. Jacques Dupont, "Les ministères de l'Église naissante dans les Actes des Apôtres," *Nouvelles Études*, pp. 133-185.

3. *Traduction Oecumenique de la Bible*, "Introduction aux Actes des Apôtres," pp. 358-59.

4. See *Traduction Oecumenique de la Bible*, p. 405, n.

5. Cf. F. Vouga, "Pour une géographie théologique des christianismes primitifs," *ETRel* 59/2 (1984):141-49. See also idem, *À l'aube du Christianisme*.

6. "All reconstructions are hypothetical. . . . They are provisional by definition" (F. Vouga, "Pour une géographie théologique," p. 141).

7. Cf. Raymond E. Brown, *La Communauté du Disciple Bien-Aimé*, LD, no. 115 (Paris, Cerf), p. 33. Brown also suggests the existence of "crypto-Christians" who

acknowledged Jesus as the Messiah but remained in the synagogue (p. 185).

8. According to E. Schuerer and G. Vermès, *The History of the Jewish People in the Age of Jesus Christ*, vol. 3/1 (Edinburgh: T & T Clark, 1986), p. 150, there is as yet no satisfactory study of Jewish proselytism in the Greco-Roman age.

9. This chronology has been called into question. See an examination of recent studies on this subject by J. Murphy O'Connor, "Pauline Missions before the Jerusalem Conference," RB 89 (1982):71-91. According to G. Lüdemann, particularly, the first Pauline missions go back to A.D. 34 or 37, and what Luke presents as the second missionary journey actually preceded the Jerusalem conference (G. Lüdemann, *Paul, Apostle to the Gentiles* [London: SCM, 1984], pp. 262-63).

10. See especially J. Jervell, *Luke and the People of God: A New Look at Luke-Acts* (Minneapolis: Augsburg Press, 1972); A. George, "Israël," in *Études sur l'oeuvre de Luc* (Paris: Gabalda, 1978), pp. 87-125.

11. See the various studies by Jacques Dupont collected in *Études sur les Actes*, pp. 245-365.

12. As in the wisdom literature, wisdom radiates from the Temple: cf. Sir. 24:10-12.

13. "It is not the city as such, but the Christian community that lives there, that forms the center.... The increase of the Word at Jerusalem is not to be understood in a purely statistical sense. It has a meaning in the order of salvation history. The thousands of believing Jews constituted the nucleus of the Christian community, in which the divine blessing was concretely manifested" (P. Zingg, *Das Wachsen der Kirche*, p. 153).

14. Cf. Jacques Dupont, "Le nom d'apôtres a-t-il été donné aux Douze par Jésus?" *OrSyr* 1 (1956):425-44. Let us observe, in Mark 3:14, that the parenthetical expression, "He named twelve whom he called apostles," is not authentic, and that it has not been retained in recent translations.

15. P. Grelot, "Les Épîtres de Paul: La Mission Apostolique," in *Le Ministère et les Ministères selon le Nouveau Testament* (Paris: Seuil, 1974), p. 48.

16. Ibid., p. 49.

17. Jacques Dupont, "Le logion des douze trônes (Mt 19,28; Lc 22,28-30)," in *Études sur les Évangiles Synoptiques*, BETL, no. 70-B (Leuven: University Press, 1985), pp. 706-43 (= *Bib* 45 [1964]:355-92).

18. Ibid. (*Études*), pp. 741-42.

19. B. Gerhardssohn, *Memory and Manuscript: Oral Tradition and Written Transmission in Rabbinic Judaism and Early Christianity* (Uppsala: C. W. K. Gleerup, 1961).

20. Ibid., p. 245.

21. Ibid., p. 248.

22. Jacques Dupont, "Le logion des douze trônes," p. 732.

23. Raymond E. Brown, K. P. Donfried, and J. Reumann, *Saint Pierre dans le Nouveau Testament*, LD, no. 79 (Paris: Cerf, 1974), p. 199.

24. As a result, the question of the Roman primacy must be rethought from the viewpoint of mission. Indeed, Paul VI's "Apostolic Exhortation on Evangelization in the Modern World" does so: "The Successor of Peter is thus, by the will of Christ, entrusted with the preeminent ministry of teaching the revealed truth.... This is also why the voice of the church shows the Pope 'at the highest point—*in apice, in specula*—of the apostolate'" (Paul VI, *Evangelii Nuntiandi*, no. 67). The document cites the expression used by St. Leo the Great to designate the Roman

primacy: "the primacy of the apostolate" (ibid.). It likewise cites the decree of Vatican Council II *Ad Gentes*: " 'Christ's mandate to preach the Gospel to every creature (cf. Mk. 16:15) primarily and immediately concerns the Bishops with Peter and under Peter' " (ibid., quoting *Ad Gentes*, no. 38).

25. Cf. F. Bovon, "L'importance des médiations dans le projet théologique de Luc," in *L'Oeuvre de Luc*, pp. 181-203 (=*NTS* 21 [1974-75]:23-39).

26. *Evangelii Nuntiandi*, no. 30.

## 9. PAUL

1. E. Haenchen, *The Acts of the Apostles* (Oxford: Blackwell, 1971), p. 530. Cf. Jacques Dupont, "Le Discours à l'Aréopage (Ac 17,22-31), lieu de rencontre entre Christianisme et Hellénisme," in *Nouvelles Études*, pp. 380-423; Lucien Legrand, "The Missionary Significance of the Areopagus Speech," in *God's Word among Men: Theological Essays in Honour of J. Putz*, ed. G. Gispert-Sauch (Delhi: Vidyajyothi, 1974), pp. 59-63.

2. Cf. A. J. Festugière, *La Révélation d'Hermès Trismégiste*, vol. 2: *Le Dieu Cosmique* (Paris: Gabalda, 1949), pp. 332-40. Festugière emphasizes that unlike the hymn to Cleanthes, Aratos' viewpoint is still very pragmatic: God's universal manifestation orientated to a self-revelation, but is merely for the purpose of rendering us service by informing us what we are to do in each season. One sees "no trace of mysticism here, of union with God" (p. 340). In *L'Idéal Religieux des Grecs et l'Évangile* (Paris: Gabalda, 1932), p. 72, Festugière, once more, observes that Paul obscures the doctrinal meaning of the Stoics' words, reinforcing the "inconsistency of persons who are better than their teaching": from both sides, the dialogue issues in a larger vision.

3. I have addressed the question in "Aratos est-il aussi parmi les prophètes?", in *La vie de la Parole: Mélanges Grelot* (Paris: Desclée, 1987), pp. 257-58.

4. Jacques Dupont, "La conclusion des Actes et son rapport à l'ensemble de l'oeuvre de Luc," *Nouvelles Études*, p. 510.

5. Cf. Jacques Dupont, "La conclusion des Actes," pp. 457-511 (= *Les Actes des Apôtres: Tradition, Rédaction, Théologie*, ed. J. Kremer, AEThL, no. 48 [Gembloux: Duculot, 1979], pp. 359-404).

6. F. Bovon, "Israel, l'Église et les Nations," in *L'Oeuvre de Luc: Études d'Exégèse et de Théologie*, LD, no. 130 (Paris: Cerf, 1987), p. 255.

7. This is the title of this section both in *Traduction Oecumenique de la Bible* and *Bible de Jérusalem*.

8. W. Sanday and A. C. Headlam, *The Epistle to the Romans*, ICC (Edinburgh: Clark, 1907), p. 3.

9. Cf. J. Murphy O'Connor, *La Prédication selon Saint Paul*, pp. 68-75; Lucien Cerfaux, "St Paul et le 'Serviteur de Dieu' d'Isaïe," in *Recueil Lucien Cerfaux*, vol. 2 (Gembloux: Duculot, 1954), pp. 439-54 (=StAns 27-28 [1951]:351-65).

10. Does he mean a priestly function in the proper sense of the word, or only the liturgical function of the layperson who brings the offering to the Temple, inasmuch as Christ is the only Priest? The latter hypothesis is defended by C. Wiéner, "*Ierourgein*: Rom 15,16," in *Studiorum Paulinorum Congressus*, vol. 2, AnBib 18/2 (Rome: PIB, 1963), pp. 399-404. For the opposite opinion, see A. M. Denis, "La fonction apostolique et la liturgie nouvelle"; A. Vanhoye, *Prêtres Anciens, Prêtre*

*Nouveau selon le Nouveau Testament* (Paris: Seuil, 1980), pp. 299-301. C. E. B. Cranfield, *Romans* (Edinburgh: T & T Clark, 1979), thinks that Paul saw himself as the Levite, in an intermediate position between the laity and Christ the Priest.

11. Reconstructions of Paul's journeys according to Acts map out three great apostolic tours, each returning him to Jerusalem. It is not clear that Luke had such a topographical arrangement in mind: in Acts 18:22, the possible reference to Jerusalem, at the end of the "second apostolic journey," is very tenuous.

12. Paul "will now write to Rome, in order to create with the Church of the capital that bond of spiritual and material solidarity without which mission would be at once false and impossible, because it would become an individual undertaking. Paul writes to Rome with his mind filled with his Spanish project. . . . He has always taken up the pen in function of the needs of his apostolate. There is nothing of the ivory-tower theologian about him. . . . His stopover . . . provides him with the opportunity to step back from his task of extending the gospel and see it as a whole. At the same time, his meditation on his project for the West enables him to subject these past accomplishments to an examination in the light of the absolutely open-ended future of which his missionary zeal affords him a glimpse. The Epistle to the Romans is born of this meditation. It is a missionary writing as are all the others; but it is a better expression of certain basic aspects of this missionary problem" (F. J. Leenhardt, *L'Épître de Saint Paul aux Romains*, CNT, no. 6 [Neuchâtel: Delachaux et Niestlé, 1957], pp. 9-10). See also F. Vouga, "L'épître aux Romains comme document ecclésiologique," *ETRel* 61 (1986):485-495.

13. There are some rare exceptions: in Romans 4:7, 7:5, 11:27, Paul uses *hamartia* in the plural. But in the first and last cases he is citing the Old Testament.

14. See *Traduction Oecumenique de la Bible*'s notes on Romans 7:7-11, and Stanislas Lyonnet, "Liberté chrétienne et Loi de l'Esprit selon Saint Paul," in *La Vie selon l'Esprit: Condition du Chrétien*, Unam Sanctam, no. 55 (Paris: Cerf, 1965), pp. 169-95.

15. In different terms, we might also mention the Hindu and Buddhist analyses of Māyā, the inanity, vanity, illusion, and ontological lie that infects the whole of human existence. Cf. Lucien Legrand, "The Tragedy of Man according to St Paul," *Jeevadhara*, 1975, pp. 135-47.

16. André Feuillet, "Le plan salvifique de Dieu d'après l'épître aux Romains," *Revue Biblique* 57 (1950):489-529.

17. The most recent study is that of F. Refoulé, *"Et ainsi tout Israël sera sauvé": Romains 11,25-32*, LD, no. 117 (Paris: Cerf, 1984).

18. The third part of the letter to the Romans, in chapters 12-15, also enters into this plan of a missionary document. Introduced by the invitation to make the life of faith the true "spiritual worship" (Rom. 12:1-2) and concluding with a description of the apostolic ministry in liturgical terms (15:14-21) followed by a call to prayer, the third part of Romans proposes the image of a community whose entire life is constituted by prayer, by the "calling on" that Romans 10:13-17 had posited as the pinnacle of missionary action. The intention, then, is not precisely parenetic: Paul scarcely has the right to counsel a community he has not evangelized and does not know personally. The "grace that God has given him to be a minister among the Gentiles" and that gives him the "boldness" to address the Romans (cf. Rom. 15:15-16) does not permit him to interfere in the labors of another (Rom. 15:20). In terms borrowed from the experiences of other communities, he seeks to propose to the Romans that they project the image of a spiritual worship in which

the nations may offer their faith in the new liturgy according to the Spirit—the goal of his entire apostolic activity. As "minister of Christ Jesus among the Gentiles, with the priestly duty of preaching the gospel of God," he would like to be able to present this offering to God (15:16) and this example to human beings (15:18).

19. Cf. F. Bovon, "L'importance des médiations dans le projet théologique de Luc," in *L'Oeuvre de Luc*, pp. 181-203 ( = *NTS* 21 [1974-75]:23-39). In the language of sociological analysis, we might say that Paul's position is more protesting, while Luke's is more attesting; or again, that Paul's language is a language of paradox, while Luke's is one of logic and reinforcement.

20. "What is the Israel of God? Is it to be identified with the new people of God, the Church, in contradistinction to the Israel according to the flesh spoken of in 1 Cor. 10:18? There are two difficulties with this. First, far from confusing the Israel of God with the ensemble of believers, Paul is precisely juxtaposing them here, and thereby implying a distinction. Second, nowhere does this lover of antitheses, Paul, explicitly distinguish the Israel of God from Israel according to the flesh. Nor does he ever call the Church the 'new Israel.' It seems to us, then, that, for Paul, the Israel of God is the ensemble of the Israelites who have believed in Christ crucified, and who, together with the converted pagans, form the true people of God (cf. Rom. 9-11)" (*Traduction Oecumenique de la Bible*, p. 567, n. on Gal. 6:16).

21. Cf. Lucien Legrand, "There is neither slave nor free, neither male nor female," *IndTSt* 18 (1981):135-63.

22. Lucien Cerfaux, "L'Apôtre en présence de Dieu: Essai sur la vie d'oraison de Saint Paul," *Recueil Lucien Cerfaux* 2:469-81.

23. Ibid., p. 475.

24. These literary genres of prayer are analyzed by B. Rigaux, "Saint Paul et ses Lettres," *StNeoTest* 2 (Paris and Bruges: Desclée De Brouwer, 1962), pp. 169-70, 182-96. On Paul's ecstatic prayer, see Lucien Cerfaux, "L'Apôtre en présence de Dieu," p. 478. For the question as a whole, see L. Monloubou, *Saint Paul et la Prière: Prière et Évangélisation*.

## 10. THE GOSPEL OF JOHN AS A MISSIONARY SYNTHESIS

1. Doubtless we must distinguish various stages in the composition of the Fourth Gospel. Several of the most recent hypotheses are to be found in E. Cothenet, *Petite Bibliothèque des Sciences Bibliques: Nouveau Testament, Les Écrites de Saint Jean*, no. 5 (Paris: Desclée, 1984), pp. 49-52. The authors agree that an essential stage in the process of composition is represented by "the evangelist," who stamps the materials he uses with his personal imprint. *Traduction Oecumenique de la Bible*, for its part, concludes: "These roots in the Christian milieu of the age have not prevented the evangelist from creating a profoundly original work, the product of long maturation. . . . Everything is adopted and assimilated in function of a complex, yet simple, view of the reality and role of Jesus, the Christ, the Son of God (20:30)" (*Traduction Oecumenique de la Bible*, p. 286).

2. E. Cothenet, *Les Écrites de Saint Jean*, p. 43.

3. Let us recall, however, the interesting translation of the lectionary in French: "Au commencement était le Verbe, la Parole de Dieu" ("In the beginning was the Word, the word of God").

4. If we integrate this aspect of the Word into the interpretation of John 1, the

verses of the Prologue referring to John the Baptist seem less erratic. If the Verbum is only the transcendent Verbum, then it becomes difficult to see why the precursor should be spoken of twice, in verses 6-7 and 15. A "later gloss," we are told. So be it. But a gloss must follow a certain logic, at least from the point of view of the author of the gloss. If the Word is the word of the gospel proclaimed by Jesus, the reference to the witness of the Baptist becomes easier to explain: the gospel begins with the Baptist (cf. Mark 1:1-2, Acts 13:24).

5. Cf. Raymond E. Brown, *La Communauté du Disciple Bien-Aimé*, pp. 187-200; E. Cothenet, *Les Écrites de Saint Jean*, pp. 37-38. The discussion is often based on a problem of textual criticism bearing on the words, "to help you believe." The manuscripts propose two different readings. Some read a present subjunctive (*pisteuēte*), and according to the nuance expressed by this tense in Greek, we should have to understand: "to help you continue to believe." Here, the Gospel of John will have been written for readers who already believe, in order to help their faith to become stronger and deeper. The main intent would be "the progress of the faith in them" (*Traduction Oecumenique de la Bible*, p. 354). Other manuscripts read an aorist subjunctive (*pisteusēte*), which, in Greek grammar would express an inchoative action: "to help you to come to believe." In this case, the Gospel would have a missionary intent: it would be addressed to non-Christians, to bring them to faith. At least this is the nuance between the present and the aorist in good Greek grammar. But is Johannine syntax really so precise? On the one hand, in John 11:15, 13:19, and 14:29, Jesus tells his disciples that he is doing such and such *hina pisteusēte*, using the aorist subjunctive, as if the disciples would only now begin to believe, despite 2:11 and 6:69. On the other hand, in 17:21, according to the best manuscripts, he says *hina ho kosmos pisteue*: "that the world may believe," in the present subjunctive, as if the world had already begun to believe and now needed only to be strengthened in faith. It seems, then, that we need not attribute too much weight to the problem of textual criticism and to the syntactic nuances it supposes, in order to resolve the question of the addressees of the Gospel.

6. Cf. Raymond E. Brown, *La Communauté du Disciple Bien-Aimé*, pp. 65-69.

7. "Any partial and fragmentary definition which attempts to render the reality of evangelization in all its richness, complexity and dynamism does so only at the risk of impoverishing it and even of distorting it. It is impossible to grasp the concept of evangelization unless one tries to keep in view all its essential elements" (*Evangelii Nuntiandi*, no. 17). The following chapter of the same apostolic exhortation, entitled "The Methods of Evangelization," thereupon lists, besides the witness of life: direct preaching and the utilization of the mass media (regarding the latter, as well, as strictly missionary), but also the liturgy of the word, catechetics, sacramental practice, and popular piety (which would be classified rather under "pastoral ministry").

8. We sometimes encounter a hesitation to admit a missionary intent in John because of the rarefied atmosphere of the Johannine teaching. "The overall tenor of the Fourth Gospel clearly favors the second meaning ('that you may make progress in faith'). What could even a well-intentioned reader understand of this Gospel without an antecedent genuine Christian formation? John is seeking to strengthen the faith of Christians undergoing trial" (E. Cothenet, *Les Écrites de Saint Jean*, p. 39). In other words, the profoundly mystical content of John's Gospel could only have been intended for Christians already far advanced in the ways of faith. It is not clear that this argument is decisive. This way of seeing things cor-

responds to a Christian milieu: for someone born a Christian, the mystical experience is the fruit of a long journey in Christian faith. But such was not necessarily the context of the Fourth Gospel, which was addressed to a milieu familiar with a non-Christian Greek mysticism. We may refer to the analysis of this milieu and its components in the beautiful book by C. H. Dodd, *L'Interprétation du Quatrième Évangile*, LD, no. 82 (Paris: Cerf, 1975), pp. 13-172. The prevalent culture included Stoicism, Philonic Neoplatonism, Gnostic and Hermetic tendencies, and, on the part of Judaism, themes inherited from Palestinian as well as Hellenistic Judaism — all developing in the symbiosis of the Hellenistic world of the first century and its swarm of ideas. In this context, the evangelizing approach could not but be a mystical one. Mysticism was not the special crown reserved for the term of a long Christian journey; it was the required starting point for a relevant proclamation of the Christian message. There is a parallel in today's India, where the mystic depths of the Hindu soul call for a dialogue and a proclamation of the Gospel in the diapason of the spiritual wealth in those depths. We think of the experience and writings of a Monchanin or a Le Saux (Abhishiktananda). In India, the Gospel of John is the best received part of the Bible (after the Sermon on the Mount, popularized by Gandhi), among Christians and non-Christians alike.

9. C. H. Dodd, *L'Interprétation du Quatrième Évangile*, p. 557.

10. The title given to this part in the commentary of Raymond E. Brown, *The Gospel According to John*, AncB, no. 29 (New York: Doubleday, 1970), 1:29, 2:541-43.

11. Let us cite the statistics in C. H. Dodd, *L'Interprétation du Quatrième Évangile*, p. 503:

|                          | Chaps 1-12 |          | Chaps 13-17 |          |
|--------------------------|:----------:|----------|:-----------:|----------|
| *Zōē*                    | 32 ⎫       |          | 4 ⎫         |          |
| *Zēn*                    | 15 ⎬       | 50 times | 2 ⎬         | 6 times  |
| *Zöopoiein*              | 3 ⎭        |          | 0 ⎭         |          |
| *Phōs*                   | 23 ⎫       |          | 0           |          |
| *Phōtizein*              | 1 ⎬        | 32 times | 0           |          |
| *Skotos, skotia*         | 8 ⎭        |          | 0           |          |
| (in the "spiritual" sense) |          |          |             |          |
| *Agapē*                  | 1 ⎫        |          | 6 ⎫         |          |
| *Agapan*                 | 5 ⎬        | 6 times  | 25 ⎬        | 31 times |
| (with a false love, 2)   |            |          |             |          |

"The synonym *philein* is used four times in each of the two parts, and *philos* is used twice in chaps 1-12 and in chaps 13-17. But (except in 5:20, 16:27) *philein* does not have the richness of *agapan*" (ibid.).

12. Ibid., p. 504.

13. On this subject, see, for example, the remarks by C. Duraisingh, *India's Search for Reality and the Relevance of the Gospel of John* (Delhi: ISPCK, 1975); S. Ryan, "Jesus and the Poor in the Fourth Gospel," *Bible Bhashyam* 4/3 (1978):213-19.

14. Cf. Oscar Cullmann, *Le milieu Johannique: Étude sur l'origine de l'évangile de*

*Jean* (Neuchâtel: Delachaux Niestlé, 1976), pp. 63-87; Raymond E. Brown, *La Communauté du Disciple Bien-Aimé*, passim.

## 11. THE WAYS OF MISSION

1. Prescinding, for the moment, from the question of the relationship between Israel and the church, to which we shall return in the section on Israel or the Mongols of this chapter.

2. Is it out of the question that, for lands deprived of concrete contact with the Jewish people, a substitutive role is providentially assigned to Islam, which also bears witness to the God of Abraham? I am thinking, in particular, of India, but doubtless this could apply to other countries of Asia or Africa, which have no, or almost no, Israelite population. With very few exceptions, Indian Christians pass almost their whole lives without ever encountering a descendant of Israel. Must we thereupon—indeed, even theologically—leave Asia to the "Mongols" and resign ourselves to seeing, outside the Mediterranean and Western world, only second-zone churches, deprived of the privilege of an encounter with the people of Abraham? But are not the Muslims also representatives of the faith of Abraham, and may we not see, in the spread of Islam in Asia, even China, a positive factor? In India, Christian theology has entered into a protracted dialogue with Hinduism and has been enriched thereby. Like any human adventure, this exciting undertaking is fraught with risk—especially, that of allowing oneself to come under the spell of the mystical depths of Hindu thought in such a way as to lose a sense of, on the one hand, the transcendence of the God who is the only God, and on the other, of the reality of the corporeal things that are the history of human beings. It is important that the Indian theological dialogue bear in all directions, and Islam can play an equilibrating role here. So it was in the time of the Fathers. Judaism and Islam provided a salutary balance to the encounter with Greek thought: Maimonides and Averroës helped Thomas Aquinas formulate his Aristotelian Christian synthesis.

3. "The books of the Old Testament present to all, according to the situation of the human race before the salvation brought by Christ, a knowledge of God and man. . . . Thus these books, which express a living sense of God, a profitable wisdom upon the life of men, and a magnificent treasury of prayers, . . . should be received with piety by Christians" (Vatican II, Constitution *Dei Verbum*, no. 15).

4. See especially Lorenzo de Lorenzi, ed., *Die Israelfrage nach Röm 9-11* (Rome: Abbaye de St Paul, 1977); F. Refoulé, *"Et ainsi tout Israël sera sauvé,"*: op. cit., chap. 9, n. 17.

5. Lorenzo de Lorenzi, ed., *Die Israelfrage nach Röm 9-11*, p. 179.

6. R. Grousset, *L'empire des steppes: Attila, Gengis-Khan, Tamerlan* (Paris: Payot, 1948). Cf. Charles Lemercier-Quelquejay, *La Paix Mongole* (Paris: Flammarion, 1970).

7. St. Ignatius of Antioch, *Letter to the Ephesians* (15:2), which also says: "It is better to be still and to be than to speak and not to be. It is well to teach if the teacher acts: thus there is only one Master, the One who has spoke and everything came into being, and the things he wrought in silence are worthy of his Father" (15:1). Elsewhere he speaks of the "Word emerging from silence" (*Letter to the Magnesians* 8:2).

# Index of Scriptural References

## OLD TESTAMENT

### Genesis

| | |
|---|---|
| 1:1 | 5 |
| 1:26-28 | 4 |
| 2:4 | 11 |
| 5:10 | 14 |
| 11:31 | 26 |
| 12:1 | 3 |
| 12:1-2 | 152 |
| 12:1-4 | 3 |
| 12:2 | 26 |
| 12:3 | 3, 26 |
| 12:4 | 26 |
| 13:14-17 | 4 |
| 23 | 4 |

### Exodus

| | |
|---|---|
| 4:22 | 9 |
| 6:7 | 9 |
| 7:17 | 26 |
| 9:29 | 26 |
| 10:2 | 26 |
| 13:3, 14 | 3 |
| 14:4, 18 | 26 |
| 15:1-21 | 153 |
| 18:11 | 26 |
| 19:5 | 8 |
| 19:6 | 30 |
| 32:1 | 42 |

### Leviticus

| | |
|---|---|
| 26:12 | 9 |

### Deuteronomy

| | |
|---|---|
| 4:32-39 | 26 |
| 7:6 | 8, 9 |
| 7:13-16 | 11 |
| 10:18-19 | 36 |
| 14:2 | 8 |
| 26:18 | 8 |
| 32:8-9 | 8, 9 |

### Joshua

| | |
|---|---|
| 24:2 | 3 |

### Ezra

| | |
|---|---|
| 10:2-8 | 9 |
| 10:16 | 9 |
| 10:19 | 9 |

### Tobit

| | |
|---|---|
| 13:10-18 | 22 |

### Job

| | |
|---|---|
| 42:5 | 25 |

### Psalms

| | |
|---|---|
| 19:5 | 121 |
| 23 | 9 |
| 29:1-2, 9 | 16 |
| 47 | 15 |
| 48:3 | 17 |
| 68 | 17 |
| 68:25-27 | 17 |
| 68:27-28 | 17 |
| 68:33 | 17 |
| 80:2 | 9 |
| 80:9-17 | 9 |
| 87 | 36, 152 |
| 87:1, 4, 5, 7 | 17-18 |
| 95:1-2 | 31 |
| 95:4 | 11 |
| 95:7 | 9 |
| 96 | 11 |
| 96:7-8 | 15 |
| 96:8-9 | 16 |
| 96:7, 8, 10, 12-13 | 37 |
| 96:11-12 | 16 |
| 98 | 16, 163-164 |
| 98:2 | 16, 37 |
| 98:4-6 | 15 |
| 98:7 | 11 |
| 98:8-9 | 16 |
| 99:2 | 11 |
| 99:2-3 | 16 |
| 110:2 | 58 |
| 117 | 15 |
| 122 | 152 |
| 135:4 | 8 |
| 138:4-6 | 15 |
| 148:11-12 | 15 |

### Proverbs

| | |
|---|---|
| 8:22-36 | 5 |

### Ecclesiastes

| | |
|---|---|
| 1:2 | 25 |
| 12:13 | 25 |

### Sirach

| | |
|---|---|
| 24:3-22 | 6 |

### Isaiah

| | |
|---|---|
| 1:2 | 9 |
| 2:2-3 | 97 |
| 2:2-5 | 21, 26, 152 |
| 2:3 | 21-22, 37, 45 |
| 5:1-6 | 9 |
| 6:9-10 | 113 |
| 6:10 | 112 |
| 8:23 | 51 |
| 10:24 | 14 |
| 11:1 | 76 |
| 11:10 | 22 |
| 13-23 | 11, 12 |
| 14:1 | 22 |
| 14:3-21 | 14 |
| 15:1-6 | 13 |
| 16:1-4 | 13 |
| 16:3 | 13 |
| 16:3-4 | 13 |
| 16:6 | 14 |
| 16:9-11 | 13 |
| 18-19 | 13 |
| 18:2 | 13 |
| 18:4 | 13 |
| 18:7 | 22 |
| 19:4 | 14 |

| | | | | | |
|---|---|---|---|---|---|
| 19:5-6 | 14 | 53:11-12 | 59 | 20:9 | 18 |
| 19:5-7 | 13 | 54:4-7 | 9 | 25-32 | 11 |
| 19:8-14 | 13 | 55:4-5 | 20 | 34:11-31 | 9 |
| 19:13 | 14 | 55:8-9 | 147 | 36:20 | 18 |
| 19:19-23 | 23 | 60 | 22 | 36:23 | 18 |
| 19:25 | 23 | 60:1-17 | 152 | 36:28 | 9 |
| 21:13-15 | 13 | 60:2-3, 6 | 20-21 | 37:27 | 9 |
| 25:6-8 | 22 | 60:6-13 | 21 | **Daniel** | |
| 31:3 | 14 | 60:16 | 21 | 7 | 13 |
| 40-55 | 19 | 60:17 | 21 | 7:14 | 58 |
| 40:6-8 | 25, 77 | 60:18 | 21 | **Hosea** | |
| 40:7-8 | 37 | 60:19-20 | 21, 37 | 2:25 | 9 |
| 40:9 | 19 | 61:1 | 44, 45, 46, 47, 63 | 10:1 | 9 |
| 40:9-10 | 44 | 62:4-5 | 9 | 11:1 | 9 |
| 40:10 | 19 | **Jeremiah** | | **Joel** | |
| 40:10-11 | 37 | 1:9-10 | 37 | 4:13-14 | 60 |
| 41:1 | 19 | 3:17 | 22 | **Amos** | |
| 41:8 | 9 | 3:19 | 9 | 1:3-2:3 | 11 |
| 41:8-9 | 9 | 11:4 | 9 | 1:3-2:4 | 12 |
| 42:1 | 9 | 16:19-21 | 22 | 2:6-16 | 12 |
| 42:6 | 19 | 20:7 | x | 4:4-5 | 12 |
| 42:7 | 20 | 23:1-6 | 9 | 5:21-27 | 12 |
| 42:10-12 | 19, 20 | 24:7 | 9 | 8:2 | 60 |
| 43:21 | 30 | 25:14-38 | 11 | **Jonah** | |
| 44:1 | 9 | 31:31-34 | 32 | 4:11 | 24 |
| 44:23 | 19 | 31:33 | 154 | **Micah** | |
| 44:28 | 19 | 32:38-40 | 32 | 4:1-3 | 21 |
| 45:1 | 19 | 46-51 | 11 | 4:3 | 22 |
| 45:14 | 19 | **Ezekiel** | | 7:14-15 | 9 |
| 45:14-16 | 20 | 11:20 | 9 | **Zephaniah** | |
| 49:6 | 19, 58, 97, 113 | 12:14-15 | 10 | 2:4-15 | 11 |
| 49:6-7 | 17 | 12:15 | 36 | 3:10 | 22 |
| 49:7 | 20 | 12:16 | 10 | **Zechariah** | |
| 49:8-11 | 20 | 14:11 | 9 | 2:15 | 22 |
| 50:1 | 9 | 15:1-8 | 9 | 8:20-23 | 22 |
| 52:7 | 89 | 16:3 | 36 | 9:9-10 | 58 |
| 52:10 | 20 | 16:6-8 | 9 | **Malachi** | |
| 52:15 | 59 | 17:6-10 | 9 | 1:11 | 23 |
| | | | | 3:17 | 8 |

## NEW TESTAMENT

| | | | | | |
|---|---|---|---|---|---|
| **Matthew** | | 5:1 | 71 | 7:29 | 71 |
| 1:23 | 81 | 5:1-2 | 78 | 8:11 | 59 |
| 4:8 | 48 | 5:3-11 | 59 | 8:11-12 | 57 |
| 4:12 | 49 | 5:14-16 | 87 | 9:6, 8 | 71 |
| 4:12-16 | 71 | 5:17 | 32 | 9:37-38 | 59, 60 |
| 4:15 | 51 | 6:10 | 59 | 9:38 | 86 |
| 4:24-25 | 62 | 6:10, 13 | 61 | 10 | 131 |
| 5-7 | 78 | 6:23 | 87 | 10:5-6 | 54, 55, 79 |

| | | | | |
|---|---|---|---|---|
| 10:5-16 | 100 | | 81, 87, 151 | 16 | 72 |
| 10:6 | 71 | 28:19-20 | 69, 81 | 16:1-8 | 74, 75, 76, 77 |
| 10:15 | 57 | 28:20 | 71, 81 | 16:5 | 75 |
| 10:23 | 55 | **Mark** | | 16:6 | 73, 76 |
| 10:40-42 | 82 | 1 | 72 | 16:7 | 77 |
| 10:1-7 | 59 | 1:1 | 41, 77, 82 | 16:14-20 | 74 |
| 10:10 | 43 | 1:4, 6 | 64 | 16:15 | 39, 65, 69, 72, 79 |
| 10:40 | 45 | 1:14 | 41, 43, 48, 49, 64, | 16:16 | 72, 140 |
| 11:2-6 | 46 | | 72, 76, 87, 134 | 16:17 | 72 |
| 11:4-5 | 59 | 1:14-15 | 43, 65 | 16:18 | 72 |
| 11:6 | 48 | 1:15 | 41, 59, 61, 72 | 16:20 | 72, 87 |
| 11:21-24 | 61, 62 | 1:15-16 | 49 | **Luke** | |
| 11:22 | 57 | 1:23-28 | 72 | 1:5 | 97 |
| 11:24 | 57 | 1:29-34 | 72 | 1:5-6 | 113 |
| 11:25 | 47 | 1:38 | 45, 53, 72, 163 | 1:6 | 155 |
| 11:25-27 | 153, 161 | 1:38-39 | 49 | 1:26-38 | 105 |
| 11:27 | 66, 71 | 1:45 | 64 | 1:27 | 113 |
| 12:25-27 | 47 | 2:2 | 132 | 1:32 | 76 |
| 12:25-28 | 59 | 3:14 | 64 | 1:32-35 | 76 |
| 12:41-42 | 56 | 4:3-8 | 59 | 2:25, 36 | 113 |
| 13:8, 23, 30 | 60 | 4:14-17, 20, 33 | 132 | 2:25, 37 | 155 |
| 13:16-17 | 47 | 4:26-29 | 59 | 2:32 | 97, 113 |
| 13:19 | 132 | 5:1-20 | 49 | 2:49 | 97 |
| 13:39-41 | 60 | 5:20 | 64 | 4:14 | 72 |
| 13:52 | 78 | 6 | 94 | 4:14-9:50 | 50 |
| 14:23 | 71 | 6:1-6 | 56 | 4:18 | xi, 160 |
| 15:24 | 54, 55, 71 | 6:7-9 | 54 | 4:18-19 | 72 |
| 15:28 | 61 | 6:8-9 | 43 | 4:18-27 | 113 |
| 16:13 | 50 | 6:12 | 64 | 4:21 | 45 |
| 17:1 | 71 | 7:24 | 49 | 4:22 | 132 |
| 18:20 | 82 | 7:26 | 49 | 4:25-27 | 56 |
| 19:28 | 99, 151 | 7:27 | 49 | 4:43 | 45 |
| 22:2-10 | 58 | 7:31 | 49 | 6:1, 7 | 92 |
| 23:15 | 54, 87 | 7:33-35 | 49 | 6:13 | 98 |
| 24:14 | 54 | 7:36 | 64 | 6:20-22 | 59 |
| 25:40-45 | 82 | 8:23-9:1 | 48 | 6:24-26 | 63 |
| 26:13 | 54 | 8:27 | 50 | 7:4 | 155 |
| 26:28 | 58 | 8:32, 38 | 132 | 7:18-23 | 46 |
| 26:39 | 66 | 8:33 | 102 | 7:21 | 47 |
| 28:6 | 76 | 8:34-35 | 66 | 7:23 | 48 |
| 28:16 | 71, 85 | 8:35-38 | 48 | 9:2-5 | 54 |
| 28:16-17 | 79 | 10:32 | 163 | 9:31 | 92 |
| 28:16-18 | 81 | 10:43-45 | 48 | 9:51 | 97, 114 |
| 28:16-20 | 77 | 10:45 | 66 | 9:51-19:28 | 50 |
| 28:18 | 48, 79, 81, | 13:10 | 54, 65 | 9:52 | 51 |
| | 82, 141 | 13:27 | 60 | 10:2 | 59 |
| 28:18-19 | 79 | 14:9 | 54, 65 | 10:4-12 | 100 |
| 28:19 | 1, 39, 55, 78, | 14:24 | 58 | 10:21 | 47 |
| | | 14:36 | 66 | 10:22 | 66 |

| | | | | | |
|---|---|---|---|---|---|
| 10:23-24 | 47 | 3:17 | 155 | 12:20-33 | 151 |
| 10:33 | 51 | 3:19-20 | 140 | 12:31 | 139 |
| 11:17-22 | 47 | 3:31-36 | 66 | 12:31-32 | 73 |
| 11:31-32 | 56 | 4:1-42 | 151 | 12:32 | 144 |
| 13:22-30 | 57 | 4:22 | 151, 156 | 12:37-43 | 135 |
| 13:32 | 33 | 4:23 | 131 | 12:46 | 87 |
| 14:16-24 | 58 | 4:23-24 | 32 | 12:46-50 | 133, 135 |
| 16:5 | 92 | 4:34-38 | 131 | 12:48 | 133 |
| 17:10 | 86 | 4:35 | 59 | 13-20 | 138 |
| 17:11 | 51 | 4:35-38 | 60 | 13:1, 34 | 138 |
| 17:16 | 51 | 4:41 | 133 | 13:19 | 137 |
| 19:45 | 97 | 4:42 | 51, 131 | 14:3-5 | 82 |
| 19:47-48 | 97 | 4:46-54 | 131, 134 | 14:10 | 66 |
| 20:1 | 97 | 4:50 | 133 | 14:17 | 140 |
| 21:13 | 54 | 4:53 | 131 | 14:23 | 133 |
| 21:24 | 113 | 5:17 | 66 | 14:24 | 133 |
| 21:37 | 97 | 5:19-20 | 66 | 14:26 | 140 |
| 22:20 | 58 | 5:24 | 5, 133 | 14:26-27 | 140 |
| 22:21-30 | 101 | 6:1, 23 | 52 | 14:29 | 137 |
| 22:24-27 | 101 | 6:14 | 135 | 14:31 | 138 |
| 22:28-30 | 99 | 6:60-68 | 135 | 15:3 | 133 |
| 22:29 | 101 | 7:16 | 66 | 15:9, 13 | 138 |
| 22:42 | 66 | 7:31 | 135 | 15:10 | 138 |
| 24:44-49 | 74 | 7:35 | 131, 151 | 15:20 | 133 |
| 24:47 | 96 | 7:49 | 53 | 15:26, 27 | 81, 140 |
| 24:47-49 | 69, 72 | 8:12 | 87 | 16:5, 19-20 | 82 |
| 24:48 | 87 | 8:19 | 66 | 16:7 | 82 |
| 24:49 | 81, 85, 160 | 8:31-32 | 5 | 16:7-11 | 85 |
| 24:51 | 82 | 8:31, 37 | 133 | 16:8-11 | 139 |
| 24:53 | 97 | 8:43 | 133 | 16:29 | 138 |
| **John** | | 8:51, 52, 55 | 133 | 16:33 | 140 |
| 1 | 138 | 8:51-52 | 5 | 17 | 141-143, 152, |
| 1:1 | 5 | 9 | 6 | | 153, 161 |
| 1:4 | 5, 134 | 9:5 | 87 | 17:1-5 | 141-142, 144 |
| 1:10 | 134 | 9:16 | 135 | 17:2 | 141 |
| 1:14 | 66, 67, 138, 144 | 9:39 | 155 | 17:6 | 133 |
| 1:14, 17 | 5 | 10:16 | 151 | 17:6-19 | 142 |
| 1:16-18 | 5 | 10:30 | 66 | 17:11 | 139 |
| 1:18 | 132, 138 | 10:35 | 133 | 17:14 | 133 |
| 1:29 | 73 | 10:36 | 139 | 17:14-18 | 6 |
| 1:29, 32 | 73 | 10:36-38 | 66 | 17:17 | 132, 133, 139, 144 |
| 1:32 | 138 | 10:41-42 | 134 | 17:17-19 | 5 |
| 1:39, 46-50 | 138 | 11:15 | 137 | 17:18 | 141 |
| 1:50 | 134 | 11:16-24 | 158 | 17:19 | 144 |
| 2:11 | 134, 135, 137 | 11:49-52 | 151 | 17:20 | 133 |
| 2:22 | 133 | 11:49-54 | 139 | 17:20-26 | 142-143 |
| 2:23-24 | 135 | 11:52 | 151 | 17:21 | 151 |
| 3:2 | 135 | 12:18 | 135 | 17:23 | 144 |
| 3:16 | xii, 138, 155 | 12:20, 23 | 131 | 17:23-24 | 160 |

| | | | | | | | |
|---|---|---|---|---|---|---|---|
| 17:24 | *159* | 4:29 | *133* | 13:22-37 | *76* |
| 19:5 | *139* | 4:32 | *104, 105* | 13:26 | *132* |
| 19:20 | *132* | 4:32-35 | *103, 106, 125* | 13:42-45, 48-51 | *112* |
| 19:30, 34-35 | *140* | 4:33-35 | *92* | 13:47 | *97, 113* |
| 19:35 | *138* | 5:3-9 | *102* | 14:1 | *112* |
| 20 | *75, 138* | 5:12 | *97, 100* | 14:3 | *132* |
| 20:8, 18 | *138* | 5:17-42 | *102* | 14:15-17 | *110* |
| 20:19-23 | *69* | 5:29-32 | *102* | 14:17 | *161* |
| 20:20 | *140* | 6:1-6 | *93* | 15 | *92, 125, 158* |
| 20:20-23 | *140* | 6:1-7 | *92* | 15:3 | *113* |
| 20:21 | *xv, 5, 73, 75, 87,* | 6:3-5 | *93* | 15:4, 6, 22 | *92* |
| | *140, 141, 144* | 6:4 | *100, 129, 133* | 15:7 | *132* |
| 20:21-22 | *69* | 6:7 | *41, 92, 133* | 15:28 | *111* |
| 20:22 | *73, 81* | 7-8 | *51* | 16:3 | *93* |
| 20:23 | *75* | 7:2-8 | *4* | 16:6-7 | *109* |
| 20:26 | *75* | 8 | *151* | 16:6-10 | *81, 92, 111* |
| 20:29, 31 | *137* | 8:1 | *93* | 16:9 | *109* |
| 20:30-31 | *136* | 8:14-17 | *102, 104* | 16:12 | *109* |
| 21:1 | *52* | 9:1 | *94, 95* | 16:13 | *112* |
| **Acts** | | 9:11-16 | *111* | 16:14-15 | *108* |
| 1:7-8 | *124* | 9:15 | *114* | 16:25 | *129* |
| 1:8 | *51, 68, 74, 89,* | 9:22 | *95* | 17:1-2, 10 | *112* |
| | *91, 96, 128, 160* | 9:31 | *51* | 17:11-12 | *113* |
| 1:10-11 | *82* | 10-11 | *103, 104, 158* | 17:16 | *109* |
| 1:21-22 | *103* | 10:1-11:18 | *50* | 17:18, 21 | *109* |
| 2 | *81* | 10:2 | *106, 155* | 17:18-32 | *108* |
| 2:1-13 | *74* | 10:3-7 | *22, 30, 158* | 17:22-29 | *106* |
| 2:9-10 | *119* | 10:3-42 | *76* | 17:22-31 | *108* |
| 2:14-41 | *74, 102* | 10:13-15 | *102* | 17:23, 27-28 | *108* |
| 2:29 | *96* | 10:19, 44-48 | *158* | 17:28 | *110, 155* |
| 2:36 | *85* | 10:36 | *133* | 17:32 | *108* |
| 2:41 | *113* | 10:36-37 | *41* | 17:32-34 | *112* |
| 2:42 | *92, 104* | 11:2 | *95* | 17:34 | *109* |
| 2:42-47 | *103, 125, 153,* | 11:7-9 | *102* | 18:4-8 | *112* |
| | *154* | 11:12 | *102* | 18:4, 19 | *112* |
| 2:44-45 | *106* | 11:12, 15-16 | *158* | 18:8 | *113* |
| 2:46 | *97, 100* | 11:13 | *158* | 18:18 | *93* |
| 2:47 | *74* | 11:20 | *55* | 18:22 | *114* |
| 3:1 | *100* | 12:1-9 | *102* | 19:8 | *112* |
| 3:6 | *102* | 12:21-28 | *50* | 19:8-10 | *112* |
| 3:12 | *102* | 12:24 | *41, 92, 133* | 19:20 | *41, 92, 110, 133* |
| 4:1-22 | *102* | 13-20 | *114* | 19:23-40 | *108* |
| 4:4 | *113* | 13:1 | *92, 95* | 19:33 | *113* |
| 4:7-12 | *102* | 13:1-3 | *81, 91, 128* | 20:17 | *92* |
| 4:8 | *102* | 13:2 | *111* | 20:18-35 | *129* |
| 4:9-12 | *102* | 13:2-3 | *111* | 20:22 | *111, 114* |
| 4:10 | *76, 102* | 13:2-4 | *158* | 20:28 | *92* |
| 4:13, 29 | *96* | 13:5, 14, 44 | *112* | 20:28-32 | *133* |
| 4:23-30 | *102* | 13:7 | *155* | 20:29-32 | *103* |

| | | | | | | |
|---|---|---|---|---|---|---|
| 20:32 | 132 | 6:19 | 122 | 15:18-19 | | 127 |
| 20:36 | 129 | 7:5 | 122 | 15:19-29 | | 63 |
| 21-28 | 114 | 7:18 | 122 | 15:20, 21 | 121, | 128 |
| 21:4-10 | 111 | 8:2 | 32 | 15:30 | | 129 |
| 21:5, 20 | 129 | 8:2-11 | 32 | 16:7 | | 98 |
| 21:20 | 113 | 8:3 | 122 | *1 Corinthians* | | |
| 21:23-24 | 93 | 8:6 | 122 | 1:4 | | 153 |
| 22:1-4 | 111 | 8:6, 13 | 125 | 1:7-10 | | 129 |
| 22:3 | 97, 111 | 8:11 | 32 | 1:14-15, 16 | | 120 |
| 22:3-21 | 114 | 8:15 | 129 | 1:17-18 | | 108 |
| 23:5 | 111 | 8:15-16 | 129 | 1:18 | 48, | 66 |
| 23:6 | 97 | 8:20-22 | 122 | 1:18-25 | | 67 |
| 23:6-9 | 111, 114 | 8:21 | 122 | 1:24 | | 134 |
| 23:9 | 111 | 8:24 | 160 | 2:1-2 | | 108 |
| 24:10 | 114 | 8:26 | 129 | 2:2 | 154, | 160 |
| 24:14 | 112 | 8:26-27 | 129 | 2:10 | | 160 |
| 24:21 | 111 | 9-11 | 157 | 3:6 | | 121 |
| 25:2-8 | 114 | 9:1-3 | 128 | 3:7 | | 120 |
| 25:19 | 111 | 9:1-5 | 123 | 3:16 | | 160 |
| 26:23 | 113 | 9:3 | 123 | 4:9 | | 98 |
| 26:25 | 132 | 9:4 | 9 | 4:15 | | 118 |
| 27:35 | 129 | 9:4-5 | 128 | 6:1 | | 33 |
| 28:8, 15 | 129 | 9:6 | 123 | 9:1 | | 118 |
| 28:21-22 | 112 | 10 | 126 | 9:6 | | 98 |
| 28:23-25 | 112 | 10:13 | 129 | 11:25 | | 58 |
| 28:24 | 113 | 10:13-14 | 153 | 12:4 | | 125 |
| 28:25-27 | 113 | 10:14-15 | 142 | 12:11 | | 125 |
| 28:25-28 | 56 | 10:14-17 | 127 | 12:28 | | 118 |
| 28:28 | 112, 128 | 10:14-21 | 121 | 13 | 125, | 129 |
| 28:30-31 | 112 | 10:15 | 78 | 14:15-16 | | 129 |
| 28:31 | 92, 114 | 10:18 | 121 | 15:3-7 | | 98 |
| *Romans* | | 11:11-14 | 128 | 15:5 | | 99 |
| 1-2 | 25 | 11:12 | 124 | 15:8-10 | | 118 |
| 1-3 | 155 | 11:15 | 123, 160 | 15:45 | | 32 |
| 1:1 | 142 | 11:16 | 123, 124 | *2 Corinthians* | | |
| 1:1-16 | 117-119, 121 | 11:16-24 | 126 | 3:3 | | 32 |
| 1:1-17 | 115-117 | 11:25-26 | 123 | 3:3-6 | | 32 |
| 1:4 | 32, 85 | 11:26 | 128 | 3:6-8 | | 32 |
| 1:16 | 118, 127, 152 | 11:28 | 123 | 3:12 | 118, | 159 |
| 1:18 | 122 | 11:29 | 9, 123, 128 | 3:17 | | 32 |
| 1:20 | xii | 11:32 | 25 | 4:4 | | 128 |
| 3:2 | 156 | 11:33-34 | 157 | 4:4-6 | | 128 |
| 3:9, 23-24, 27, 30 | 25, 62 | 11:33-36 | 123 | 4:6 | 118, | 134 |
| 3:22 | 62 | 13:1-7 | 33 | 4:10 | | 128 |
| 3:23-24 | 122 | 13:11-12 | 124 | 4:11 | | 160 |
| 4:18-21 | 4 | 13:12 | 86 | 5:16 | | 118 |
| 5:12-14 | 122 | 15:15-25 | 115-117 | 5:18 | | 155 |
| 5:20 | 155 | 15:16 | 118, 126, 153 | 5:20 | | 118 |
| 5:20-21 | 122 | 15:16-21 | 119-121 | 6:2 | | 124 |

| | | | | | | |
|---|---|---|---|---|---|---|
| 6:7 | 132 | 3:22 | 155 | 2:7 | 118 |
| 6:16 | 160 | 3:28 | 123, 125, 129 | 2:11-12 | 118 |
| 7:4 | 118, 159 | 4:6 | 129 | 5:17-18 | 130 |
| 8:4 | 129 | 4:19 | 118 | **2 Timothy** | |
| 8:23 | 98 | 5:20 | 122 | 4:2 | 154 |
| 9:13 | 129 | 5:23-25 | 32 | **Philemon** | |
| 10:4-8 | 118 | 6:11-18 | 117 | 10 | 118 |
| 10:13-16 | 128 | 6:14-16 | 118 | **Hebrews** | |
| 12:7-11 | 102 | 6:16 | 128 | 3:1 | 42, 153 |
| 12:9-10 | 163 | **Ephesians** | | 4:12 | 152 |
| 12:12 | 127 | 1:10 | 28 | 8:7-12 | 32 |
| **Galatians** | | 1:13 | 132 | 10:15-17 | 32 |
| 1-2 | 117 | 1:22-23 | 160 | 12:2 | 42 |
| 1:1, 11-16 | 118 | 2:14-17 | 85, 155 | 12:22 | 31 |
| 1:1, 11, 16-17 | 126 | 3:2, 9 | 28, 128 | **1 John** | |
| 1:1, 15-16 | 158 | 3:12 | 118, 159 | 1:1-4 | 138 |
| 1:7 | 62, 90 | 3:19 | 160 | 1:5 | 140 |
| 1:8, 9 | 118 | 3:20 | 86, 160 | 2:20-21 | 140 |
| 1:11-12 | 62 | 6:19 | 118, 159 | 3:14 | 75 |
| 1:15 | 118, 126, 142 | **Philippians** | | 4:8, 16 | 138 |
| 1:16 | 128 | 1:20 | 118 | 5:6-10 | 140 |
| 1:18 | 119 | 2:25 | 118 | **2 John** | |
| 1:18-23 | 127 | 3:8-11 | 160 | 7-11 | 143 |
| 2:1 | 119 | 3:10 | 128, 163 | **3 John** | |
| 2:2 | 128 | 3:12 | 163 | 9-11 | 143 |
| 2:2-9 | 158 | 4:6-7 | 130 | **Revelation** | |
| 2:7-10 | 103, 118, 119 | **Colossians** | | 2:5 | 87 |
| 2:8-9 | 126 | 1:5 | 132 | 5:9 | 85 |
| 2:9 | 128, 150 | **1 Thessalonians** | | 14:6 | 134 |
| 2:9-10 | 126 | 1:1 | 98 | 14:14-16 | 60 |
| 2:14 | 102 | 1:5 | 127 | 19:13 | 133 |
| 2:14-16 | 118 | 1:9-10 | 110 | 21:23 | 86 |
| 3-4 | 61 | 2:2 | 159 | 22:20 | 164 |

## Of Related Interest

Jacques Dupuis, S.J.
**JESUS CHRIST AT THE ENCOUNTER OF WORLD RELIGIONS**
Faith Meets Faith Series
Articulates Christian conviction about Jesus as the Christ in relation to other religious traditions, and—equally important—searches out the wisdom these other traditions bring to Christianity. Learned yet accessible to non-specialists, this book transcends narrow dogmatism while finding in the christology of the first Ecumenical Councils fresh resources and questions—both for Christians and for peoples of other religious faiths.
ISBN 0-88344-723-1 Paper
ISBN 0-88344-724-X Cloth

Donald Senior
Carroll Stuhlmueller
**THE BIBLICAL FOUNDATIONS FOR MISSION**
A thorough survey of scripture showing how universal mission became an accepted part of the Christian perspective.
   "Enables those not trained in biblical criticism to understand not only the ideas but the critical issue behind their interpretation. . . ."   —*Biblical Theology Bulletin*
ISBN 0-88344-047-4 Paper

Walbert Bühlmann
**WITH EYES TO SEE**
*Church and World in the Third Millennium*
With Franciscan zest for the inner life of the ecclesia and a willingness to challenge the powerful, the author of *The Church of the Future* offers "New Commandments for the World Church."
   "A challenging strategy for reshaping the church's mission agenda in the next century."                                                   —James A. Scherer
ISBN 0-88344-683-9 Paper

C.S. Song
**THIRD EYE THEOLOGY**
*Theology in Formation in Asian Settings*
Revised Edition
Since 1979 this classic work has been regarded as the landmark in unearthing and

exemplifying the possibilities of a new kind of Asian Christian theology—one that takes its point of departure from the folklore and cultures of Asia.
ISBN 0-88344-735-5 Paper


Louis J. Luzbetak, S.V.D.
**THE CHURCH AND CULTURES**
*New Perspectives in Missiological Anthropology*
With a wealth of scientific information for the non-anthropologist, this completely revised edition of a classic explores anthropology's relevance to pastoral work, religious education, social action, liturgy—every aspect of mission—with special attention to contextualization, by which a local church integrates its understanding of the Gospel with local culture.
ISBN 0-88344-625-1 Paper